A HISTORY OF JAPAN

1615–1867

A HISTORY OF JAPAN
1615-1867

George Sansom

STANFORD UNIVERSITY PRESS

STANFORD, CALIFORNIA

Stanford University Press
Stanford, California
© 1963 by the Board of Trustees of the
Leland Stanford Junior University
Printed in the United States of America
Cloth ISBN 0-8047-0526-7
Paper ISBN 0-8047-0527-5
Original edition 1963
Last figure below indicates year of this printing:
87 86 85 84 83 82 81 80 79 78

PREFACE

The main purpose of this, the third (and last) volume of *A History of Japan*, is to describe the political and social development of which the foundation was laid by Ieyasu, the first Tokugawa Shōgun.

Ieyasu was a genius, who combined civil and military capacity of the highest order; and although he died in 1616, after holding office as Shōgun for little more than a decade, his stamp is visible on the institutions of his country as they developed during the two hundred and fifty years after his demise.

The system of checks and balances by which he and his successors (notably Iemitsu) kept the great feudatories in order was a political feat combining strength and skill in a remarkable fashion, for Japan had its Hotspurs and Glendowers in the seventeenth century, and the central government was anxious not to take arms against them. Indeed the essential feature of government by the Tokugawa Shōguns was a determination to keep the peace. After the Shimabara rising in 1637–38 the country was free from civil war, and the energies of the nation were devoted to increasing the production of goods in agriculture, manufactures, and mining.

The government at that time was concerned more with finding occupation for unemployed samurai than with promoting the military spirit. The Ordinances for the Military Class (Buke Sho-Hatto)—first issued in 1615, soon after the fall of Ōsaka—direct the samurai to cultivate both military and civil virtues, since obviously there could not be useful military employment for all. Fortunately for the country, many of these men were absorbed into civilian employment, principally of the administrative type, since they were members of a class—it might be described as a caste—consisting mainly of men of some education, a qualification rare in other classes except the clergy. It was such men who eased the transition from an age of war to an age of peace. They occupied posts in the central and local government offices of the Bakufu or in the castle towns of the Shōgun's vassals, the daimyos.

Thus, with some exceptions of course, the whole country was tolerably well administered and the several barons, some of whom enjoyed a substantial autonomy, were kept under close watch by Censors or other intelligence officers appointed by Yedo. Furthermore, one of the main reasons for closing the country in 1639 was the determination of the Bakufu to prevent those feudatories with access to the sea from making contacts with representatives of Western powers who might supply them with powerful weapons.

It will be seen, therefore, that the country was firmly governed. It was able to enjoy for the better part of two centuries not only freedom from foreign aggression but also a steadily rising standard of living. It is true that it suffered frequently from such natural calamities as plague and famine, but on balance it prospered, as is clear from all available evidence of material progress.

More difficult to measure and assess is the moral condition of society in its various grades, from the samurai down to the farmer, the artisan and (lowest in the scale) the trader. Here there is fairly reliable evidence, for most of the serious literature of the Yedo period deals with what today we call sociology; and it is interesting to notice in this context that the Bakufu did not as a rule exercise a strict censorship of political writings. Individual scholars were in general free to criticize the government, but any attempt to form a school of political thought was usually suppressed. In such circumstances it was natural for the discontented to resort to satire, and the literature of the period is rich in shafts of wit aimed at official solemnity.

Yet from such evidence alone it is not easy to gather a fair impression of the nature of life in Tokugawa Japan. Writing early in the seventeenth century, Fujiwara Seika, a not very good poet, bewailed in verse "this dreadful age." Two centuries later—about 1800—a well-known treatise on contemporary morals strikes a pessimistic note. "The ruler is selfish," it says. "The high officials are selfish. The samurai have no idea of duty. No longer does a man sacrifice himself or his family for the sake of his Lord. . . . As the saying goes, nowadays the only members of a samurai household who do not steal are the master and his horse."

Such judgments are more entertaining than instructive; but we know a great deal about the trend of city life as the seventeenth century gave place to the eighteenth. This was the era known as Genroku, celebrated for its gay costumes, which clearly reflected the mood of the citizens, their interest in plays and novels and the plastic arts. Perhaps this was the summit of political and cultural life under the Tokugawa Shōguns. The Bakufu's prestige was high, especially under the Shōgun Yoshimune, from 1716 to 1745. After this there seems to have been a decline in its power, which may be ascribed less to a lack of competence than to the difficulty of the problems with which it was now faced.

These were new and urgent, for they resulted from breaches in the policy of isolation which were due to the arrival of foreign ships in Japanese waters. The first intruders were Russians, when in 1792 an envoy named Laxman sailed into the harbour of Nemuro in Yezo, later proceeding to Hakodate. Throughout the closing years of the century the Shōgun's officers were active in the protection of Japanese interests in Sakhalin and the southern islands of the Kuriles. Thereafter the Bakufu struggled to keep foreign ships away from Japanese ports, issuing in 1825 to local authorities a strongly worded Expulsion Order, which in fact could not be enforced. Before long the pressure of the Western powers, culminating in the naval expedition of Commodore Perry in 1853, obliged Japan to abandon her exclusionist policy and to face the dangers of international society.

Japan was then a well-governed state, fitted by past experience to take this step, for the history of the Yedo period shows a truly remarkable development in almost every aspect of the national life. It was indeed a great achievement.

G. S.

ACKNOWLEDGMENTS

I owe a great debt to my friends John Galvin and Stanley Smith, whose generosity has made it possible for me to complete this three-volume history of Japan in very favorable conditions.

For precious advice and assistance I have depended upon outstanding Japanese scholars. Among them I must mention in particular Professor Nakamura Kichiji of the University at Sendai, who came to Stanford from Japan to guide my studies for several weeks. I profited by his wisdom and enjoyed his friendship.

Professor Yukio Yashiro, an old friend, in his capacity as Chairman of the Commission for the Protection of Cultural Property (Bunkazai Hogo Iinkai), gave valuable assistance in authorizing the reproduction of important texts and pictures. In the collection of these, Professor Takeshi Toyoda and Dr. Chisaburo Yamada gave generous help.

I owe especial thanks to Dr. Madoka Kanai for authorizing the reproduction of material from the Historiographical Institute of Tokyo University (Shiryo Hensanjo), over which he presides.

I am also indebted to the Director, Mr. Leon Seltzer, and the staff of the Stanford University Press for skilled and patient editorial work.

CONTENTS

DESCRIPTIVE LIST OF PLATES

Plates 1–6 follow p. 50. Plates 7–12 follow p. 98.
Plates 13–18 follow p. 162. Plates 19–23 follow p. 194.

LIST OF ILLUSTRATIONS IN TEXT

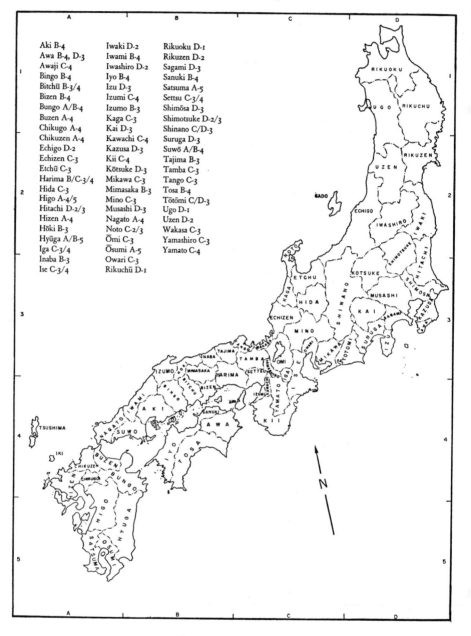

Aki B-4
Awa B-4, D-3
Awaji C-4
Bingo B-4
Bitchū B-3/4
Bizen B-4
Bungo A/B-4
Buzen A-4
Chikugo A-4
Chikuzen A-4
Echigo D-2
Echizen C-3
Etchū C-3
Harima B/C-3/4
Hida C-3
Higo A-4/5
Hitachi D-2/3
Hizen A-4
Hōki B-3
Hyūga A/B-5
Iga C-3/4
Inaba B-3
Ise C-3/4

Iwaki D-2
Iwami B-4
Iwashiro D-2
Iyo B-4
Izu D-3
Izumi C-4
Izumo B-3
Kaga C-3
Kai D-3
Kawachi C-4
Kazusa D-3
Kii C-4
Kōtsuke D-3
Mikawa C-3
Mimasaka B-3
Mino C-3
Musashi D-3
Nagato A-4
Noto C-2/3
Ōmi C-3
Ōsumi A-5
Owari C-3
Rikuchū D-1

Rikuoku D-1
Rikuzen D-2
Sagami D-3
Sanuki B-4
Satsuma A-5
Settsu C-3/4
Shimōsa D-3
Shimotsuke D-2/3
Shinano C/D-3
Suruga D-3
Suwō A/B-4
Tajima B-3
Tamba C-3
Tango C-3
Tosa B-4
Tōtōmi C/D-3
Ugo D-1
Uzen D-2
Wakasa C-3
Yamashiro C-3
Yamato C-4

The provinces of Japan

A HISTORY OF JAPAN

1615–1867

The Tokugawa Shōguns

1603–1616	Ieyasu (First Shōgun)
1616–1623	Hidetada (Second Shōgun)
1623–1651	Iemitsu (Third Shōgun)
1651–1680	Ietsuna (Fourth Shōgun)
1680–1709	Tsunayoshi (Fifth Shōgun)
1709–1713	Ienobu (Sixth Shōgun)
1713–1716	Ietsugu (Seventh Shōgun)
1716–1745	Yoshimune (Eighth Shōgun)
1745–1760	Ieshige (Ninth Shōgun)
1760–1786	Ieharu (Tenth Shōgun)
1787–1837	Ienari (Eleventh Shōgun)
1837–1853	Ieyoshi (Twelfth Shōgun)
1853–1858	Iesada (Thirteenth Shōgun)
1858–1866	Iemochi (Fourteenth Shōgun)
1866–1867	Hitotsubashi Keiki (Fifteenth Shōgun)

CHAPTER I

THE NATURE OF THE TOKUGAWA GOVERNMENT

1. *Ieyasu's Political Aims*

THE MATERIAL foundations of the Tokugawa Bakufu, as well as Ieyasu's attitude towards problems of government during the last fifteen years of his life, have been described at the end of the preceding volume of this work. The situation may be recapitulated here, while stating the main features of his policy in further detail.

The foundations of the Tokugawa government were laid between the years 1600 and 1616, the date of the battle of Sekigahara and the date of Ieyasu's death. After Sekigahara, Ieyasu's first care was to increase and consolidate his military strength to such a degree that even the most powerful warrior houses in combination would not dare to challenge him. This superiority he was able to attain, thanks to his immense prestige, by escheating the domains of his vanquished enemies and rewarding his trusted vassals, the Fudai daimyos, with fiefs in strategic positions where they could keep watch and ward upon the uncommitted daimyos, the Tozama or Outside Lords.[1]

Numerical military strength was not sufficient. It was also necessary that the wealth of the Tokugawa family should keep pace with its growing political power. The basis of the Japanese economy was the feudal village producing the staple foodstuff, rice; and the chief item in the annual revenue of the Bakufu was the rice grown in the lands owned by the Tokugawa family. This had been assessed at about 1,000,000 koku (of five bushels) in 1590, when Ieyasu first established himself in the Kantō (the eight eastern provinces). It was increased by the incorporation of new domains and had reached 2,557,000 koku by 1598, the year of Hideyoshi's death.

After the battle of Sekigahara Ieyasu was able to escheat revenues of 3,830,000 koku, thus bringing his total holding to close upon 6,400,000 koku. This was about one-fourth of the total assessed revenue of the whole country, then estimated at from 24 to 25 million koku.

The revenues escheated were not all retained by the Tokugawa family. A great proportion was distributed among their vassals and retainers as a reward for service. It is difficult to state accurately the posi-

---

[1] Large areas of land belonging to monasteries were also confiscated.

tion at a given time, since the processes of confiscation and distribution were continuous; but the following survey of the process called *daimyō no toritsubushi* ("smashing, or crushing, the daimyos") will show how Ieyasu and his successors increased the material wealth of the Bakufu during the seventeenth century:

Escheatment by	*Million koku*
Ieyasu	3.83
Hidetada	4.53
Iemitsu	3.85
Ietsuna	.77
Tsunayoshi	1.70
Total at 1690	14.68

Since Ieyasu had a revenue of close on 3 million koku before Sekigahara, the total holding of the Tokugawa family at the end of the seventeenth century was of the order of 17 million koku. At that time the total assessed revenue of the whole country was about 26 million koku, so that there was left in the hands of the Tozama daimyos some 9 million koku.[2]

Apart from the growing agrarian economy, the Bakufu profited by an accelerated development of domestic trade throughout the country, which (owing to an increased use of currency and ease of transport) had begun to create during the sixteenth century a national market in the place of a system of isolated local or regional markets. This change had favoured a national control of the mercantile economy by the Bakufu in addition to its substantial share of the country's arable land. It was obviously to the advantage of the Tokugawa Shōguns to promote domestic industry and trade; and much if not most of the recorded history of Tokugawa government after the fall of Ōsaka Castle in 1615 has to do with mercantile and industrial policy.

[2] A rough estimate of the position in 1600, after Sekigahara, is as follows:

	Million koku
Total revenue of Tokugawa family from direct domains...	8.5
Revenue from domains allotted to Fudai daimyos........	6.0
Balance for Tozama and miscellaneous holdings.........	10.0
Total revenue from fiefs of 10,000 koku or more.....	24.5

Katsu Awa, in his *Suijin-roku*, says that the revenue from domains under direct Tokugawa control rose from 3 million koku in 1603 to nearly 7 million in 1690. This does not include the revenue of the Hatamoto (direct military retainers of Tokugawa). The Code of One Hundred Articles (*O Sadame Gaki Hyakka-jō*) in its early version states that ca. 1660 the total assessed yield of the country was 28.19 million koku. The actual yield was probably greater, and by 1860 it had reached about 35 million koku of rice or equivalent produce.

Ieyasu increased his wealth at every opportunity. He confiscated the gold and silver mines of Sado and the silver mine of Iwami, and by his orders all mines were stimulated to increase their output. By 1601 he had begun to mint gold and silver coins in considerable quantities. He already had in his castles vast stores of precious metals which he had collected earlier, and when he died he left gold and silver estimated at 1,950,000 ryō.[3] Of this 750,000 ryō was bequeathed to junior branches of the Tokugawa family, and the remainder was placed in the Bakufu treasury.

A further substantial revenue was obtained from the leading commercial centres. The towns which, thanks to their immunities, had developed a flourishing trade during the sixteenth century were now transferred to the direct jurisdiction of the Bakufu, and their citizens were made subject to the absolute rule of Bakufu officers—Shoshi-dai, or Deputies, in Kyoto and Bugyō, or Commissioners, in other former municipalities. These measures abolished the privileges of the cities of Ōsaka, Sakai, Fushimi, Nagasaki, Nara, and Yamada.

In consequence, at least in part, of this harsh treatment of private enterprise, a new class of government contractor developed and enjoyed a monopoly of large-scale commercial activity. Steps were taken to apply controls to foreign as well as domestic trade. By an edict of 1604 the Bakufu assumed a monopoly of the sale of imported raw silk, then the most important item of merchandise in the trade with China; and this may be regarded as the first step towards a policy of full official control of foreign trade.

During Ieyasu's lifetime the Bakufu continued to promote foreign trade. Ieyasu maintained the strong interest in merchant shipping which he had shown when he took Will Adams into his service in 1601. He sanctioned the visits of Dutch (1606) and English (1613) ships and traders. He approved of Japanese voyages to Luzon and Annam, and welcomed envoys from those regions. In general he favoured a kind of foreign commerce which, unlike the Portuguese trade, was free from the influence of Christian missionaries; and he was gratified to learn that Portuguese vessels were being attacked and captured by the Dutch in

---

[3] The ryō was the unit of gold currency. The coin called "koban," minted in 1601 at the Fushimi Mint founded that year by Ieyasu, was worth one ryō, and the "ōban" was worth ten ryō. It weighed 44 momme and contained 67.7 per cent of gold, 27.8 per cent of silver, and 4.5 per cent of copper. The total weight of 44 momme is equal to a little over 6 oz. avoirdupois. The content and purchasing power of gold coins fluctuated widely during the seventeenth century. The largest unit in the calculation of value in gold was the "kan," a weight equal to 1,000 momme.

Asian waters.[4] Trade relations with Spain were opened from 1610, but did not flourish.

By that time Ieyasu's attention was occupied by domestic problems, since he knew that there must soon be a final reckoning between himself and the supporters of Hideyori. Since he was preparing for a decisive military struggle, the supply of munitions by foreign merchants could be of some importance, and therefore the outlook for them—the Dutch in particular—seemed promising.

Apart from the specific task of destroying the Toyotomi party, the general purpose of the Shōgun's government was to establish and maintain its authority over all the orders of society which together constituted the body politic. These were the Throne; the feudal baronies; the peasantry; the artisans; and the traders. The Buddhist Church was no longer an estate of the realm, and the Shintō establishment in the seventeenth century was lacking in political influence.

The first laws and regulations of the Tokugawa Shōgunate were addressed to each of these orders in turn, by Ieyasu and then by Hidetada and Iemitsu, the second and third Shōguns.

In an ordinance of 1611 Ieyasu exacted an oath of allegiance from the daimyos of central and western Japan, and in 1612 he required similar submission from the northern provinces. These were the first ordinances defining the duties of vassals of the Tokugawa Shōgun:

Article 1 calls upon them to obey the laws laid down generation after generation since the Shōgun Yoritomo, thus invoking such codes as the Jōei Shikimoku (1232) and the Kemmu Shikimoku (1336) as well as orders issued by Yedo.

Article 2 forbids giving shelter to persons guilty of breaking the Shōgun's laws or disobeying his wishes.

Article 3 requires a daimyo to take action against any samurai or person of lower rank in his fief who is guilty of rebellious conduct or of murder.

At this time Ieyasu was in Kyoto, and the Toyotomi forces were in Ōsaka. In exacting loyalty from the western daimyos he had especially in mind Hosokawa Tadaoki, Ikeda Terumasu, Fukushima Masanori, and Katō Kiyomasa, who had all fought for him at Sekigahara.

---

[4] But the regular Japan voyage of a Portuguese vessel known as the "Great Ship from Macao" was of special interest to Ieyasu, who habitually sent by it a large sum in silver for the purchase in China of gold and expensive silks. This vessel carried a license under the Shōgun's "vermilion seal," and the Dutch were warned not to attack it. For details of the Portuguese trade from 1555 to 1640, see C. R. Boxer, *The Great Ship from Amacon* (Lisbon, 1959).

In 1611 and again in 1613 he issued orders regulating the conduct of Court nobles and limiting the rights of the Throne. And in the years 1611–14 he gave out ordinances banning the Christian religion and ordered the expulsion of missionaries. In 1614 the Christian churches in Kyoto were destroyed and their clergy arrested. Then followed the siege of Ōsaka Castle, ending in its capture in 1615.

Now Ieyasu had only a year longer to live, but he continued to execute his policy of gaining and preserving for his successors a decisive military and economic superiority over any foreseeable combination against him. In 1615, as the supreme commander, he laid down rules for the behaviour of the whole military class. This legislation strikes the keynote of the domestic policy of Ieyasu and his successors, for it exacted from all members of that class an unconditional obedience. The document, known as Buke Sho-Hatto, or Rules for the Military Houses, was drawn up under the instructions of Ieyasu by the Zen monk Sūden, incumbent of the Nanzenji (the presiding Zen foundation), in collaboration with other scholars. It was read with a running commentary to an assembly of daimyos in Fushimi Castle in the presence of Hidetada on August 30, 1615.

It is a fundamental document, and although it was frequently revised in some particulars, it was never substantially changed. It was always reaffirmed on the accession of a new Shōgun. The principal injunctions of its thirteen clauses may be summarized as follows:

1. The study of literature and the practice of the military arts must be pursued side by side. ("On the left hand learning, on the right hand the use of weapons.")
2. Drunkenness and licentious behaviour must be avoided. ("In the Codes such conduct is forbidden. Lewdness and gambling bring the downfall of a State.")
3. Those who break the laws are not to be given shelter in any fief. ("Law is the basis of right conduct.")
4. The greater and lesser feudatories and those who hold land under them as retainers must at once expel any soldier in their service who is charged with treason or murder.
5. No sanctuary is to be given to men who plot rebellion or incite risings. Hereafter residence in a fief shall be limited to men born in that fief.
6. All building work on a castle, even if only by way of repairs, must at once be reported, and all new construction is strictly forbidden.

7. Should it be learned that in a neighbouring fief there are men who plot changes and form parties or factions to carry them out, they must at once be denounced [to the Bakufu].
8. Marriages are not to be privately contracted.
9. All daimyos in attendance at the Shōgun's court shall follow the prescribed rules of conduct. They must not bring into the City an escort of more than the number of men allowed for their respective ranks.
10. All costumes and ornaments are to be appropriate to the wearer's rank, and not extravagant in colour or pattern.
11. Common people are not to ride in palanquins without permission. ["Common people" here means the lower orders—peasants, artisans, and traders.] Exception is made for physicians, astrologers, aged persons, and invalids.
12. All samurai in all fiefs are to live frugally.
13. All daimyos are to choose capable persons to advise them in the government of their fiefs.

It is an interesting feature of this ordinance that the comments on its several clauses consist of more or less appropriate quotations from classical sources, principally Chinese. The whole document thus has a somewhat Confucian flavour, which is not characteristic of mediaeval law-giving in Japan but is common in the later legislation of the Tokugawa Bakufu. In the foregoing translation, specimen comments on the first three clauses only are given (in parentheses).

In its contents it conforms to an almost universal pattern, since an authoritarian system of government is usually accompanied, if not by an artificial state religion, at least by a code of belief and behaviour and by a certain puritanical outlook expressed in sumptuary rules. Indeed the clauses in the Buke Sho-Hatto enjoining frugality and laying down standards of dress and food are an echo of the past, since both Yoritomo and the Hōjō Regents had attempted to regulate the style of living of their vassals. Although it cannot be said that any of those rulers deliberately promoted religious beliefs, they did strive to inculcate the military virtues of obedience and sacrifice.

2. Ieyasu's Methods

This piece of legislation illustrates the determination of Ieyasu to create an absolute state, governed in perpetuity by the Tokugawa. From its beginning the Bakufu legislated against change—indeed in the seventh clause the word "change" means "revolt."

Ieyasu's cipher

This determination, according to some writers (including Rai San-yō), can be traced back to Ieyasu's challenge of Hideyoshi at Komaki and Nagakute, when (they assume) he had already made up his mind to destroy the Toyotomi family. The simple, popular view at the time was sentimental rather than critical. It was felt that Ieyasu had deliberately planned, as a matter of national policy, to kill or cause the death of Hideyori. This was deplored but understood. Ieyasu was cruel, but he had to be ruthless if he was to succeed.

This is true enough. He knew exactly what he was about, and what action was unavoidable. He meant to build a government of the kind known in recent times as "totalitarian," or at least to lay its solid foundation. The working of his mind is revealed by his acts after the fall of Ōsaka Castle in June 1615.

When the Tokugawa forces stormed through the castle apartments, a Toyotomi warrior named Ono Harunaga rescued Ieyasu's own granddaughter Sen Hime from the flames. He therefore felt justified in begging Ieyasu to spare the life of Hideyori's mother, Yodogimi. But Ieyasu was unrelenting. With Hideyori's death the Toyotomi family was destroyed save for two small children. The subsequent hunting down of the surviving defenders of Ōsaka was merciless. Day after day at least fifty or a hundred men were caught and killed, and soon their heads were exposed by the thousand on the road between Fushimi and Kyoto. Many tragic tales are told of the cruelty for which Ieyasu was responsible. The eight-year-old son of Hideyori by a concubine was decapitated on the public execution ground at Rokujō-Kawara. His elder sister was spared, but she had to end her days in a nunnery at Kamakura.

Having destroyed his principal enemy, Ieyasu still had to secure the submission of all potential rivals. This he achieved chiefly by the strategic distribution of fiefs, by constant surveillance in a far-reaching system of espionage, and by imposing upon the most powerful daimyos obligations designed to reduce their wealth and thus to limit their military strength.

But perhaps his most powerful weapon was his public reputation.

During his last years he was treated as an idol, an object of worship, almost as a deity; and although he was thought by the ordinary citizen to have murdered Hideyori, he was nonetheless regarded as supreme beyond challenge. He built the solid base of a government which was to last for more than two centuries; and his successors for generations carried out what was called "the ancestral law"—the principles laid down by him—which soon acquired the nature of holy writ. No previous Shō-gun had reached such a pinnacle of glory, in life or in death. He was buried with honours far beyond those accorded to Yoritomo or Takauji, and was posthumously deified under the sacred title of Gongen, which means an avatar of the Buddha. Gongen Sama was the name by which he was known to the people of Japan until recent times.

It may be asked how he was able to impose his will upon the prin-cipal warlords. The answer is that by his victory at Sekigahara he had settled the issue between a confused civil movement led by Ishida and a military party led by himself and his great generals. He was able to do this because unlike Hideyoshi, who had wasted his strength on the Korean campaign, he had carefully created and fostered a great disci-plined force. Upon the fall of Ōsaka, though it was perhaps still pos-sible for his strongest enemies to resume the struggle, they dared not challenge his moral ascendancy. Thereafter they abandoned hope of dividing the country, regarding it (in the words of one of them, Nabe-shima Nobushige) as "impossible, even in a dream."

Ieyasu had little interest in administrative detail. He saw his prob-lems in a broad outline and wanted bold solutions. Consequently the close organization of the Bakufu did not begin until after his death. There was an extremely active period of transition from military to civil government between 1600 and 1615, which merits close attention be-cause it reveals lively and original features of the national character and a power to invent and improvise with which Japan is not usually cred-ited. It also brings into relief the somewhat finical nature of the system developed a century later. During his last years Ieyasu depended not upon a regular civil service but upon a number of gifted individuals with whom he surrounded himself. It included such various figures as the monks Tenkai and Sūden; the Confucian scholar Hayashi Razan; rich merchants like Gotō Shōzaburō, Chaya Shirōjirō, Suminokura Ryōi, Shimai Sōshitsu, and Imai Sōkun; the Englishman Will Adams; and a few favourite vassals like Ōkubo Tadachika, who had been with him since Mikawa days, not to speak of adherents like Honda Masanobu, his onetime falconer.

All these were exceptional men, in refreshing contrast to regular office-holders, and most of them deserve some special notice for their interesting characters and the nature of the services they rendered to Ieyasu. Chaya Shirōjirō is perhaps the best illustration of the type of man whom Ieyasu found most useful. His father was a rōnin (a masterless warrior), crippled in the wars, who set up as a draper in Kyoto, where he did business for Ieyasu's father, and by arrangement sent young Shirōjirō to Mikawa to be an esquire and companion to Ieyasu. Succeeding to his father's business, Shirōjirō became the purveyor to the Tokugawa family in Yamashiro province and before long was one of the wealthiest merchants in Kyoto, living in a grand style. As a contractor on a large scale he furnished military supplies to Ieyasu, and was with him at his principal battles, from Mikatagahara (1572) to Odawara (1590).

It was this Chaya who gave Ieyasu timely notice of the death of Oda Nobunaga, and enabled him to escape from Sakai in 1582, on the dangerous journey through Iga. He also acted as an intelligence agent in Kyoto for Ieyasu; and year after year, while Hideyoshi was still in power, he took secret messages and presents from Ieyasu to the Court —a fact recorded in the Court noble Kajūji's diary for 1591, which shows that Ieyasu had long looked forward to a time when he would rise to supreme power in the state.

It was Chaya, too, who helped to lay out the city of Yedo after Ieyasu moved east from Mikawa. From 1595 he did not leave Ieyasu's side, and he more than once declined important posts as Governor of Tokugawa domains, on the ground that he was not a soldier and did not wish to change. He died in 1596 and was succeeded by his eldest son, who fought at Sekigahara, and then by his next son, who went to Nagasaki at Ieyasu's request, to supervise foreign trade and doubtless to pick up some bargains for himself and his master. He was also told to keep on eye on the Christians.

Suminokura Ryōi, Shimai Sōshitsu, and Imai Sōkun were also men who displayed great talents and accumulated great wealth as merchants and contractors. Sōshitsu (a Hakata merchant, 1537–1615) is known as the author of a testament containing injunctions to his son, a work which gives an idea of the creed of the reputable merchant in his day. He was a brewer and a moneylender—a frequent combination which created many great fortunes.

Gotō Shōzaburō, an officer of the mint, was the brain behind Ieyasu's currency policy. He had been contractor for Ieyasu's armies before Sekigahara.

A group of men including Ōkubo Nagayasu, Ina Tadatsugu, and

Itagaki Katsushige advised on the vital problems of agrarian policy—the control of the farming population and the land surveys. Ina was a particularly able man, and was handsomely rewarded. He was a skilled land surveyor and rendered remarkable service in irrigation and flood control. At Sekigahara he had been in charge of the transport of supplies. He died in 1610, and the field was left to Ōkubo Nagayasu, who now became Ieyasu's chief adviser on agrarian policy, particularly on mining matters.[5]

After his death Nagayasu was found to have engaged in peculation on a vast scale, but for a time he was able to shelter unsuspected under the protection of Ōkubo Tadachika, a trusted vassal who had no knowledge of his guilt. Ieyasu seems eventually to have become aware of Nagayasu's cupidity but until he discovered its alarming extent to have thought that the value of Nagayasu's skill outweighed his errors.

Honda Masanobu, a favourite of Ieyasu, openly charged Nagayasu's protector, Tadachika, with covering up Nagayasu's crimes. (Masanobu was also under Tadachika's patronage, but hated him.) The sad truth was that nearly all these men were guilty of embezzlement, and had no scruples.[6] It was the accepted practice among their kind, and it was made easy by the very loose control of finance in the early days of the Bakufu, before an audit office was established; but Nagayasu's offense was monumental.

His extravagance was amazing. When proceeding on tours of inspection he would be accompanied by a retinue of servants, concubines, and sangaku dancers numbering several hundred in all. Wherever they stopped for the night there would be wild dancing and drinking, and their calls upon peasants or townspeople for labour and supplies caused great distress. Yet Nagayasu, justly confident of the value of his services, merely boasted of his excesses, which continued until his death in 1613 at the age of sixty-nine.

When, according to his will, he was about to be placed in a golden coffin, and great men were about to attend his obsequies, Ieyasu suddenly ordered the funeral rites to be stopped, pending an enquiry into Nagayasu's misdemeanours. The enquiry revealed that he was guilty of treasonable conduct. His seven sons were sent to castles governed by kinsmen or vassals of Ieyasu, there to be held in custody. They were

[5] Nagayasu was the son of a sarugaku performer (a type of dance) in the province of Kai, where he was employed by Takeda Shingen. He attracted the attention of Ieyasu and was engaged by him.

[6] Honda Tadakatsu, a soldier who had fought well at Sekigahara and had a low opinion of civilians, referring to this situation observed: "A daikan [a Shōgun's deputy], like a bottle, should have a rope round his neck." The Japanese earthenware bottle, having a long neck and wide lip, could be slung on a rope.

subsequently killed or ordered to commit suicide; and the doctrine of complicity (renza) being invoked, punishment was extended to many of Nagayasu's relatives and associates. His patron, Ōkubo Tadachika, who had given him his surname, was at this time engaged in anti-Christian activities in Kyoto, and was deprived of his fief *in absentia*. Many others received similar treatment.

It is not clear why Ieyasu ordered such severe retribution, for Nagayasu's services had been of great value; but it has been suggested that Nagayasu was party to a conspiracy to overthrow Ieyasu in which a number of foreign and Japanese Christians were involved. The evidence here is not convincing, but no doubt an examination of Nagayasu's papers showed that he was dishonest in political as well as financial matters.

Another and perhaps more plausible explanation of Ieyasu's wrath is that he was appalled to discover the amount of Nagayasu's accumulation of coin and bullion. Ieyasu himself, though his personal habits were frugal, was a man of miserly temperament, in constant fear of losing his treasure, which, he rightly supposed, was essential to the maintenance of the Bakufu in its early stages. On his death it was reckoned that he had two million ryō in gold coin and about twice that amount in treasure of various kinds. When he discovered that Nagayasu had embezzled sums of the same order of magnitude he was naturally infuriated.

It was more than a fortunate accident that brought all these men into action at a critical juncture in their country's history. After Hideyoshi's death Ieyasu looked forward to an era of peace. It is true that he still had battles to fight, but he saw farther into the future than most of his contemporaries, for he had always been a man to take a long view. His vision was shared by his trusted familiars, and it is therefore of interest to trace the links which bound them to him, for although they were a heterogeneous band, they were united by one purpose, wanting nothing better than the full exercise of their talents.

Honda Masanobu (Sado no Kami) was a retainer in the Mikawa fief, and when Ieyasu was a youth he had been employed as his companion. Tadachika's uncle, Ōkubo Hikozaemon, in his *Mikawa Monogatari*,[7] relates that his elder brother, Ōkubo Tadayo, took a liking to

---

[7] Hikozaemon's *Mikawa Monogatari* is an interesting record of the relationship of Ieyasu with the Ōkubo family. It also contains a discussion of the mutual obligations of lord and vassal which may be regarded as a forerunner of Bushidō, the systematic code of chivalry developed by men like Yamaga Sokō (1622–85). Hikozaemon's treatment is individual and sentimental rather than philosophic, but it shows that with a prospect of peaceful years men had begun to consider the future of the samurai class in a new society.

Masanobu and helped him when he was in trouble for taking part in a religious uprising in Mikawa. It was another Ōkubo who introduced Masanobu to Ieyasu as a skilled falconer. Masanobu was not much of a warrior, but he displayed a political acumen that encouraged Ieyasu to make use of his talents. He was frank in the expression of his opinions, and Ieyasu was wise enough not to take offence but to trust him entirely. He was of great assistance in deciding upon the transfers and confiscations of fiefs which followed Sekigahara. He himself was without greed, and never rose beyond 20,000 koku as a small daimyo. He argued that the Fudai daimyos, the hereditary vassals, who served Ieyasu should be rewarded with important duties, rather than being given lavish allowances. He died in 1616, ravaged by syphilis.

Some Fudai daimyos were discontented, among them the most handsomely rewarded, Ii Naomasa and Honda Tadakatsu. They were proud of their lineage and despised the upstarts with whom Ieyasu was surrounding himself. The upstarts, however, continued to flourish, and Masanobu's son, Masazumi, followed in his father's footsteps. He attended Ieyasu in Sumpu, and took part in discussions of policy. He is said to have deserved a share in the credit for plans to destroy the house of Toyotomi. He naturally aroused envy among the proud military heroes, and they plotted against him. He died in exile. His family's misfortunes were regarded as condign punishment for ingratitude to Ōkubo Tadachika, their generous patron.

After Ieyasu's death the organization of the Bakufu began to lose its makeshift character. It could no longer be described as cut on the village headman pattern (shōya-jitate) or even the provincial pattern (Mikawa-jitate). Ieyasu's former comrades and associates were growing old—he had died at the age of seventy-five—and the appointments held by his intimates lapsed. New offices were created and filled, and by 1634 were clearly defined. Doi Toshikatsu and the two Sakais, Tadakatsu and Tadayo, remained as "elders," but their juniors, Matsudaira Nobutsuna, Abe Tadakatsu, and others, occupied key positions under them. A new bureaucracy was taking shape.

It is of interest in this context to quote from a document which shows what kind of ideas about government—its essence and its forms—prevailed in the minds of Ieyasu's advisers, who cannot have foreseen the complex system which developed after his death.

The document, a study of the principles of government, is attributed to Honda Masanobu on the authority of scholars like Kinoshita Junan, Arai Hakuseki, and Muro Kyūsō. It is known as *Honsa Roku,* and is said to have been drawn up at the request of Ieyasu.[8] A rather long-winded and prosy essay, its line of argument is that good government depends first of all upon the character of the ruler, who must always strive for self-improvement. Masanobu condemns as causes of disorder such systems of ethics as Buddhism, Shintō, and "modern" Confucianism, and goes back to the pristine virtue of the Sage Kings of Chinese antiquity. He makes the obvious point that greed, ambition, and other vices are obstacles to good government. He gives some examples of what is needed for the purposes of good government, dwelling upon the fact that high officials must not seek popularity. Their duty is to serve the state faithfully and unselfishly. Officials such as stewards and treasurers must combine great ability with integrity. They must prevent waste.

There is a good deal more of this kind of homily, and although it is commonplace there is no doubt that Masanobu, himself a righteous man, was convinced of the importance of high moral standards. He saw the dangers of vanity and corruption, those two ruinous evils in public and private life.

After some observations on the duties of the military class and the choice of men to hold important offices he turns to the treatment of the peasants. It is here that there occurs the often-cited statement: "The peasants (hyakushō) are the foundation of the State. There is a rule for governing them. Each man must have the boundaries of his fields clearly marked, and an estimate must be made of the amount needed for his consumption. The rest must be paid as tax. It is right that the peasants should be so treated that they have neither too much nor too little. Further, during the months of October and November [after the harvest] they must work on the roads, being maintained at official expense. But no other corvée should be imposed upon them, for if they are fatigued their crops will be poor."

He condemns luxury and says that such pastimes as *cha no yu* (the tea ceremony) are incompatible with good government. He gives an interesting brief sketch of Japanese history to show how after the honest and efficient administration of the Hōjō Regents there was a sad deterioration. The Ashikaga Shōguns were followed by Hosokawa, who had some understanding of government; but after his death the country fell into the hands of men like Nobunaga and the Taikō, great soldiers

---

[8] *Honsa* stands for *Honda Sado* (no Kami); *roku*, of course, means a chronicle. Another work attributed to him, *Ji-kokka kongen* ("on the Foundations of Government"), is of doubtful authenticity.

but ignorant of the Way (the moral law). They had no ideals. They led luxurious lives and oppressed the people.

It is not easy to trace Masanobu's influence in the legislation of the early days of the Bakufu, although it is most probable that he suggested the ordinances of 1611 and 1612 defining the duties of the vassals of the Tokugawa family. He certainly stood for impartial judgment in matters of controversy. He may also have suggested the general lines of the Buke Sho-Hatto; but it is clear that he saw the future as a simple, improved version of the past.

3. *Ieyasu's Character*

Ieyasu was loyal to both Nobunaga and Hideyoshi, but he was always careful to preserve some degree of independence. His decision not to send a contingent to take part in the invasion of Korea, though it may not have angered Hideyoshi, nevertheless showed a bold and independent spirit. It gave him a great advantage, for he was strong when other important vassals were suffering severe losses.

He was at first reluctant to move to Yedo at Hideyoshi's instance after the fall of Odawara, since it meant the loss of his former provinces, especially of Mikawa, his own home and the breeding ground of the Mikawa bushi. But he knew that he must bide his time, and patience was one of his virtues, matched only by his far-sighted determination.

Quite apart from his political wisdom, he was both a good fighter and a born strategist. He was a skilful archer, a man of robust constitution who enjoyed field sports and scarcely knew what illness meant. At the age of sixty he was extremely active, and enjoyed hunting, riding, swimming, or any other hard exercise. .His body was small, but well-developed, and he was inclined to corpulence—in this and other respects resembling Napoleon.[9]

As to his generalship there can be no doubt. He gave Hideyoshi a taste of his quality at Komakiyama and Nagakute. He is said to have fought over forty-five battles in his lifetime. He did not win them all, but at Mikatagahara he defeated a force twice as great as his own, led by Takeda Shingen, a warrior mistakenly reputed to have been the greatest commander of his day.

He was a frugal man, but devoted much attention to the accumulation of wealth. His eastern provinces were valuable, and his investments in trade and industry brought him immense profits. He admired

---

[9] He had no serious illness until after the age of seventy. Before that he suffered once or twice from boils, and once from a mild venereal complaint.

the character of Yoritomo, and read with care the *Azuma Kagami,* or "Mirror of the East," the Kamakura Bakufu's official record of the period from Yoritomo's revolt in 1180 to 1266. He intoned the Nembutsu (Buddha-calling) regularly.

The common traditional view of Ieyasu's achievement is that he ate the pie which Nobunaga had prepared and Hideyoshi had baked. Like most apophthegms, this is only half true. Ieyasu certainly built upon foundations laid by his predecessors, whose military exploits had brought about some measure of national unity, but it was Ieyasu who completed the process by a combination of military and civil talent amounting to genius. His will was as strong as theirs, his political judgment was much sounder, and in action, where they were often hasty and violent, he was cool, patient, and far-sighted. Yet his character is not attractive, for it lacked the warmth of his late sinful colleagues.

4. *The Shōgun and the Throne*

One of the first administrative orders of Hidetada on behalf of Ieyasu was a regulation of the powers and duties of the Emperor and the Court. This was of no great practical importance, seeing that the Shōgun's powers were such as he chose to assume; but it was desirable to formulate the relation of the Bakufu to the Throne, if only as a warning against conspiracy by the nobility.

There had been an order communicated in 1613 by Ieyasu to Itakura Shigenori, one of his officers (the Shoshi-dai or Deputy) in Kyoto, in which brief rules were laid down for the conduct of the nobles. They must devote themselves to study and behave with decorum, eschewing loose living, especially gambling and association with disorderly characters. Disobedience would be punished by exile.

A much more detailed ordinance was issued in 1615, soon after the fall of Ōsaka, when Ieyasu's position was impregnable. Known as *Kinchū Kuge Sho-Hatto* (Rules for the Palace and the Court), it is of great interest, because it shows clearly the attitude of the Tokugawa Shōguns to the reigning Emperor and his nobles. The principal points in its seventeen articles may be summarized as follows:

The Emperor [to emphasize his birth but not his office, he is called Tenshi, not Tennō] is to devote himself to learning. He must follow the teaching of the classics and uphold the tradition of poetry.

Correct gradations of rank must be observed. The Great Ministers [Dajō-Daijin, Sa-Daijin, and U-Daijin] are to have precedence over princes of the blood royal.

The Court ranks and offices of members of the military houses are to be additional to those held by the nobles.

Whatever their standing at Court, offenders shall be banished. The scale of offences shall accord with the terms of the ancient codes [ritsuryō].

Ecclesiastics of the highest rank [Daisōjō] must be appointed according to precedent, but a man of great talent, even if he is of the common people, may be raised to the rank below.

It will be seen that although attention is paid to the dignity of the Sovereign and his nobles, they are deprived of almost all but ceremonial functions. The hereditary claims of the great families are recognized, but there is no freedom of action. All from the Emperor down are at the mercy of the Shōgun and his officers. Nevertheless the Emperor is regarded as the fountain of honour, but it is a fountain of which the Bakufu directs the flow. The revenues of the Throne had fallen very low in Ashikaga times, but they were raised by Hideyoshi and Ieyasu in turn.

In addition to its onerous regulations the Bakufu took steps to strengthen its control by arranging marriages, notably that of Hidetada's youngest child, Kazuko, to the Emperor Go-Mizunoo in 1620. At this time military "aides" were assigned to the Emperor and to retired Emperors, to keep a close watch on the Court.

5. The Shōgun and the Vassals

Although Ieyasu was prompt to resolve those disputes among vassals which were of direct concern to him, he left most such matters to the Hyōjōsho, a judicial council which consisted of a number of his trusted officers. When he handed the title of Shōgun to his son Hidetada, he enjoined the Council to be loyal to both Hidetada and himself, and to judge all suits with complete impartiality. In 1614 the members of the Council subscribed to an oath by which they swore to pronounce sentence on any person whatever—even their own parents or relatives— found guilty of treason against the Shōgun or his family or of any breach of his ordinances. The signatories were Sakai, Doi, and other high officers.

In 1615 Doi, Sakai, and Andō sent a letter to Matsudaira Nagato no Kami (the western daimyo Mōri, upon whom Ieyasu had conferred the name of Matsudaira) instructing him to destroy all the castles in his fief except one, which was to be kept as his residence. Similar orders, he was informed, were being sent to all provinces. This was a cardinal feature of Bakufu policy and the sort of measure which, one might suppose, would be announced in a solemn edict; but the simple method here employed is characteristic of the early days of the Bakufu, when the government of the country was likened to the rule of a village by its headman.

After Ieyasu's death in 1616, however, the organization of the Bakufu proceeded apace. The Bakufu being the headquarters of the Tokugawa government, it was necessary first to decide upon the rank and function of the various branches of the Tokugawa family and to determine the classification of their feudatories. The principal Tokugawa families were the Three Houses (Go-Sanke) of Owari, Kii, and Mito provinces, respectively the domains of Ieyasu's sons Yoshinao, Yorinobu, and Yorifusa. Below them in rank came the cadet branches known as Go-Kamon (the Kinsmen), established after Ieyasu's death and granted the name of Matsudaira. Among them were Hideyasu, a son of Ieyasu, with a fief of 670,000 koku, and Hoshina, a son of Hidetada, with a fief of 230,000 koku. Additions to this class were made by later Shōguns.

The vassals of the Tokugawa were of two kinds, the Fudai and the Tozama. The distinction between them depended upon their relationship with Ieyasu after the death of Hideyoshi. Those who held the eastern seaboard provinces, as well as others who had followed Ieyasu at Sekigahara, were regarded as hereditary vassals and styled Fudai. Those who had belonged to the Toyotomi faction but had submitted to Ieyasu after Sekigahara and the fall of Ōsaka were regarded as vassals who though presumed loyal must be kept under surveillance. These were called Tozama ("Outside Lords").

The Fudai daimyos were for the most part holders of fiefs of 50,000 koku or less. Exceptional cases were those of the Ii family at Hikone (150,000 koku, later raised to 250,000), the Sakai, the Ōkubo, and a few others who had more than 100,000 koku; but the average revenue was about 50,000. The number of Fudai vassals was from time to time increased by promotions. It was 37 before Sekigahara, and reached 145 at the end of the eighteenth century.

The Tozama, or Outside Lords, were powerful chieftains who had been neutral or hostile to Ieyasu after the death of Hideyoshi. They included the great houses of Maeda (1,020,000 koku), Shimazu of Satsuma (770,000 koku), Hosokawa, Kuroda, Asano, and Daté, all of whom had territories in provinces remote from Yedo. As a matter of policy the Fudai were placed in strategic situations where they could keep watch upon the Tozama and threaten their rear or flanks should they begin to move troops; but the Fudai were frequently transferred from province to province lest they should develop local connexions unfavourable to the Bakufu.

It was a cardinal feature of Bakufu policy to guard against any increase in the strength of Outside Lords and indeed whenever possible to impose upon them duties which would weaken them. The custom of exacting a period of residence in Yedo was one of the methods by which the Bakufu could involve rich Tozama daimyos in great expense while at the same time keeping them under observation. These visits were at first voluntary, and were paid by a number of daimyos from central and western Japan who travelled to Yedo to declare their allegiance to Ieyasu at the time of his appointment as Shōgun in the spring of 1603. A letter from Kuroda Nagamasa to a kinsman describes a visit to Yedo in that year, when he was received and entertained by Hidetada. He accompanied Ieyasu to Kyoto for the ceremony of investiture as Sei-i-Tai-Shōgun, and then returned to Yedo, where he was received in the castle by Ieyasu.

The regular attendance of vassals had its remoter origin in the system of political hostages, of which the first example under the rule of the Tokugawa Bakufu was the journey to Yedo in 1600 as a hostage of the mother of Maeda Toshinaga, the most powerful of the Tozama daimyos and a man greatly mistrusted by Ieyasu. Thereafter the vassals were encouraged to journey to Yedo to declare fealty; and the practice, once voluntary, became obligatory. It was laid down in specific terms in the amended version of the Buke Sho-Hatto issued in 1635. The relevant clauses provide that vassals shall establish residences in Yedo, which they are to occupy each year, or in some cases in alternate years, for a period of four months, leaving their wives and children in Yedo when they returned to their fiefs. This system of "alternate attendance" (Sankin Kōtai) was an effective method of keeping the daimyos under observation. It also placed a heavy burden upon the wealthy Tozama, who were expected to keep up a grand style.

The construction and repair of castles for the Bakufu was one of the tasks imposed upon daimyos by the Bakufu with the object of reducing their financial strength. Thus the daimyos of seven adjacent provinces were called upon to assist Ii Naokatsu in building the great castle of Hikone,[10] which was designed to hold down the Home Provinces and surrounding territory; and during the years from 1602 to 1614 the leading daimyos had been called upon to contribute labour and materials for the repair or enlargement not only of Bakufu strongholds but also

---

[10] It took the place of Ishida Mitsunari's castle of Sawayama.

of a number of Imperial residences. Work on the castle at Yedo went on for ten years, while much effort was expended on Fushimi, Sumpu, Nagoya, and other great edifices. Certain public works, such as the construction of roads and harbours, were also undertaken by vassals under orders from Yedo.

The Hatamoto. Below the daimyo in the feudal scale stood the Hatamoto or Bannerman. The name (which originally stood for the headquarters of a commander in the field) came to signify the bodyguard of a general. In the Yedo period the hatamoto were those minor vassals under the direct command of the Shōgun whose revenues were less than 10,000 koku—usually much less. When Ieyasu was in Mikawa they formed the mainstay of his armies, for they owed him a personal allegiance. Their number is not exactly known, but after 1635, when rules were laid down for their duties, their strength was about 5,000. They had a right of direct access to the Shōgun. When they were called to active service by him, they had to join the colours with 13 men for the first 500 koku of their revenue, and a similar number for each additional 500 koku. It was estimated that they could put into the field a total force of 80,000 men. This figure included a lower grade of direct retainer, the unfeoffed samurai called Go-kenin, who numbered about 17,000.

The Bakufu disapproved of any close association between the lower grade hatamoto and the peasants working on their land. For fear of uprising, or even of the formation of a class of local gentry like the kokujin, who had caused trouble to previous governments, it was the policy of most daimyos to withdraw the hatamoto of less than 500 koku from the land by offering them a fixed stipend. This was as a rule willingly accepted, and many of the hatamoto took to residence in the castle towns, where they created a new problem, since being unemployed they tended to make mischief.

Hatamoto of the highest rank had a revenue of 3,000 koku or even more. They had to take part in the alternate attendance, and a number of them obtained responsible official posts. The process of withdrawing hatamoto and go-kenin from the land had gone so far by 1722 that only about one-tenth of the total number (estimated at 22,000) were not drawing stipends. The land of the hatamoto thus withdrawn was then incorporated in Bakufu domains.

6. The Administrative Machine

The administrative system, as we have seen, was built up gradually. It took its more or less permanent form under the rule of the third Shōgun, Iemitsu (1623–51). For the convenience of readers, however, it seems best to anticipate the later additions and to set forth in this preliminary chapter the main features of the system as it was developed under the first three Shōguns.

The principal offices were the Tairō, or Great Elders; the Rōjū, or Council of Elders; and the Hyōjōsho, or Judicial Council. Their respective functions were as follows:

The Tairō. The function of the Tairō, or Great Elders, was to advise upon high policy and to act as Regents during the minority of a Shōgun. In Hideyoshi's day there had been five such elders (Go-Tairō), but under the Yedo Bakufu the number was reduced to three (in 1633), then to two, and later to only one. The first holders of this office were Doi Toshikatsu, Sakai Tadakatsu, and Sakai Tadayo. Subsequent appointments were not made regularly, but only for some special purpose. On such occasions an experienced Fudai daimyo of not less than 100,000 koku was selected.

The Rōjū. The functions of the Rōjū were both advisory and administrative. Under Ieyasu there were only two Rōjū. There was little change under Hidetada, but under Iemitsu, in a thorough revision of the system of government, their number was increased to five and later reduced to four. Their functions were clearly defined in an ordinance of 1634, which may be summarized as follows:

1. Relations with the Throne, the Court, and the Prince-Abbots.
2. Supervision of daimyos of 10,000 koku and above.
3. Prescribing the forms of documents in official communications.
4. Supervising the internal affairs of the Shōgun's domains.
5. Gold and silver coinage.
6. Public works.
7. Enfeoffments.
8. The control of monasteries and shrines.
9. The compilation of maps, charts, etc.

The four Rōjū served in rotation, each for one month. They communicated with the Shōgun through the Soba-yōnin, chamberlains in personal attendance upon him. They have sometimes been described as constituting a sort of cabinet, but such analogies are misleading, for when there is an elaborate organization of bureaux and councils, military men in authority are apt to find short cuts to action.

The Hyōjōsho was a council composed of the Rōjū and certain Commissioners (Bugyō) in charge of executive departments of the Bakufu. Such were the Machi-Bugyō (City Commissioners); the Jisha-Bugyō

(Commissioners for Monasteries and Shrines); the Kanjō-Bugyō; and the Ō-Metsuke, the Chief Inspectors or Censors. The function of the Hyōjōsho was partly administrative and partly judicial, since at this time there was no clear distinction between the executive and legal functions. It might be described as the Supreme Court.

Lower in the scale came certain officials with specific rather than general functions. They were the Wakadoshiyori, the Ō-Metsuke, the Jisha-Bugyō, the Yedo Machi-Bugyō, the Kanjō-Bugyō, and the officers of various local government organs.

The Wakadoshiyori were first appointed (the date is uncertain) in 1631. As their title ("Junior Elders") indicates, they were subordinate to the Rōjū. In 1634 an instruction was sent to them, stating their duties. Usually from four to six in number, they were to supervise the hatamoto; to control craftsmen and physicians; to inspect public works and buildings; and to regulate the activities of persons holding office in the great castles of Kyoto, Ōsaka, Suruga, and elsewhere. They were also to keep watch on vassals (other than hatamoto) of less than 10,000 koku of revenue. Their appointment was irregular until 1662.

The Ō-Metsuke were officials who may be described as Chief Inspectors or Censors. They were intelligence officers whose duty it was to keep watch on all daimyos. They were directly responsible to the Rōjū. There were four Ō-Metsuke, and under them sixteen subordinates called Metsuke, who were responsible to the Wakadoshiyori. It was part of their duty to keep watch on the hatamoto.

The Jisha-Bugyō were Commissioners, four in number, responsible for the control of religious establishments, both Buddhist and Shintō, and for the supervision of the clergy.

The Yedo Machi-Bugyō were Commissioners, two in number, responsible for city government, police and justice.

The Kanjō-Bugyō were Finance Commissioners, four in number, who supervised the administration of Tokugawa domains. They also dealt with suits or petitions from the eight Kantō provinces.

Local Government Organs. Since the country consisted of the direct Tokugawa domains and the self-governing fiefs of vassals, there was limited scope for local government officials appointed by Yedo. There were four officers called Gundai, who administered Tokugawa estates in certain key provinces, and there were forty or fifty officers, called Daikan, or Deputies, exercising similar powers in other Tokugawa estates. Apart from these there were Governors of castles, who, in Ōsaka, Kyoto, and Sumpu, went by the title of Jōdai.

Local government posts in the strict sense were those of the Shoshi-dai in Kyoto, who was the military governor of the city, with jurisdiction in the Home Provinces; and of the Bugyō or Commissioners in other important towns, such as Nagasaki, Yamada, Nara, and Nikkō. All such posts were held by Fudai daimyos or by men of the rank of hatamoto. No Tozama daimyos were employed.

CHAPTER II

HIDETADA AND IEMITSU

1. *Hidetada, 1616–23*

HIDETADA nominally succeeded to the office of Shōgun in 1605, but he did not decide policy during the lifetime of Ieyasu. From 1616, however, he proceeded boldly with the consolidation of the Bakufu by the "squeeze" of certain great feudatories, including his younger brother Matsudaira Tadateru; the powerful daimyos Fukushima Masanori and Honda Masanobu; and his nephew Matsudaira Tadanori. The total revenue escheated by Hidetada amounted, as we have seen, to more than four and a half million koku.

Hidetada did not remain long in office. He retired in favour of his son Iemitsu in 1623, but retained authority until his death in 1632. While in power he reaffirmed and developed certain important policies introduced during Ieyasu's last years. He repeated in 1616 the ban upon Christianity and the orders confining the entry of foreign ships other than Chinese to the ports of Nagasaki and Hirado. In 1622 he ordered the execution of fifty-five Christians in Nagasaki, and in 1628 he issued a similar decree. He also banned the importation of books concerning the Christian religion. He continued the organization of the Bakufu, as, for instance, by instituting the appointment of Wakado-shiyori.

Although he seems to have been firm in his conduct of public affairs, he was bullied by his wife, who favoured her second son as Hidetada's successor. Thanks, however, to the determination of the wet-nurse of Takechiyo, the first-born, Ieyasu had ordered that he should not be passed over. He succeeded in 1623 as the third Shōgun, Iemitsu; and the wet-nurse, O-Fuku, acquired much influence in the Shōgun's Court, where she was on familiar terms with the leading Bakufu officers of the day. She somehow contrived to obtain the Court title of Tsubone, or Lady-in-Waiting.

2. *Iemitsu, 1623–51*

Iemitsu while in office showed considerable self-confidence, conducting himself as if to the manner born, especially in his attitude towards the great Tozama vassals, whom even Ieyasu had treated with some measure of amiability. According to the Abbot Tenkai he was intelligent and determined, but difficult to approach. He had a certain showy side to his character. While ordering daimyo and hatamoto to economize, and while expelling from his service persons whose dress was especially gay, he maintained a fantastically numerous suite in the inner apartments of the Yedo Castle—so numerous that after his death some three thousand superfluous attendants, mostly women, were dismissed. He was lavish in his expenditure. Once when a number of hatamoto petitioned for loans, he ordered the contents of some chests full of gold in his treasury to be distributed among them, saying that the gold was doing no good shut up in a vault. This incident is recorded less as an example of his generosity than as evidence of his ignorance of money matters, for unlike his calculating grandfather he could not understand the simple arithmetic which his accountants tried to explain.

Whether Iemitsu deserves credit for the administrative measures introduced during his term of office is a matter of small concern. It was a period of importance in the development of Bakufu policy, and he was no doubt guided by capable men, such as the Tairō Doi Toshikatsu and the leading Bakufu members of the Council of Elders. His behaviour is of interest chiefly for the light it throws on the disciplinary powers which the Shōgun exercised over the vassals. One of Iemitsu's first acts was the punishment of his younger brother Tadanaga (Kunimatsu) for outrageous treatment of his vassals. Tadanaga was stripped of his great fief of half a million koku. He was probably insane, and this drastic action was taken not by way of retribution for a crime but rather because the first three Shōguns had no mercy for a daimyo guilty of high-handed action. They were always on the lookout for insubordinate behaviour which might be the first step to active disobedience. It was for such reasons that Iemitsu announced that no special favours would be granted to the Outside Lords, who had been treated with some show of courtesy by his predecessors. In 1634 Iemitsu led an army of over 300,000 men to Kyoto to impress the Court and to remind the Tozama of his military strength.

In 1632 the rights and duties of the Hatamoto (Bannermen) were laid down. They were to cultivate the warlike arts; to keep to their station in life; to avoid gambling and extravagance; not to join factions; not to engage in trade; and not to nominate heirs without permission. In 1633 the rules for military service were made stricter than those that applied in 1600. For instance a daimyo of 100,000 koku had (when ordered) to mobilize the following: 350 men with firearms; 60 men with bows; 150 men with spears; 20 men with banners; 170 mounted men; and 2,150 foot soldiers.

It was as part of the policy of keeping the daimyos under control that in 1635 a new version of the Buke Sho-Hatto, or Rules for the Military Houses, was issued from Yedo. It was framed in more specific terms than the original ordinance of 1615. One of its important changes was a provision making the alternate atendance of feudal lords at the Shōgun's Court compulsory instead of optional.

At about the same time (1634) the organization of the Bakufu was strengthened by the establishment of elders (Rōjū and Wakadoshiyori) and Commissioners (Bugyō) and by the formation of the Judicial Council, the Hyōjōshū. This was equivalent to the Monchūjo in the Kamakura system. In 1636 its Council Chamber, the Yedo Hyōjōsho, was established as a permanent office inside the castle enclosure.

The Bakufu continued to reduce the authority and even the dignity of the Throne after the death of Ieyasu. In 1627 great offence was given to the Emperor, Go-Mizunoo, whose powers had already been severely diminished by the ordinances of 1615. Appointments to the highest ecclesiastical rank and office had for long been a prerogative of the Crown, but in 1627 the Kyoto Shoshi-dai, under orders from Yedo, cancelled a number of such appointments and withdrew the Emperor's power to select and nominate candidates for the "purple robe."

Go-Mizunoo was deeply wounded and threatened to abdicate in protest, but the Bakufu, far from giving way, deprived some seventy prelates of their titles and vestments. Go-Mizunoo was helpless, and on abdicating in 1629 expressed his despair in a verse which may be translated:

> O Land of Reed Plains,
> If you must grow rank and wild
> Then grow wild at will,
> For this world is grown a wilderness,
> In which the True Path can no longer be seen.[1]

This is an interesting political document, recognizing the bitter truth that the Imperial House was at the mercy of the warlords and that righteous government was at an end.

Go-Mizunoo was humiliated in several ways. His abdication was forced, and he can hardly have been happy about the matter of the

---

[1] The translation is kindly furnished by Robert Brower and Earl Miner. The text is:

> Ashihara yo
> Shigeraba shigere
> Ono ga mama
> Totemo michi aru
> Yo ni araba koso

succession. He had at first intended to name his son by Hidetada's daughter to succeed him, but when the young man died, he was obliged to name the Princess Oki-ko, another child of the same marriage, and she succeeded in 1630 as the Empress Myōshō, the first female sovereign since the Empress Shōtoku (d. 770). Thus the Throne was occupied by a grand-daughter of a Tokugawa Shōgun.

It was not, however, the intention of Iemitsu entirely to humiliate the Court or to deprive the Throne of all prestige, for that would have offended many loyal subjects, in the military class as well as in the priesthood. (Despite their superior power, the leaders of the military society were anxious to be received at Court, and indeed insistent.) When he arrived in Kyoto with his great army in 1634, he gave fairly liberal assistance to the Imperial family and to a number of Court nobles. He raised the land revenue of the retired Emperor from 7,000 to 10,000 koku, and was lavish in his gifts to the citizens of Kyoto, where he wished to make a good impression.

From this point on, though, the Throne had no political power, but only the right to confer Court ranks and the duty to perform the traditional ceremonies throughout the year. Since the Throne was short of funds, the condition of the nobility was poor. The nobleman of the highest rank was the head of the Konoye family, and his income was about 2,000 koku, while most of the other noble families, numbering about one hundred and thirty, were in a state of indigence and reduced to earning a livelihood by teaching their respective arts or crafts, such as painting, calligraphy, music, poetry, and embroidery, or by giving instruction in deportment. More profitable in the long run was the marriage of a daughter to a wealthy daimyo.

Further events during the rule of Iemitsu are described in the three following chapters, which deal with the growth of urban societies; the persecution of Christians; foreign trade; and the seclusion policy which by 1640 closed the country to all but a limited quantity of imports and a handful of Dutch merchants.

CHAPTER III

THE FEUDAL SOCIETY

1. *The Social Order*

THE SOCIAL SYSTEM of the Tokugawa government was based upon a rigid division of classes. In principle no man could rise above the class in which he was born, for it was the purpose of the rulers by legislating against change to found a self-perpetuating state.

This was by no means a new concept. It was implicit in the policy of Hideyoshi, who by his Sword Hunt (a measure of disarmament decreed in 1588) fixed the separation of the farmer from the soldier; but in the Tokugawa regime the distinction between classes, though not strict at first, was most definite by the time of Iemitsu, the third Shōgun. It was regarded as hereditary and unchangeable.

The four classes were in descending order the Soldier, the Farmer, the Artisan, and the Trader. Of these the soldiers numbered less than one-tenth—probably not much more than one-twentieth—of the total population, and the peasants about eight-tenths. In Japan's war-ridden Middle Ages it had been natural that the mass of the people should have been divided into warriors and producers, but the division went further back, to the Yōrō and Taihō codes of the eighth century, which adopted Chinese social groupings of a similar nature. A strong feeling for rank and social status is a marked characteristic of the Japanese people throughout their history.

There were gradations within each class, so that there was room for some social movement, though the division between classes was not easily disregarded. The military class included all members of arms-bearing families, from the great warlords to the poorest samurai.

Below the military class came first, as we have seen, the cultivators of soil, a class which included the poor peasant labourer and the well-to-do farmer. In the peaceful times that followed the fall of Ōsaka the peasant was safe in his holding, but his life was hard and he was subject to oppression by a harsh landlord. The attitude of the ruling class was grimly expressed by an observation attributed to the Tairō Doi Toshikatsu, who was the greatest man in the land after the Shōgun. In 1640 he is said to have visited his estate after an absence of ten years and, finding the villagers in well-built houses instead of the hovels which he remembered, to have exclaimed: "These people are too comfortable. They must be more heavily taxed."

Since the mediaeval economy of Japan was agrarian, the peasant was the most numerous element in the population and, it might be argued, the most important. Certainly Japanese history cannot be understood without some knowledge of the part played by the great rural communities of which the workers on the land were the principal members.

The general trend of the policy of the military class was to keep the peasant on the land, and to prevent him from leaving the particular fields which he cultivated. The early Tokugawa legislation was not severe, and it showed some concern for protection of the peasant against oppressive landlords. An order issued by the Yedo magistrates in 1603 laid it down that a peasant might leave his land if the steward in a Tokugawa domain, or the landlord of a private domain, should be guilty of "excessive" conduct. In such cases the peasant must before leaving make arrangement for the payment of tax due. He was then free to live where he chose. A second clause in this order prohibited the use of violence by a landlord against a peasant, and ordered that disputes about tax must be taken to a magistrate's court for settlement.

It is clear that the treatment of peasants tended to grow more severe, although some landlords used persuasion rather than force. The Bakufu took a moderate line. In 1643 an order was issued which contained the following interesting clause: "If the punishment inflicted by a Steward or Daikan [Deputy] is wrongful and unbearable, the peasants may leave as soon as their tax payments are completed, and they may reside in a neighbouring village, where they are to be free from interference by those officers." But it is clear that by this time the orders of the Bakufu did not prevent the ill-treatment of peasants by harsh landlords. Absconsion of peasants became more and more frequent, and we find, for example, in the year 1642 a law (hōrei) issued by the daimyo of Okayama which places the responsibility for absconsion upon the Five-Man Groups (Gonin-gumi),[1] and obliges the village to cultivate the deserted plots.

Not all absconders were driven by ill-treatment, but most of them saw prospects of less back-breaking employment in the towns. They thus created a class of manual labourers or servants, which grew in size as the peacetime economy expanded, or if they could develop some special skill they were absorbed into the third social class, that of the artisans.

The artisans—the workers in various handicrafts—were regarded as

[1] Gonin-gumi were groups of citizens or villagers who were entrusted with keeping the peace in town and country.

lower in the social scale than the farmers, but those who possessed special knowledge and capacity were treated with some respect, particularly if their craft was of direct service to the military class. The ar-
mourers in general, the swordsmiths in particular, were given special
treatment—well paid and well housed—by the Bakufu and the great
daimyos. The carpenter, too, was high in the scale, and we learn, for
instance, that the chief carpenter in Kyoto in 1698, one Nakai Mondo,
was given a stipend of 500 koku and allowed to wear one sword, thus
being half-way to the status of a samurai. Similar rights were granted
to specialists, such as goldsmiths, silversmiths, artists, clothiers, and
even confectioners who directly served the Shōgun's court.

The ordinary workers were not so fortunate. Those settled in a
castle town usually worked for the daimyo with little salary, in return
for the privilege of an assured market for their goods. Below them
came the journeymen, workers on call for a daily wage. These artisans
formed guilds to protect their interests—one guild for one trade, such
as guilds of carpenters, sawyers, smiths, tilers, masons, plasterers, and
so forth. Their system of apprenticeship was severe, but efficient.

Tradesmen—merchants and shopkeepers—came lowest in the social
scale,[2] but as the economy of Japan developed and expanded in times
of peace, merchants in particular were to gain increasing power, until
by the eighteenth century they were able, by their financial strength,
to break down barriers in the social structure which the Tokugawa
Shōguns had erected. By then the rich merchants were employed regularly as government contractors, and their services were indispensable
to the members of the military class. Even trade guilds, to which the
government was in principle opposed, were used to collect certain taxes.

It should be added that there were multiple gradations in each class,
from the daimyo down to the lowest rank of samurai; from the rich
farmer down to the day labourer; from the skilled artisan down to the
apprentice; from the rich merchant down to the peddler. All such distinctions were scrupulously observed, precedence and modes of address
at a meeting of village elders, for example, being matters of great concern. The complex social hierarchy demanded a strict etiquette in social
relations, which was burdensome but had the merit of encouraging
courteous behaviour.

Although the four classes here described included most of the population, there were certain persons or groups who did not fit into the
official categories. We have already noticed the floating population of

---

[2] Except for the "hinin," or "not men," who were outcasts.

manual labourers—the porters, navvies, boatmen, palanquin bearers, and others who did work requiring strength rather than skill. They were as a rule men who, like the absconding peasants, had escaped the obligations of their class either from preference or from necessity. But a more striking departure from social convention is that of members of the military class who, through misfortune or through discontent, rebelled against the established authority of their day. These were the masterless samurai known as rōnin, figures in feudal history who deserve special study.

2. *The Rōnin*

Although the ordinances of the Tokugawa Shōguns placed members of the military class under strict discipline both in Bakufu service and in all feudal domains, there was one category which did not respond to systematic treatment.

The process of organizing the feudal state had an unfortunate sequel, an internal contradiction which was revealed by the problem of the Rōnin, the unemployed samurai. The problem began with the distinction made by Hideyoshi between the soldier and the farmer, a distinction which debarred the soldiers from living in the villages. This was part of the purpose of Hideyoshi's land surveys; for he wanted the farms to furnish national revenue and not to support a class of local warrior-landlord who might foment rebellion. A more immediate cause, however, was the reduction or abolition of the fiefs of Ieyasu's antagonists. Since the rōnin thus created had as a rule no local attachment, they raised no urgent problem until after the battle of Sekigahara, because so long as the wars continued they could follow their calling. But after Sekigahara the problem became acute, since the abolition or reduction of fiefs and the transfer of daimyos now took place on a large scale. The number of soldiers expelled, or otherwise deprived of masters and livelihood, is said to have reached 500,000.

This great number is not surprising. In the fifty years from 1601 to 1650 the aggregate revenue from confiscated fiefs amounted to over 12 million koku, which gives an idea of how many daimyos were moved. The Tokugawa Shōguns had a voracious appetite for land, and they seized upon most specious excuses for confiscating fiefs, without regard for the welfare of their inhabitants. At one time, for instance, they had refused to recognize the adoption of an heir by a daimyo or hatamoto in his last years, and thus they were able to exercise the right of confiscation in cases of intestacy. On this account alone some sixty fiefs with a total revenue of five million koku fell to the Shōgun.

By such devices the number of samurai thrown out of employment was swollen, as is clear from the fact that when, in 1651, the Yedo government at last decided that it must take drastic action to reduce the number of rōnin, one of its first steps was to moderate the practice of escheatment and to recognize the adoption of an heir by a daimyo or a hatamoto not more than fifty years of age. All previous measures had been ineffective.

In the early days of the Yedo Bakufu, not long after the fall of Ōsaka, the Shōgun's council had already been alarmed by the difficulty of controlling the soldiers who, now out of employment, were restless and inclined to make trouble. About 100,000 men are said to have fought on the Toyotomi side, and since their casualties are reckoned at 30,000, there were 70,000 in the Kinai, or Home Provinces, alone, mostly in Kyoto, all hoping and some praying for more disturbance in the state. The number who had fought on the Tokugawa side was even greater. All these were a constant source of anxiety to the government, some of whose members favoured a violent policy of repression, designed to solve the problem by expelling rōnin from the cities. This ruling was at first applied indiscriminately, but later only to men who showed no intention of taking service with a new master or of earning a livelihood in some kind of civil employment.

An interesting example is that of men who had been retainers of Fukushima Masanori, one of Ieyasu's most trusted generals. He was stripped of his fief of some 500,000 koku for disobeying an order of the Shōgun. His retainers were thus out of employment, but those of the highest rank were known to be capable men, and other daimyos competed for their services. Such cases were not usual, but in general a vassal taking over a vacated fief would not dismiss all its former samurai residents. Thus the real number of unemployed is difficult to estimate; but it was sufficient to embarrass the Bakufu, which at first handled the situation in a clumsy fashion, for as well as ordering expulsion from the towns, it instructed the daimyos to eject rōnin who sought employment in their fiefs. Similar action was enjoined upon monasteries and other places where such men had taken refuge for the purpose or under pretence of preparing to enter holy orders by a course of study.

An order of 1623, issued by the Shoshi-dai Itakura, referred especially to rōnin living in Kyoto, where they were most numerous. Notices were to be posted up in the city, warning people not to take such men into their service. Rōnin who had long been settled in the city in trade or other legitimate occupation, and had a wife and children living there, need not be expelled. The same rule applied to men in other regular employment, provided that they sought the approval of the city authorities. Similar rules were embodied in the Buke Sho-Hatto of 1631 and 1635, and both urban and rural officers throughout the country were instructed to refuse accommodation to strangers.

To avoid such orders a number of rōnin took refuge in the countryside, where they returned to farming, sometimes as hired workers, sometimes as small holders, in the fief to which they had originally belonged. There they were usually free from interference so long as they went unobtrusively about their own business.

Some of the Bakufu's orders were aimed at Christian rōnin, who were among the most intractable. They played a leading part in resistance to the anti-Christian policy of the government as it was carried out in Kyūshū. They were known as Amakusa Rōnin or Shimabara Rōnin after the places where they had fought against Bakufu troops in 1637. Most stubborn among them were the Christian samurai who had been followers of Hideyoshi's general, the Christian daimyo Konishi Yukinaga, whose fief was in southern Higo. They were known as Konishi Rōnin.

Despite all the oppressive measures of the Bakufu the number of rōnin was not sensibly reduced. It may even have increased, for certainly the grievances of the majority were not removed. The danger of uprising was real, as is clear from the large-scale revolt that was being planned by the rōnin under the leadership of Yui Shōsetsu, in the last years of Iemitsu.

CHAPTER IV

FOREIGN RELATIONS

1. *The Phase of Expansion*

I E Y A S U, as we have seen, was enthusiastic in the promotion of foreign trade, and the first decades of the seventeenth century saw a rapid expansion of Japanese activity abroad. The Bakufu issued licenses for the voyages of Japanese merchant vessels under the Shōgun's vermilion seal, while individual Japanese traders and other adventurers found their way to most countries in the western Pacific and beyond the Malacca Straits to Burma. The number of licenses issued between 1604 and 1635 was of the order of three hundred, or an average of ten voyages out and home each year. This was a fairly large number in a period of very slow transport by sea. In addition to these licensed carriers, Portuguese and Chinese ships carried both imports and exports, while the western daimyos, especially Shimazu, Matsuura, Nabeshima, and Ōmura, traded in licensed vessels on their own account from time to time.

The behaviour of some of the licensed ships was almost piratical. They would attack any ship or place for booty, and they were feared in all parts of South-East Asia. Several countries protested and pressed the Japanese government to take measures of control. At the request of Luzon the visits of the licensed ships were reduced to four a year. Some writers regard this action as a prelude to the exclusion policy developed in the 1640's.

The export cargoes consisted mainly of silver, copper, iron, sulphur, camphor, rice, and other grains, as well as substantial quantities of lacquer goods, fans, and similar works of handicraft. In return traders brought to Japan raw silk (the most important item), silk fabrics of high quality, cotton, shark skin, deer skin, scented woods, dyes, sugar, lead, and tin.

There were Japanese settlements in most parts of eastern Asia, from Formosa and Macao to the Moluccas, the Philippines, Borneo, Celebes and Java, Siam and the Malay Peninsula. The largest were in Luzon, Siam, and Indo-China. Many of the settlers were soldiers who could find no suitable employment at home after the wars. Among them was one Yamada Nagamasa (d. 1633), who lived in the Siamese capital of Ayuthia, where he was trusted as an adviser by the King and appointed

to high office. He was able by his military skill to suppress an outbreak
of revolt during a succession dispute.

2. *The Exclusion Policy*

This thriving and promising phase of expansion came to a surprising
end upon the issue of certain orders closing the country to foreign trade
and travel with a few strictly limited exceptions. These orders, of 1633,
1635, and 1639, are often loosely described as the three Exclusion Decrees. This is not quite accurate, since in form they were not public
notices but letters of instruction to provincial officers directing them
how to carry out the policy of the central government.

It is of especial interest to examine and compare the contents of
these documents, since they show the gradual development of a policy
of almost complete isolation—an historical phenomenon which, while
simple in appearance, is by no means easily explained. They are akin
to the anti-Christian orders issued by Ieyasu in the years 1611–14, but
they are much more drastic and much wider in scope.

The order of 1633 is in the form of a memorandum addressed to the
two Governors of Nagasaki by the Rōjū Sakai Tadakatsu and three
other high officers of the Bakufu. Its main provisions (there are seventeen articles in all) are as follows:

1. It is strictly forbidden for any vessel without a valid license to
   leave Japan for a foreign country.
2. No Japanese subject may leave for a foreign country in any vessel without a valid license.
3. Japanese subjects who have resided abroad shall be put to death
   if they return to Japan. Exception is made for those who have
   resided abroad for less than five years and have been unavoid-
   ably detained. They shall be exempt from punishment, but if
   they attempt to go abroad again they are to be put to death.

The remaining articles deal principally with the search for Christian
converts and for missionaries already in hiding in Japan or being
smuggled in at Japanese ports. The treatment of foreign vessels apply-
ing for entry is to be decided by reference to Yedo.

The order of 1635 is also addressed to the two Governors of Nagasaki. It contains seventeen articles, which resemble those of the 1633
order, but are stated in somewhat more specific terms. Thus Japanese
ships are strictly forbidden to make voyages abroad; Japanese subjects
may not go abroad, and those who are found secretly taking passage

will be put to death, the ship concerned, with its master, to be held pending reference to Yedo. The remaining articles deal chiefly with the search for Christians and with the treatment of cargo. The last article deals with the handling of consignments of raw silk from China. This was the most valuable single item of import trade, and the order provides that the Bakufu, or more specifically the Shōgun, should enjoy a monopoly of the sale of all raw silk. A further provision of interest (Article 14) lays down rules for the treatment of foreign vessels entering Japanese ports, and grants some special privilege to Portuguese and Chinese vessels.

An order of 1636 (not counted separately in our designation of three orders) is substantially the same as that of 1635, except for three clauses dealing with the children and grandchildren of foreigners by Japanese mothers. By another notice of the same year all foreign residents were ordered to move to Deshima, at the head of Nagasaki Bay, where lodgings had been prepared for them. This applied at first only to a few Portuguese, who were expelled from Japan not long afterwards (1638). Later Deshima was to become the permanent home of all Dutch residents in Japan, who moved there from Hirado in 1641. They were confined to a restricted area, and their families were obliged to leave the country.

These documentary orders of 1633–36 together completed the isolation of Japan, except for an indirect contact with the outside world through Chinese, Portuguese, and Dutch ships entering only designated ports and subject to rigorous inspection and control. It will be seen that most of the prohibitions are related to the anti-Christian policy as it had developed since the death of Ieyasu, and it should be noted that in addition to these orders issued to officials in Bakufu domains a clause in the Buke Sho-Hatto of 1635 requires all daimyos strictly to forbid the practice of Christianity in their fiefs.

The third and final measure in the exclusion policy, taken in 1639, seems to have been stimulated by a rising in Kyūshū in 1637–38 which was regarded by the Bakufu as a revolt of Japanese Christians. This was the Shimabara Revolt, in which an army of peasants from the island of Amakusa and the near-by Shimabara peninsula held out for several weeks against a powerful force mobilized by western barons at the order of the Yedo government. The slaughter was dreadful. The insurgents were for the most part poor country people, but they were joined by a number of disaffected samurai and led by some soldiers who had fought under Christian generals in the civil wars. Their total number is usually given as 37,000 and it is said that only a hundred or so escaped. These figures have been challenged, and it is probable that the number of combatants on the rebel side was not more than 20,000. The government forces are put at about 100,000, and their casualties must have amounted to 10,000 or more. They appear to have fought without much courage or skill, and they were not competently led. Their failure to achieve an easy victory seems to indicate a decline in the military spirit during the two decades after the siege of Ōsaka.

The revolt was not primarily a religious uprising, but a desperate protest against the oppressive rule of feudal lords in a remote and backward region. Yet there can be no doubt that many of the insurgents were inspired to feats of courage by the Christian faith of their leaders. Their banners were inscribed with the names of saints and with such legends as "Praise to the Blessed Sacrament." Whatever its true nature, this rebellion led to the end of overt Christian worship in Japan. It doubtless hastened and redoubled the efforts of the authorities to track down believers and to hunt out missionaries; and it must have strengthened the trend towards exclusion which was already apparent in the orders of 1633 and 1635.

The final exclusion order of 1639 was issued over the signatures of the seven senior councillors. It states that in view of the continued arrival of foreign priests and their teaching of the forbidden Christian faith, the formation of leagues plotting against the government (a capital offence), and the fact that prohibited articles from abroad can be sent to priests in hiding and their converts, no galliot (Portuguese vessel) shall from now on be admitted to a Japanese port. Should this order be disobeyed the offending vessel will be destroyed and its crew and passengers put to death. The substance of these orders is to be communicated to Chinese and Dutch vessels arriving at a Japanese port, with a promise of rewards for information regarding persons illegally entering the country.

In spite of this unqualified ban a Portuguese vessel entered Nagasaki Bay in July 1640. The 1639 expulsion had struck a serious blow at the Macao trade, and the Senate of the island had decided to take the great risk of sending a mission to Japan begging the government there to reconsider its policy. But no sooner had the vessel arrived than it was dismantled, and its crew and passengers taken into custody pending the receipt of instructions from Yedo. Early in August the reply came. It was communicated to the Portuguese envoys in a solemn and ceremonial manner. Accused of defying the laws of Japan, the envoys replied that they were not a trade mission and had brought no cargo but only a diplomatic memorial to the Japanese government. The Japanese Commissioners then ordered the sentence to be read to them. It was a sentence of death for disobeying a decree of the Shōgun which had been pronounced for the purpose of putting an end to Christianity in Japan.

Early next morning the envoys, bound and imprisoned, were offered their lives if they would renounce the Christian faith. They all refused, and were thereupon taken to the execution ground, where fifty-seven of their number were decapitated. The remaining thirteen were spared, so that they should carry a report of the punishment to Macao. Their ship was burned.

Evidently the exclusion policy of which this drastic action was a clear display was in some way connected with fear of foreign aggression; yet the texts of the relevant exclusion orders all seem to indicate that their main purpose is the destruction of Christianity in Japan. This view, however, is not easy to reconcile with the condition of Christian evangelism in 1635–39, the years during which the orders were issued. It is therefore worth while to examine the development of anti-Christian policy in Japan from the early days of Ieyasu's government with a view to understanding its motives.

3. *The Anti-Christian Movement*

It will be remembered that the first anti-Christian pronouncement was made in 1611; this was a notice instructing officials to take steps against converts. It was followed in 1612 by an order to Hasegawa Fujihiro (Sahyōe), Governor of Nagasaki from 1606 to 1614, to punish certain specified offenders. Then came a long decree in June 1613, addressed to all monasteries and shrines, calling upon them to beware of the Evil Sects, which were Christianity and a certain unorthodox branch of the Nichiren or Lotus Sect. Finally in January 1614 the monk Sūden presented a memorial in which he described the evils of Christian belief and the harm done by its teaching to the native religious tradition. This document, in which a certain Confucian flavour can be detected, called for the expulsion of foreign missionaries. It was approved by Hidetada under his vermilion seal, and thus became the law.

It must be said that Ieyasu was quite patient with the foreign missionaries until 1612, and even then his action was relatively mild. He would not allow his officers, the members of the military class, to become Christians, but he did not interfere with the beliefs of the classes beneath them—the farmers, craftsmen, and traders. It is true that in 1613 twenty-seven Japanese evangelists and catechists were executed; but this was punishment for a deliberate breach of the law in the Shōgun's capital by a Spanish missionary named Sotelho, who in 1612 built a chapel in Yedo and publicly celebrated mass. Sotelho was condemned to death, but the sentence was not carried out.

In 1614, however, the ban on Christianity was stated in positive terms.[1] At this time Ieyasu was willing to expel the Jesuits and other missionaries, especially since he could now rely upon Dutch and English traders, who were not subject to missionary pressure. Most of the missionaries now left, but a few remained in hiding and others returned to Japan secretly. It is known that there were several Fathers in the castle at Ōsaka during the siege. Yet despite this flouting of the edicts no foreign priest was punished by death during Ieyasu's lifetime. There is indeed good reason to suppose that Ieyasu, preoccupied as he was with the coming trial of strength at Ōsaka, was not much perturbed by the Christian propaganda in Japan. The decrees issued during his lifetime do not bear the marks of his authorship, and those of 1613 and 1614 were thought by the Jesuits and by the resident English traders to be the work of Hasegawa, the Governor of Nagasaki, who was bitterly anti-foreign and responsible for cruel persecution of Christians in the Arima fief, which he secured by mean trickery in 1614.

Ieyasu was a man of broad mind and calm judgment. He was more interested in the expansion of trade than in the punishment of missionaries. It was not until after his death that stringent action was taken against Christians in Japan. A new edict was issued in October 1616 by the Rōjū. It was addressed to all daimyos and ordered them to prevent all their people, down to the farmers, from adopting the Christian faith. Also in 1616, shortly after Ieyasu's death, certain restrictions were placed on the voyages of Japanese vessels licensed under the vermilion seal. They were to obtain a special approval from the Rōjū.

This measure was the first step in a policy of seclusion which was presently to be rigorously enforced by the Tokugawa Bakufu. In the same year all foreign vessels, except Chinese, were forbidden to enter any ports other than Hirado and Nagasaki. The anti-Christian movement, however, still had not reached its height, and at about this time two Jesuit Fathers, de Angelis in 1618 and Carvalho in 1620, travelled to Yezo and visited newly discovered gold mines. They said mass in settlements of miners brought there from the mainland by a "gold rush" of some 50,000 men a year.[2] In the years from 1618 to 1621 a large

---

[1] In 1606 there were about 120 Jesuits (66 Fathers and 56 Brothers) and some 30 members of Franciscan and other orders. The total number remaining or returning after the edict of 1614 is put at 47, and more were smuggled in from time to time.

[2] See H. Cieslik, *Hoppō Tankenki* (Tokyo, 1962).

number of Japanese Christians, both priests and converts, were executed in Kyoto and Nagasaki—over fifty in 1619—but no foreign Christian was done to death until 1622, which was the year styled in the reports of the missions the year of the Great Martyrdom. At this time thirty Christians were beheaded and twenty-five burned at the stake. Of the latter, nine were foreign priests, the first to suffer the death penalty in Japan.

The tragic scene was described by an eyewitness, the English trader Richard Cocks, a man who had no liking for the "papistical" missionaries. He wrote: "I saw fifty-five of them martyred at one time at Miyako. Among them were little children of five or six years, burned alive in the arms of their mothers, who cried 'Jesus, receive their souls!' There are many in prison who hourly await death, for very few return to their idolatry." No wonder that Cocks called the government of Japan "the greatest and the most puissant tyranny the world has ever known."[3]

In 1624 a number of missionaries from Luzon were allowed entry, but Hidetada refused to approve the requests of an official mission from the Philippines seeking for privileges for Spanish evangelists and traders. In 1625 he forbade Spanish subjects to reside in Japan for purposes of trade, though he did not prohibit trade as such. His order did not, however, prevent the smuggling of missionaries into Japan, and at a somewhat later date Matsukura Shigemasa actually proposed an expedition to destroy what he described as the missionary base in Luzon.

This may have been only a specious excuse for buccaneering voyages, but it is evident that some Bakufu officials were moved by a genuine fear of the influence of Christian doctrine. It is true that most of the converts were poor country people, but there were also among them many samurai and city dwellers. Converts of every kind were subjected to such fierce oppression that in the towns all the Christians seem either to have recanted or to have vanished into obscurity. But the countryfolk clung to their faith and disobeyed the edicts, meaning to resist at the cost of their lives. The Bakufu resorted to cruel persecution, seeking out believers in the remotest corners of the poorest provinces and subjecting them to torture. Yet while some recanted, many withstood the agony inflicted upon them by ruthless pursuers. In some parts of Kyūshū the peasants formed leagues to prolong their revolt, especially in poor regions where religious fervour was strongest.

---

[3] The total number of Christians executed in Japan between 1613 and 1626 is given in missionary reports as about 750; and of course thousands more must have suffered and died from imprisonment or exile and destitution.

By 1625 the persecution had reached its peak, and Christianity had been either eradicated or driven underground in most parts of Japan, though there were sporadic revivals and martyrdoms for two or three decades more. In some places the peasants continued to worship in secret, encouraged by missionaries in hiding.

In 1640 a board of enquiry was established in Yedo—a kind of Inquisition—called Shūmon-Aratame, the Examination of Sects. In 1664 all daimyos of 10,000 koku and above were ordered to establish a similar office. The test of trampling on the Cross (fumie) was introduced. In order to trace the religious beliefs of the people all monasteries and chapels were ordered to keep a register of persons resident in their parish, with particulars of birth, death, marriage, travel, occupation, and so forth. Thus the Buddhist clergy were called upon to act as police agents for the Bakufu in the pursuit of Christians.

It will be noticed that documents of 1633–39 clearly state that the purpose of the exclusion edicts was the suppression of Christianity in Japan. Since the teachings of the missionaries were incompatible with the feudal principles upon which the power of the Bakufu was based, the persecution of the priests and their converts, though morally evil, might be defended on political grounds; but it could scarcely be argued that it was necessary to close the country altogether in order to keep out the influence of a foreign religion.

Evidently there are some anomalies here. In the first place, the exclusion policy was not thoroughgoing, since it made exceptions for China and Holland, in fact for any country that did not send Christian missionaries to Japan. The Dutch, anxious to capture the Japan trade, had been at pains to warn the Japanese against the Portuguese and the Spanish, whom they accused of planning to seize Japanese territory or at least to use force against Japan. The English traders would not have been excluded, but they had already left Hirado (the centre of their activities) in 1623, before the exclusion orders. Thus the effect desired by the Bakufu could have been secured by the existing ban upon the entry of Portuguese or Spanish persons, whether traders or missionaries.

The Spanish had been denied entry after 1624. And, as mentioned, all foreign residents were ordered in 1636 to move to Deshima at the head of Nagasaki Bay, where lodging was prepared for them. This applied only to a few Portuguese, who were expelled from the country in 1638, following the Shimabara rising. Moreover, by the time of the third and final exclusion order of 1639, Christianity had been all but entirely stamped out, and it would have been possible to prevent the entry of missionaries by a systematic control at the ports. This, however, would have required the collaboration of the daimyos in whose territory the ports were situated; and here we have a further clue to the policy of the Bakufu.

The Tozama daimyos in western Japan and Kyūshū profited by foreign trade, and if they were allowed to continue their trading they might easily grow strong enough to endanger the primacy of the Bakufu and even bold enough to call upon Portuguese or Spanish assistance. The only way of preventing such rivalry was to prohibit all foreign trade at ports other than Nagasaki, which was under the direct jurisdiction of the Bakufu. In this way the Bakufu obtained not only a control of foreign trade but also a monopoly of its profits; and whatever other result was expected from the exclusion policy, it is quite clear that this is exactly what the Shōgun had been aiming at since Ieyasu's day. In retrospect it becomes evident that Tokugawa policy was directed to creating a dictatorship, an authoritarian state, exercising full control over all aspects of the national life, economic as well as social and moral.

Was the Bakufu's fear of Christian propaganda genuine, or was it a pretence by which the exclusion policy was justified? The number of Japanese Christians, probably of the order of 300,000 before the great persecutions, may have fallen by death and apostasy to far less than 100,000 men and women who practised their devotions in concealment. It is hard to believe that a man of the stature of Ieyasu would have been deterred from his policy of expansion by fear of the influence of so small and weak a community as the scattered Christians after 1625. But neither Hidetada nor Iemitsu was cast in the heroic mould, and it is probable that they and their advisers genuinely feared foreign aggression. They were not men to take a great risk. They had no trust in the loyalty of the Outside Lords, and what they had heard of the activities of European states did not encourage them to join in the struggle for territories and trade which was disturbing the Pacific Ocean.

There is an illuminating passage in a report of François Caron, the head of the Dutch trading station in Japan, who had given some lessons in world geography to Iemitsu. Writing in 1641, Caron says that "after investigating the size of the world, the multitude of its countries and the smallness of Japan . . . he [Iemitsu] was greatly surprised and heartily wished that his land had never been visited by any Christian."[4]

---

[4] This and other interesting data on the geographical conceptions of the Japanese at that time are to be found in C. R. Boxer's *Jan Compagnie in Japan*. The Japanese learned a great deal about navigation from the Dutch, and before the exclusion orders Dutch pilots were frequently carried by ships licensed under the Shōgun's vermilion seal.

Reflecting upon the history of the persecution of Christians in Japan one cannot avoid the question of cruelty. The descriptions of torture to which the converts were subjected are heart-rending, and evoke a detestation of the very memory of those who ordered such atrocities. It appears at first sight that religion calls forth bitter hatreds compared with which secular animosities are almost gentle. In Japan, men, women, and children died after agonies prolonged with a fiendish ingenuity that, it seems, could not be matched elsewhere.[5] But the record of the Christian Church in mediaeval Europe is no less sickening. It even gains an increment of horror from the fact that the pain of the victims was enjoyed. We learn of Savonarola that he suffered "many and assiduous tortures" for many days; and that the Albigensian crusaders burned "innumerable heretics with immense joy—[cum ingenti gaudio]."

It should be noted that the persecution of Christians in Japan was not primarily of religious origin. It was not proposed by the Buddhist Church nor did the Buddhist clergy play an important part in it. The antagonism of the ruling class to Christianity was mainly political. Socially, Christianity was inconsistent with the feudal hierarchy, and ethically it was opposed to the code of the warrior class. It was the faith of potential enemies of Japan.

But it is unlikely that fear of Christianity was the compelling reason for the seclusion policy. There is interesting evidence on this point in an account by a Ming scholar, Huang Tsung-hsi, of his visit to Japan in about 1646, when he sought to obtain help for resistance against the Manchus. He discusses the Japanese seclusion policy and agrees that fear of Christianity and of Europeans was a motive, but says that the underlying reason was the determination of the Tokugawa to secure internal peace and prosperity, and to avoid any foreign involvement likely to jeopardize those aims.

The lengths to which the Bakufu went in enforcing this policy seem to confirm Huang's view. The measures they took were typical of Confucian China, which was always isolationist and preoccupied with internal security, and especially typical of Ming China, which dismantled its navy, closed its ports, and restricted trade to stations where it could be closely regulated.[6]

One point which is often overlooked in considering the seclusion

[5] In some cases, it is said, the executioners were ordered or bribed to finish off the victim without such preliminaries.
[6] The substance of these two paragraphs was kindly furnished by Professor Theodore de Bary. Huang was a scholar, and also a great patriot. Receiving no encouragement from Japan, he returned to China to take part in guerilla activities.

policy is the nature of Japan's foreign trade in the seventeenth century. The Portuguese, Dutch, and English vessels entering Japanese ports did not carry Western goods, but articles from other parts of Asia, principally China. When trade was limited to one port, Nagasaki, Japan was not deprived of any essential articles, since these could still be brought in by Dutch and English vessels and also by Chinese vessels as before. Trade between China and Japan was not interrupted by the Tokugawa Bakufu, although certain articles were at times excluded.

CHAPTER V

THE GOVERNMENT OF THE FIEFS

1. Fudai and Tozama Daimyos

THE CENTRALIZED feudal government, developed during the process of national unification begun by Nobunaga and completed by Ieyasu, rested upon the overlordship of all land in the country exercised by the Tokugawa Shōgun. Every daimyo was subject to the power of the Shōgun. He could be deprived of his fief or obliged to exchange it for another fief, and in principle he was bound to govern his fief in accordance with the laws and orders of the Shōgun.

In practice there were two classes of daimyo, distinguished by a difference of origin and of treatment by the Bakufu. These have already been described in Chapter I as the Fudai, hereditary vassals of Ieyasu and his successors, and the Tozama, lords of great domains inherited from their ancestors and not granted them by the Tokugawa family. Let us now consider the situation in more detail.

Although the most trusted and in some ways the most protected of all daimyos, the Fudai were not well treated, being frequently moved about, while others were free. The practice was a bad one, since by changing a ruler's province (kunigae), the Bakufu deprived him of the opportunity to get well acquainted with his people, and his fief was therefore unlikely to be well governed, while the cost of moving was a burden.

As the name suggests, the Tozama, or Outside Lords, were not within the sphere of Ieyasu's direct control during the years when he was building up his power to the point which it reached after Sekigahara. They had been adherents of Hideyoshi, but after the destruction of the Toyotomi family they had no national leader to follow, and were therefore obliged to accept, however reluctantly, the dominance of the Tokugawa family. They were potential enemies, and had to be carefully watched; but Ieyasu treated them generously, rewarding them with more land than they could have expected from Hideyoshi. He reserved for himself and Fudai vassals the greater part of the Kantō (the eight eastern provinces) and the whole of Kinai, or Home Provinces, with Kyoto and Ōsaka. The Tozama were for the most part traditionally strong in the remoter provinces, chief among them being such barons as

Daté in the North, and Nabeshima and Shimazu in Kyūshū.[1] The Fudai daimyos were placed mainly at points where they could, if required, hamper any hostile movements that the Tozama daimyos, either singly or in combination, might make.

The Bakufu, having made its strategic dispositions, gradually increased its pressure upon the Outside Lords, and their subjection was completed by the measures already described—the Buke Sho-Hatto and the rule of alternate attendance, or Sankin Kōtai. By this rule, it will be remembered, all daimyos were compelled to spend four months of every other year in attendance at Yedo, returning to their fiefs in the interval but leaving their wives and families behind as hostages. The rule applied to Fudai and Tozama alike, but in the case of the former obedience to it may be regarded as an expression of loyalty, and in the case of the latter as an act of submission. The practice began soon after 1615, but, as we have seen, it was made a definite obligation from 1635. It was a burdensome duty involving the daimyos in double expenditure; and in some cases of hardship exceptions were made.

The success of the methods by which the Bakufu imposed its authority becomes clear if one compares the somewhat cautious approach of Ieyasu just after Sekigahara to the attitude expressed in a speech said to have been addressed to the Tozama by Iemitsu upon his installation as the third Shōgun in 1623. He is reported to have used these words: "My ancestor and his son regarded you as equals, and you have had special privileges. But now I am the Shōgun by right of succession, and you will henceforward be treated as hereditary vassals [Fudai]. If you do not like this, go back to your fiefs, and make up your minds. Then, as tradition dictates, the clash of arms shall decide who is to be supreme in the country." This may not be true, but it is consistent with the firm attitude taken by the Bakufu at that time.

---

[1] The general position of Fudai in relation to Tozama was as follows:

1. Along the Tōkaidō, the main road from Kyoto to the eastern provinces, was a string of Fudai vassals to Suruga and westward, protecting Kyoto, Ōsaka, and the Kinai from attack.

2. In the North (Mutsu and Dewa), Tozama such as Daté, Gamo, Uyesugi, and Satake were screened by Tokugawa supporters in Mito, Utsunomiya, and the like, thus protecting the Kantō from attack from the North.

3. Northwest from the Tōkaidō lay the powerful Maeda, holding Kaga, Echizen, and Noto. To guard against incursions by him into the Eastern seaboard region or the Kinai, Yūki Hideyasu was placed at Fukui and Matsudaira Tadateru at Takata.

4. In the central provinces (Chūgoku) were placed Fukushima, Mōri, Ikeda, Asano, and others, protecting the Kinai against attack from the West.

5. In Kyūshū the great barons were as far as possible separated from one another by daimyos friendly to the Bakufu. Before Ieyasu's rule there had been no Fudai in Kyūshū.

The total assessed revenue of all daimyos midway in the seventeenth century was approximately 19 million koku, or seven-tenths of the total national assessment of 27 million koku. In the first decades of the Yedo Bakufu, there were some 200 fiefs. The number was under 200 in 1614, but rose subsequently. The distribution of revenue among the daimyos fluctuated as fiefs were escheated or restored, but on a basis of 200 fiefs the proportion was of the order of 50 with revenues of 100,000 koku and over, to 150 with revenues of from 50,000 koku to 100,000 koku.

In return for their fiefs the daimyos had certain obligations to the Bakufu, since in principle each fief was a grant which might be withdrawn, reduced, or exchanged. At a change of Shōgun all vassals were obliged to submit an inventory of their holdings and to renew their oath of loyalty by swearing to observe the Buke Sho-Hatto. Their tenure was then confirmed by a document under the vermilion seal. They were committed to render specified military service, and they were also liable to certain emergency services, such as contributing labour and materials to the building of castles and other undertakings. Finally, they were obliged to observe the rule of alternate attendance.

Apart from these obligations the daimyo was at liberty to govern his fief at will, except when Bakufu interests were directly concerned, or when there was a gross breach of the principles laid down in the Buke Sho-Hatto and other fundamental documents. It is true that the 1635 version of the Buke Sho-Hatto established the rule that "in all matters the laws of Yedo must be observed and applied at all places in all provinces"; but in practice most of the daimyos issued laws and regulations suitable to conditions in their own domains, and acted as independent rulers. Admittedly, the Tozama daimyos were given greater freedom than the Fudai, the Bakufu being generally reluctant to interfere in Tozama affairs once the great "crushing" (toritsubushi) which ended in Iemitsu's day had taken place. Nevertheless, it can still be said that the internal government of each fief, whether Fudai or Tozama, was as a rule left to the daimyo. Oppressive government was frowned upon but not punished as such; it was only in extreme cases of bad government which might lead to dangerous quarrels within a fief, or grave suspicion of disloyalty, that Yedo intervened.

The political intelligence system of the Bakufu was efficient. Intelligence officers (Metsuke) visited, and at times resided in, Tozama fiefs, giving advice to the daimyo and information to Yedo. As for the Fudai daimyos, it was not difficult for the Bakufu to ensure that they governed their fief's competently, since punishment for misbehaviour could be prompt and severe, including either transfer to a less desirable fief or plain dismissal. Such treatment could not be applied to Tozama daimyos, whose fiefs were usually distant from Yedo and who might resist the Shōgun by force if he pressed too hard. They could in most cases have been overcome without great difficulty, but the mere fact of open revolt would damage the Shōgun's prestige. It was easier to keep the Tozama in order by such indirect methods as imposing costly tasks upon them. The Tozama daimyos for their part were generally careful to avoid action likely to offend the Tokugawa family. Those who were ruling their fiefs during Ieyasu's lifetime seem to have had friendly feelings towards him, for Daté, Maeda, and Shimazu were in tears by his bedside during his last hours.

2. The Internal Administration of the Fiefs

The inauguration of an era of peace in a society dominated by a warrior class presented to its leaders a number of contradictions not easily resolved. If the feudal character of that society was to be preserved, the Shōgun must be able to ensure the loyalty of his vassals while granting them a large measure of autonomy. He must have overwhelming strength at his command, but he must be careful not to get into a situation where he has to use it, for that might wreck the whole structure so patiently erected; and therefore he was obliged to aim in practice at maintaining an apparent balance of power. There might be a threat in the background, but it was concealed once Iemitsu had made his gesture by marching a great army to Kyoto for purposes of demonstration.

Consequently the autonomy enjoyed by most daimyos was considerable. Each had full control over the people in his domain, who had to obey his laws and pay the taxes which he imposed. It is difficult to define more exactly the powers and functions of a daimyo, since they varied from place to place and from time to time; but his chief duties were to develop the economic resources of his fief, to keep order among its people, and to be prepared on call from the Shōgun to mobilize an armed force.

The daimyo's task was not simple, for it usually involved reconciling varied interests within a wide area. Each daimyo, whether Fudai or Tozama, possessed and governed his domain. His retainers (and by this term only the warrior class is intended) received from him either land or rice. Those who received land were known as chigyō-tori (recipients of land revenue), and those who received rice as kuramai-tori (recipients of rice from the daimyo's storehouse).

The chigyō-tori, who consisted of the upper class of family retainers, received land (and control of the peasants) from the total holding of the daimyo, and this was known as kyūchi, or granted land. Granted land was not necessarily all in one locality. It was often composed of scattered lots, in respect of which the grantee could impose tax and labour service upon the farmers. From all such lands the tax rice was collected by the daimyo's officers and made over to the respective grantees; and the dimensions of the grant were expressed not in measurements of area but in terms of bushels of rice—the kokudaka.

The kuramai-tori, a lower level of retainers, received a fixed amount of rice from land under the direct control of the daimyo, such land being commonly described as kurairi-chi (storehouse land), because its product went direct to the daimyo's storehouses. Samurai of lower rank received a small allowance of rice from this source, the land under the daimyo's direct control, and were usually referred to as fuchimai-tori, a term which means stipendiaries. There were several social grades among the warrior class, its members being distinguished by the amount of their allowances or stipends.

The proportions of the cultivated area reserved for these two types of tenantry varied from fief to fief, but the following table may be regarded as showing a normal range:[2]

Date	Fief	Kurairi-chi (under daimyo's control)	Kyūchi (under retainers' control)	Kyūchi (as percentage of total cultivated area)
1625	Hagi	370,000 koku	280,000 koku	41%
1631	Ōmura	42,000	19,000	31
1632	Owari	150,000	450,000	75
1643	Mito	180,000	180,000	50

As a rule, the land held by the upper class of retainers ("kashin," relatives of the daimyo) represented a smaller part of the total area available for cultivation than that allotted for furnishing stipends to the kuramai-tori, who were generally far more numerous than the holders of granted land. For example, in the Hagi fief cited in the table above, there were in 1625 a total of 1,764 grantees as against 4,465 stipendiaries.[3]

This division of a fief into two classes of tenantry naturally raised

[2] Based on figures given in an article by Fujino Tamotsu in Shigaku Zasshi, Vol. LXV, No. 6.
[3] Miwa on the Hagi fief, Keizaishi Kenkyū, Vol. XII, No. 3.

1

2

4

自・日本到

呂宋國舟也 三苫

右

慶長九年甲辰八月十八日

3

異國渡海船之圖

5

6

武家諸法度

一 文武弓馬ノ道専ラ可相嗜事
左文右武古ノ法也不可不兼備矣弓馬ハ武
家ノ要枢也平兵為凶器不得已而用之況不
忘乱何不願修錬乎

一 可制群飲佚遊事
ノ基也

一 可制諸國武巌制殊重祇好色業博奕是亡國
令條所載武巌制殊重祇好色業博奕是亡國

一 肖法度業不可隠置於國之事
法是礼節ノ本也以法破理不破法肖法
ノ類其科不軽矣

questions of jurisdiction. The holders of land by subinfeudation were free, within reasonable limits, to administer their land according to their own ideas. They could decide what crops were to be grown, and what tax in kind should be collected from the peasants. They could also conscript labour for such work as clearing ground, cutting channels, or sweeping snow. They could, and often did, punish delay in payment of tax by torture or other harsh treatment, for which the peasant had no redress.

It was the tendency—though rarely on humanitarian grounds—for the daimyo to reduce the area of land grants and increase the number of stipendiaries. This was a natural trend, since every acre of granted land reduced *pro tanto* the power of the daimyo. The process was not rapid, but changes were carried out in most fiefs between 1640 and 1660. An illuminating example is a reform of the system of subinfeudation introduced in the domains of the Kishū clan in 1646. It ended in an arrangement by which, although the grantee retained direct control of the farmers on his land, the rate of tax was fixed by the daimyo, and punishment for offences was not left to the grantee but made the responsibility of a magistrate appointed by the daimyo. Further, the grantee was forbidden to reside in the farm area, except in special cases.

The reform (if it may be so styled) of the subinfeudation system was carried out in other fiefs at about the same time. Of special note are those in Mito and Owari, which not only had particularly large areas of granted land (see the table above), but were held by members of the Tokugawa family and therefore came under the direct notice of the Bakufu.

The purpose of this so-called reform of the system of subinfeudation (it is known as "chigyōsei no kaikaku," or "reform of the land revenue system") was to reduce the area cultivated by grantees, so that they should not, by remaining on the land, create a class of small landed gentry in close touch with the peasants. This was a revival of the fear of the jizamurai or dogō (yeoman farmers) which had moved Hideyoshi to order his Sword Hunt. But in many cases the grantees did remain on the land and cultivated the fields themselves, this type of arrangement being called tedzukuri, or real digging (in contrast to kosaku, or tenant farming). In 1653, however, the Bakufu issued an order to all daimyos, instructing a general reorganization similar to that introduced in the Kishū domains in 1646: grantees were to live in the castle town and become stipendiaries, receiving the amount of rice for which the land was assessed—so many koku less a fixed percentage for tax. Most daimyos had put this order into effect by 1660.

All such "reforms" resulted in strengthening the authority of the daimyo and reducing the danger of local uprisings. It will be noticed in this context that the great revolt planned by the rōnin in 1651, under the leadership of Yui Shōsetsu, was of urban and not rural origin, although it is true that the rising was a protest against conditions caused by an increase in the number of unemployed soldiers. Men taken from the land to live in a castle town were likely to get restless.

The foregoing description of the fiefs should be supplemented by some particulars of the administration of the Tokugawa domains, the so-called Tenryō, a high-sounding name which might be translated as "celestial estates."

The government of towns in Tokugawa domains (including the capital city) was in the hands of the machi-bugyō, city commissioners appointed by the Bakufu. The Tokugawa lands were administered by the officials known as "gundai" or "daikan" (deputies). The gundai, of whom there were four, had charge of lands assessed at 10,000 koku or more. The daikan, of whom there were from forty to fifty, had control of lands assessed at from 5,000 to 10,000 koku. They may be regarded as a sort of inferior daimyo, and in fact where their area was assessed at 10,000 koku they were equal to daimyos, living in castles and in other ways enjoying the rights of a feudal lord, although they received fixed salaries and were paid officials. Originally they were appointed for their knowledge of local conditions and were not necessarily members of the military class. Ieyasu gave such posts not only to Fudai vassals but also to certain rich merchants, and even to big farmers like Ina and Hikozaka, who figure prominently in the history of Tokugawa fiefs.[4]

---

[4] Ina Tadatsugu, who has already been mentioned as one of Ieyasu's trusted assistants, came from a warrior family in Mikawa. He was rewarded for valuable services to Ieyasu by the post of Kantō Gundai, which gave him control of the eight eastern provinces on behalf of the Shōgun. He was at the same time Daikan in the province of Kai, and was thus in charge of Tokugawa domains assessed at one million koku. Ieyasu owed him a special debt for his handling of the transport of supplies in the Sekigahara campaign.

CHAPTER VI

IETSUNA, SHŌGUN 1651–80

1. *The New Bakufu*

THE THIRD Shōgun, Iemitsu, died in 1651, and his place was taken by Ietsuna, his son by a secondary wife. The boy was a minor, and the task of guiding the nation through a transition from military to civil principles in the conduct of its affairs fell to the high officers of the Bakufu. At that time there were two Tairō, Sakai Tadakatsu and Hotta Masamori, and three Rōjū, chief of whom was Matsudaira Nobutsuna. To these, in accordance with Iemitsu's directions, there was added Hoshina Masayuki, a Tokugawa and the half-brother of Iemitsu, a man of recognized gifts and strong character.

Tadakatsu was growing old, and was therefore not well suited to head the government in a difficult situation. Hotta, a younger man, might have filled the office of Tairō with success, but he was one of several retainers chosen by Iemitsu to follow their overlord in death, according to the barbarous custom known as "junshi."[1] Thus Nobutsuna was left to conduct government with Abe Tadaaki, an upright and experienced man, who was the remaining Rōjū.

The first important problem with which they had to deal was the discontent of the rōnin, a problem illustrated in a vivid way by the circumstances of the rising of Yui Shōsetsu, which took place only a few weeks after Ietsuna's accession. The Bakufu reacted by introducing certain reforms which may in a general way be described as a departure from the hitherto severe attitude of the ruler to his vassals. The concession to daimyos of the right to adopt heirs at a late age is one example of this charge; and another is the general moderation of the official attitude towards the rōnin, as it became constructive rather than punitive.

When Ietsuna was named Shōgun he was only ten years old. During the remaining thirty years of his life he continued poor in health and mild in spirit, but showed an engaging, gentle character, if one may judge from some of his letters which have been preserved. The government remained almost entirely in the hands of his ministers, who were advised by Hoshina, a learned man who was no doubt partly re-

---

[1] It was abolished in 1663.

sponsible for the civil trend of policy during the next two decades. He encouraged scholarship, respecting such men as Yamazaki Ansai, a Confucian of the Sung school, and in general it may be said that learning was highly esteemed in official circles.

This new government was faced with a new situation, not dangerous but difficult, and dealt with it in a somewhat negative manner, quite unlike the decisive policy of its predecessors, who had inherited something of the dictatorial manner of a commander-in-chief addressing his troops. Ietsuna's advisers, in dealing with the rōnin or the gangsters and rowdies in the city streets, were cautious but adequate, and their treatment of the great daimyos was on the whole firm but understanding.

The leading Bakufu officers at this time (ca. 1651–71) were as follows:

Tairō	Sakai Tadakatsu	died 1656
	Sakai Tadakiyo	1666–1680
Rōjū	Itakura Shigenori	1665–1677
	Sakai Tadakiyo	1656–1666
	Abe Tadaaki	1633–1671
	Inaba Masanori	1657–1696

Of these men, Abe was distinguished by strong will, high principles, and good administrative ability. Sakai Tadakatsu was growing old, and Sakai Tadakiyo was experienced but crafty and of doubtful integrity. Fortunately for Ietsuna his guardian Hoshina, thanks to his ability as well as his family connexions, was able to exert influence in political matters and to prevent great blunders; but the administration was timid by the standards of some of his critics. It was, however, soon to be tested by a very difficult problem raised by the discovery of a plot to overthrow the Shōgun's government by force in 1651. This movement, in which a number of rōnin played the leading parts, may be dismissed as a failure, for it was detected and suppressed with ease; but a study of its growth and of the attitude of the authorities towards the rōnin as a class furnishes some useful evidence of the nature of government at the end of the rule of Iemitsu.

2. The Rōnin Conspiracy

The ringleaders of the conspiracy were two remarkable men, Yui Shōsetsu and Marubashi Chūya. Yui was a man of humble origin, who had as a child been sent by his parents to a village school where he displayed remarkable talents. He was taken up by some rōnin who lived near by, and from them he learned much about the history of the recent past. Moved by an ambitious spirit, he determined to rise to heights of power, following the example of Hideyoshi, a poor lad who had become master of all Japan. Marubashi was a samurai of good family, a man of moderate talent and immense bodily strength, burning with a wish to avenge the death of his father, who had been captured and executed by soldiers of the investing army during the siege of Ōsaka castle.

Each of these men was in his way a characteristic product of the times, part of the flotsam and jetsam carried on the ebbing tide of war in the early seventeenth century. Each was a man of parts, thwarted by lack of opportunity; for, owing allegiance to no feudal superior, they were both without place or emoluments. Many men in this predicament, looking for a means of livelihood, sought to make use of their only asset by teaching military science. It seems at first sight strange that so soon after long years of slaughter there would be a demand for such instruction. But since most adult members of the warrior caste had no other occupation, and since all were ordered by the Shōgun's edicts to cultivate the arts of war alongside the arts of peace, there was a demand for teachers of experience. In most cities and towns there were flourishing schools where students could practise the use of weapons or learn the principles of tactics and strategy.

Such establishments naturally provided a meeting place for active men, and became social as well as educational centres, where they could exchange views on political matters. Some of these schools—academies, they might be called—were attended by hundreds of disciples or pupils, and they were obviously advantageous places for the ventilation of grievances and the discussion of current affairs. They were attended by men of all ranks in the warrior class, from small daimyos and bannermen down to the lowest grade of samurai and even to the leaders of bands of ashigaru (foot soldiers). Their number increased as the Bakufu took measures to guard against subversive conduct by ordering feudatories to expel from their fiefs men who were not in their service. These provisions (which are to be found in the Buke Sho-Hatto) were aimed at the rōnin, and of course tended to increase the number of masterless men gathered together in cities and towns.

Both Yui Shōsetsu and Marubashi Chūya found employment as instructors. Chūya, with his great strength, gave lessons in the use of the halberd, a deadly weapon but not easy to wield, while Shōsetsu joined a flourishing academy in which his talents soon brought promotion and the trust of its master, whom he presently murdered and succeeded.

Shōsetsu even established an ironworks and an armourer's shop, selling its products to well-placed samurai, and thus increasing his connexions with persons of importance in both town and country. His establishment naturally attracted many rōnin and other discontented persons. One of these was Chūya, whom Shōsetsu took into partnership. At what point Shōsetsu began to plot a rising and to gather support in secret is not quite clear, but it was during the rule of Iemitsu, and probably soon after 1645. His plan was to choose a windy night and by an explosion of gunpowder in the government magazine to start in the inflammable city of Yedo a conflagration which would afford opportunity of raiding the Castle and murdering high officials in the confusion. Similar action was to be taken in Kyoto, Ōsaka, and other cities.

This bold and desperate *coup d'état* might have succeeded but for the unforeseen obstacles that ruin most conspiracies. It had been intended to strike very soon after the death of Iemitsu, in June 1651, but a delay was caused by a sudden illness of Chūya, who began to shout secrets in his delirium. Action was postponed until the first days of September. By that time details of the plot had come to the knowledge of the Bakufu. Chūya was arrested in Yedo, and in Sumpu (Shizuoka) Shōsetsu disembowelled himself, along with several of his comrades, on being surrounded by police. The corpse of Shōsetsu was subjected to the usual base indignities, while his aged parents and many close relatives were crucified. Chūya and his accomplices, after cruel tortures, were crucified; their wives and children were decapitated.

Apart from its dramatic quality, this uprising of members of the military class is of peculiar interest as evidence of the development of the domestic policy of the Bakufu, which was bound to run into difficulties so long as it aimed at conserving the military spirit while promoting industry and trade.

The senior councillors, taken unawares by the conspiracy, met soon after its suppression to discuss its origins and to decide what action should be taken to prevent further disturbances. The majority opinion was at first in favour of strong measures, including the expulsion of all rōnin from Yedo, but finally the view of the Rōjū Abe Tadaaki prevailed. He argued that the sensible course was not to use force against the movement but to take steps which would reduce the number of rōnin. It was on his advice that the practice of escheatment was brought to an end, and that an effort was made by Bakufu officials to find openings

for employment suitable to the rōnin. Prominent among such functionaries was the City Commissioner (Machi-Bugyō) who had arrested
Chūya. This was a man named Ishigaya Sadakiyo, who had been
wounded in fighting in Kyūshū and understood the feelings of old
soldiers. He was able to find good places for more than a thousand
rōnin in the next twenty years or so, and other veterans gave the same
kind of help.

These were not great numbers, but the fact that the Bakufu saw fit
to take a moderate line shows that it was inclined to move from a strict
military outlook and to develop a stronger civil administration. One of
the difficulties that had to be overcome was the distaste of many samurai
for clerical work. There were posts in the central and local government
offices which required a knowledge of composition and accounting, but
few of the older rōnin had these qualifications. The celebrated scholar
Arai Hakuseki (1657–1725) was himself a rōnin, and he held important
official posts, but he said that of the samurai he had known since his
childhood hardly one in ten had sufficient knowledge of writing and
arithmetic for even modest duties in the bureau of a minor Commissioner, whereas when he reached mature years almost all samurai even
of the lowest order had the necessary education.

Soon after the unsuccessful plot of Yui Shōsetsu, another conspiracy
was discovered by a Bakufu agent in which several hundred rōnin were
involved, and in the same year (1652) there was a small disturbance on
the island of Sado. But these were of little significance, for the problem of the rōnin was being solved as much by the lapse of time as by
the efforts of the government. The samurai who as youths had fought
at Ōsaka in 1615 were now between fifty and sixty years of age. They
had given place to their sons, who, having the advantage of some school-
ing, could find posts in the numerous offices of a government which was
becoming increasingly bureaucratic in its constitution and its outlook.

By the close of the century the number of rōnin was small. Most of
them were men who by temperament were not fitted to regular employment and a quiet life. Some became fencing masters or teachers of military science, finding no lack of pupils in the rowdy element of urban
society; others were frankly disreputable characters, often on the edge
of crime. The word rōnin is frequently used in a pejorative sense, but
it must be remembered that we learn not of the well-behaved majority,
but of the vagabonds and wastrels. They were few in number, but they
were conspicuous sources of trouble in the cities, where they stalked the
streets seeking quarrels, "flown with insolence and wine." In striking

contrast to such ne'er-do-wells were rōnin scholars like Ogyū Sorai and poets like Matsuo Bashō, leaders of philosophical or literary movements in the late seventeenth century.

3. *The Townspeople*

The rōnin were not the only people who gave trouble to the government. After the battle of Sekigahara there was a long interval of peace—broken, it is true, by the siege of Ōsaka—a half-century covered by the rule of Ieyasu, Hidetada, and Iemitsu, lasting from 1601 to 1651, during which the government devoted itself primarily to perfecting a civil administration. This task involved some diminution of the privileges which the military class had enjoyed at the expense of the civilian society.

In this period the economy of the whole country developed apace, since all but the area of hostilities in the Ōsaka region was busily engaged in the increase of trade and industry for civil rather than for military purposes. As we have seen, both domestic and foreign trade flourished under the encouragement of Ieyasu, and much new wealth was created by the increasing output of mines and the manufacture of goods for peacetime consumption.

One of the results, or the concomitants, of this new activity was a flow of population from the country to the towns, and this was especially true of the eastern seaboard, since the Shōgun's choice of residence, first in Sumpu and then in Yedo, shifted the centre of military and political power away from the ancient capital of Kyoto. Once the system of alternate attendance (sankin kōtai) was established, the vassals from all parts of Japan built houses in Yedo and brought there considerable retinues. They spent large sums annually, and gave employment to many tradesmen, artisans, and labourers. The size of the population of the city thus grew rapidly, while its character changed as life became more varied and, on the whole, more attractive, especially to men who wished to avoid hard work and a drab style of living.

Many such found their way to Yedo soon after 1615, and by the mid-century the city population included a considerable element of ne'er-do-wells, living on the fringe of respectable society and subsisting upon dubious occupations. Such men were known as "kabukimono," a term which approximates to "eccentrics," because their behaviour was of an unusual and striking kind.[2] Some of them were military men of good

---

[2] "Kabuku" means to lean or to incline.

standing who for lack of occupation in a time of peace sought excitement in street-fighting and robbery.

Forerunners of the kabukimono began to occupy the attention of the Bakufu as early as 1612, that is before the siege of Ōsaka, when certain members of the manservant class known as chūgen killed a high officer in revenge for his murder of a page. On enquiry it was found that there were companies of these chūgen throughout the city, banded together for illicit purposes. In order to deal with them the Bakufu set up barriers in the streets, and in a battue were able to capture and kill several hundred. They were men who had formed bands under leaders known by such names as Arashi no Suke (Captain Tempest), and were sworn to protect one another in any circumstances, even against their own parents or masters. They professed certain moral principles superior, they said, to those of their elders, and they were in fact loyal to their comrades.

The Bakufu was at first disposed not to treat them as criminals, and no doubt their intentions were not entirely evil; but they wanted to attract notice and for that purpose they resorted to extremes, challenging the authority of the government by engaging in robbery with violence and murderous street-fighting. The government was forced to restore order by drastic measures. In 1628 watches were placed at all cross-roads, and large numbers were thus cut off and arrested, some to be put to death. But the abuses continued. A lampoon current in Yedo about 1645 refers to two hatamoto of high rank (10,000 koku and 3,000 koku) as leaders of bands of yakko (varlets or underlings) known as hatamoto-yakko, who would rove the streets after nightfall to rob and murder unwary citizens. Their leaders wore fanciful costumes, and their hair was dressed in fanciful styles. It was this departure from ordinary habits that gained them the sobriquet of kabukimono. They grew sidewhiskers (whereas the ordinary practice of the samurai was to be cleanshaven to the crown of the head), and they carried extremely long swords. Their bands had preposterous names, such as "Daishō-jingi-Gumi," meaning the Band of all the Gods, great and small, or the Pantheon Band.

In considering the part played by hatamoto in these highly irregular movements, it should be recalled that the Bakufu, in organizing the hatamoto after 1635, had withdrawn from the land hatamoto of 500 koku or less, and given them a fixed stipend, which proved inadequate. It was men of this kind who became rōnin and leaders of gangs.

Opposed to the hatamoto bands were bands of young townsmen known as machi-yakko who claimed to remedy injustice and to punish evil-doers. They had the same kind of habits in behaviour and costume as the hatamoto-yakko, but their leaders were of a different social origin, being for the most part members not of the military caste but of the class of clerks, shopkeepers, innkeepers, and superior artisans. Their business brought them into contact with military circles because many of them acted as employment agents, finding body servants (chūgen) for samurai who had been brought to Yedo by their daimyo. In literature the most celebrated of the machi-yakko was one Banzui-In Chōbei, a man of great physical strength and courage who was killed in 1657 by the leader of a band of hatamoto-yakko in a quarrel over some trifling matter. Chōbei owes his reputation to a stage play of much later date, in which he is presented as being sliced to death "like a carp on a chopping board."[3] In the play he is a heroic character, a champion of the weak and a scourge of the wicked.

For what reason it is not quite clear, the yakko are credited in romantic literature with remarkable virtues. They are depicted as patterns of chivalry, and styled Otokodate, a word which means a brave who stands up against injustice. It is true that some of the bands of yakko were governed by severe codes of loyalty among themselves, and no doubt from time to time they performed quixotic acts; but in real life, if not in legend, they seem to have been disorderly rogues and to owe their reputation chiefly to the eighteenth-century stage plays in which they figure as heroes. It is indeed a curious fact that the theatre in Japan owed its development to its portrayal of the kabukimono and their exploits. A play in which the Otokodate is the principal character is akin to the Beggar's Opera.

The roving bands of yakko continued to harass the Yedo government until late in the seventeenth century. In 1686 three hundred members of the band called "Daishōjingi-Gumi" were rounded up and its ringleaders executed. Thereafter the yakko seem to have lost their courage and their influence, degenerating into groups of gamblers and loafers. The formation of these youthful bands and the "gang warfare" in which they engaged constitute a phenomenon which has its counterpart in the great cities of Western countries today. The standard of behaviour of the young men seems to be common to both societies. The attention to costume and coiffure, the jargon, and the obedience to leaders are essentials, and what is perhaps most striking of all is the strict observance of a code of loyalty within the band, concurrent with the pursuit of illicit aims.

[3]The story of Banzui-In Chōbei is told at length in that excellent work, Bertram Mitford's *Tales of Old Japan*, under the title "A Story of the Otokodate of Yedo." In this version he is parboiled in a hot bath and finished off by spear-thrusts.

The yakko also furnish an interesting sidelight on the trend of urban life in Japan after the wars. They, like the rōnin (they were in fact often led by rōnin) were the product of a rapidly growing city population and a rise in the cost, or it might be better to say the standard, of living. The policy of the Bakufu inevitably moved from meeting wartime needs to building up an efficient civil administration; and of necessity it sacrificed some of the privileges of the military class—especially its weakest members—for the benefit of the lower orders.

One of the first causes of discontent among the hatamoto was a fall in the purchasing power of their revenue, which, as we have noted, in many cases was converted from a basis of the product of land under cultivation to a fixed stipend. They were often left with no land to farm and no duties to perform. An interesting episode in the year 1651 throws light on the condition of samurai living upon a fixed income. A daimyo named Matsudaira Sadamasa, holder of a fief in Mikawa, returned it together with all his possessions to the Bakufu, with a memorial requesting that all his property should be distributed among hatamoto in distress, and that the Shōgun should also make money payments to them out of his treasure. He himself shaved his head and walked through the streets of Yedo carrying a begging-bowl. The Bakufu treated Sadamasa as a madman, and confiscated his fief, which they transferred to his elder brother. It was only a few weeks after this that Yui Shōsetsu's revolt took place.

During the years from 1660 to about 1670 the government saw to it that nearly all land formerly held or cultivated by hatamoto and go-kenin in the provinces adjacent to Yedo was incorporated in the direct Tokugawa domains. The occupants thus became stipendiaries, and most of them moved to Yedo. By the end of the century nearly nine-tenths of the total number of hatamoto and go-kenin were living on rice allowances from the Bakufu granaries. Some of them found well-paid employment as officials, but the openings available were not nearly sufficient to absorb the great numbers of people who were now forced to live on a small fixed stipend.

4. The Great Fire of Meireki

The early years of Ietsuna's minority were saddened by a great disaster in the Shōgun's capital. In 1657 a conflagration lasting for three days destroyed more than half the city, with a loss of life estimated at 100,000. The fire started on the eighteenth day of the new year, in the Hongo district. At that time a north-west gale was blowing with hurricane force and the flames spread with appalling speed from street to street, consuming the wooden houses (dry from a year of drought) from Kanda, south to Kyōbashi, east to Fukagawa, and showed no sign of abating. On the evening of the second day the wind veered and drove the flames back from the southern outskirts of the city towards the centre. Reaching Kōjimachi they destroyed all the houses of the retainers and servants of the daimyos resident in the vicinity of the Shōgun's castle, and presently attacked the castle itself. Part of the outer citadels was destroyed, but the keep, though damaged, was saved. The mansions of the great daimyos which were adjacent to the castle were all burned to the ground. The wind and the flames abated by the end of the third day, though the smoke was so thick and the smouldering ruins so widespread that it was difficult to move about the city for some time; but by the 24th day of the month it was possible to collect a great number of corpses and carry them by boat along the Sumida river and then to a point beyond the situation of the Ryōgoku bridge in the suburb of Honjō. There great pits had been dug, and in these the bodies were deposited as monks of different sects recited masses for the souls of the dead. Here a memorial chapel was built. It was called the Ekō-In, the Hall of Prayer for the Dead, and it stood there until recent times, a vulgar, gaudy structure, used for the spring and autumn wrestling matches.

The city was restored, with wider streets and better planning, under the supervision of Bakufu officials. The work took two years to complete. The Bakufu, taking a practical view, gave particular care to that part of the city which had been the centre of wholesale trade. The daimyos had been sent home, and the rebuilding of the Shōgun's castle and palace was the last important undertaking to be completed. By 1659 the Shōgun was installed with imposing ceremonies. Meanwhile the government had paid special attention to the needs of the ordinary citizen. They promptly organized the supply of food on a very generous scale, and they advanced funds to the townspeople for rebuilding their shops and dwelling houses. The Bakufu also advanced funds to daimyos for rebuilding their residences, and made grants to hatamoto who had suffered loss. Much of the credit for organizing measures of relief and reconstruction was due to Matsudaira Nobutsuna, the leading Rōjū at the time, who proved himself a very able administrator.

5. Sakai Tadakiyo in Office

Strictly speaking, Ietsuna's minority ended in 1663, but Hoshina Masayuki continued to advise him until 1672. By that time able men like

Nobutsuna, who would have resisted bad government, had died, and the field was left to Sakai Tadakiyo, the senior Rōjū, who became Tairō in 1666. Under him were the Rōjū Itakura Shigenori, Tsuchiya Kazunao, Inaba Masanori, and Kuze Hiroyuki.

These men were of only mediocre ability, and Tadakiyo was not a man of solid capacity, but rather an easy-going, self-indulgent, clever man who rose to the highest office thanks to the decease of the stalwarts who had served Iemitsu. The only survivor of that reliable band was Abe Tadaaki, who had a low opinion of Tadakiyo and frequently rebuked him. But Tadaaki was growing old, and died in 1671, after thirty-eight years of faithful service. It was Tadaaki, it will be remembered, who prevailed upon his colleagues not to persecute the rōnin but to take steps which would lessen their numbers by providing decent employment.

Tadakiyo was not a man to devise and execute a policy of his own. He dealt with problems as they arose. Notoriously given to taking bribes, he was the object of scurrilous lampoons by the citizens of Yedo, accusing him of greed and corrupt practices. Apart from Tadaaki's rebukes he was reproached by a powerful daimyo, Ikeda of Okayama, for his ignorance of the people's needs and his failure to show an example by simple living. There was discontent throughout the country, said Ikeda, and signs of popular uprisings. If these should take place, he boldly hinted, some powerful daimyo might join them. Relations between the Shōgun and the daimyos were at that time of special importance, because changes were taking place in the aims and methods of administering the fiefs. It was natural that there should be disagreements among the advisers of the daimyos, conflicts of opinion between progressive and conservative parties within the clan, and it was the duty of the Bakufu to avert such troubles by cautious but firm diplomacy.

One of the most celebrated of such cases was a prolonged succession dispute in the domain of the Daté family, whose seat was at Sendai. It was a difficult case, in which the Bakufu intervened at a time when Sakai Tadakiyo was in office, and as such it deserves some detailed description.

6. *Politics in the Fiefs*

As the daimyo of a fief, particularly a Tozama fief, progressed with his plans for improving its organization and for that purpose strengthening his own control, he was bound to arouse opposition from those who thought their own interests to be in danger or who were on general grounds conservative. Thus the more land was taken under the daimyo's direct control, the less was the relative strength of the important rear-vassals, even if their own holdings were not interfered with; while the smaller tenants, on becoming stipendiaries, lost their local influence to the officers of the daimyo.

The class of landholder known as "family retainers" (kashin) was not homogeneous. It included, as well as relatives of modest standing, kinsmen equal in rank and influence to the daimyo or his direct heir. It was to be expected that the powerful rear-vassals would at any prospect of change readily believe that they were losing privileges to which they were entitled. This feeling naturally became acute when a question of succession arose upon the death or retirement of a daimyo, and during the seventeenth century several fiefs were disturbed by violent quarrels between two or more parties, each supporting a different claimant.

These disputes (known as On-Iye Sōdō or Noble Family Discords) were the chief political events of the era, since after 1615, thanks to the strict discipline of the Bakufu, they were virtually the only form of political disturbance with which the country was troubled. Accordingly such quarrels were regarded seriously by Yedo, since they occurred principally in the great Tozama domains and threatened serious consequences if they were not peacefully settled. Several of these disputes took place in the latter half of the seventeenth century. They were rousing affairs, attracting popular attention throughout the country and supplying the themes of numerous stage plays which stirred the groundlings in the eighteenth century. In particular, the prolonged succession quarrel in the domain of the Daté family deserves some notice because it throws light upon the attitude of the Bakufu towards the Outside Lords, and in general upon the clan politics of the period.

The succession to this fief (of 620,000 koku) was not necessarily decided by primogeniture in a direct line from Daté Masamune, the founder, who had been favoured by Ieyasu. There resided in the Daté domain a number of kinsmen and hereditary vassals, all of whom were related, some closely, some distantly, and some by marriage, to the actual head of the clan. Among them were holders of estates of 10,000 koku or more, who could justly claim to be qualified both by birth and by capacity to rule the fief.

In 1658 Tadamune (who had followed his father Masamune) was succeeded by his son Tsunamune, at that time in his eighteenth year. A kinsman and an accomplished vassal was named to advise him. Some two years later, in 1660, Tsunamune was in Yedo, engaged in the task of clearing and deepening a waterway in the city—a corvée of the kind customarily imposed by the Bakufu on Tozama daimyos. He was suddenly dismissed and placed under house arrest. The grounds for this action are not quite clear, and there is a flavour of intrigue in the story; but it seems that Tsunamune was accused of drunkenness and debauchery, and that the charge was correct. The accusation no doubt came from home, for leading vassals had arrived from Sendai, the capital of the Daté country, and appealed to the Bakufu to force Tsunamune's resignation and to appoint in his place his infant son Kamechiyo.

This was agreed, but the Bakufu did not take this step without careful consideration. They were tolerably well-informed, since their Censor (the Sendai Metsuke) visited Sendai regularly year after year from 1658 to 1674; and the Tairō Sakai Tadakiyo took a personal interest in the case. He had been on friendly terms with Tadamune and was well disposed towards the Daté family. He was therefore loth to take extreme steps against the delinquent Tsunamune, but the pressure from Sendai was very strong. In the summer of 1660 the Council of Elders in Yedo received from Sendai a memorial signed by fourteen leading vassals recommending the retirement of Tsunamune on grounds of health; and accordingly the son Kamechiyo (now named Tsunamura) became the daimyo under the guardianship of Munekatsu, his great-uncle, and Muneyoshi, his uncle. The genealogy of the Daté clan is as follows:

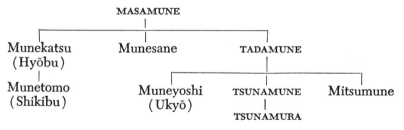

During the next ten years there was much violent dissension in Sendai, reaching a climax in the spring of 1671, when a prominent member of the Daté family, Aki Muneshige, complained urgently to the Bakufu of the misgovernment of Munekatsu and others acting in the name of Tsunamura. The Sendai Metsuke tried to mediate between Aki and Munekatsu, but Aki was obdurate, and began a lively campaign against Tsunamura's guardians. The Metsuke reported the situation to the Bakufu, and soon Aki was ordered to appear before a commission of enquiry in Yedo. He duly proceeded and on arrival was summoned to a meeting in the mansion of the Tairō, Sakai Tadakiyo. There were in Yedo now present also several other visitors from Sendai, notably Harada Kai Munesuke, one of the principal retainers of the Daté family.

Aki Muneshige reached Yedo on the 13th day of the second month and was directed by Harada to the Daté mansion in the Azabu district. On the 16th an officer from the Bakufu examined him there. Aki at once sent word of this to Sendai and was, in a roundabout way to avoid leakage, advised by his friends to hold firm and to defeat Munekatsu at all costs. From the 16th onwards Muneshige, Harada, Shibata, and other officials from Sendai were time after time closely interrogated. Early in the following month Muneshige was sent for and submitted to a close examination by Itakura, the Rōjū on duty. Harada and Shibata were again questioned, and whereas Shibata's statements were accepted, Harada made a poor impression. He left in a despondent mood.

Towards the end of the month Harada, Aki, and others were summoned to Itakura's house early in the morning. At midday they were told that an enquiry would be held at the Tairō's mansion. They were to be examined separately, by the Rōjū and by the Metsuke. Harada found that his answers did not agree with those of Muneshige and others, and was in a state of great distress and excitement. According to one version of this trial, Harada after his examination was waiting in an anteroom, when Aki approached and shouted insults. Then swords were drawn. In a wild struggle Aki was killed by Harada, and Harada was cut down by men who rushed in from the next room. Shibata died of wounds.

Harada appears to have drawn first. The offence was aggravated by having taken place in the house of a high Bakufu official. A trial was held without delay, the issue being not the succession question but the murder of Aki by Harada. The verdict was severe. The Harada family was destroyed, and the family of Munekatsu was punished. The rule of Tsunamura was confirmed. Harada's four sons and two grandsons were executed at Sendai in the summer of 1671, and his two grand-daughters were punished. No action was taken against Aki's family, since he was regarded as a paragon of loyalty—a view with which many of his contemporaries could not agree.

This is the usual version of the Daté affair, based upon reputable chronicles; but some modern Japanese historians tend to disagree with the treatment in which Aki is the hero and Harada the villain. The question is of no great interest, since the existence of serious disagreements within the clan is proved and it is shown that a solution was reached by the intervention of the Bakufu. It is in the theatrical versions of the Daté Sōdō (Disturbance) that the parts of hero and villain are most clearly allotted, and the play called *Meiboku Sendai Hagi* was the most successful of its kind during the eighteenth century. It is an interesting phenomenon in the history of the Japanese theatre that of the forty or so plays written by the great dramatist Chikamatsu Monzaemon (1653–1724) more than thirty deal with the succession quarrels in the great fiefs. They are called On-Iye Kyōgen (Noble Family Plays).[4]

There was no lack of material, for succession feuds like that which split the Daté family were common throughout the country, the best known of them being those in the great fiefs of Kuroda, Kaga, and Nabeshima. Although they often took the form of revolt by discontented vassals, they should be regarded as an expression not of disloyal, rebellious sentiment but rather of a genuine desire to reform and improve the administration of the great fiefs. The natural trend was to strengthen the daimyo, to concentrate power in his hands, and to remove weaknesses which arose from a diversity of rights and functions within his territory. Such a policy was bound to bear hard upon certain vested interests, such as those of rear-vassals holding broad acres as almost independent rulers, and it might, if not carefully carried out, injure the small cultivators and the peasantry. But the process was inevitable, since administrative reform was in the air, and a due regard for economic needs exacted some unity in the control of the material resources of the fief. Competition in trade and industry was taking the place of rivalry on the battlefield.

The Daté affair is also interesting in that it illustrates the nature of the relationship of the Bakufu with the Tozama daimyos. The Yedo government was kept informed of conditions in the fiefs by its Censors, who also at times acted as mediators. Whether the dispute could have been settled more promptly is hard to say. There is no direct evidence that Tadakiyo took bribes from Sendai, but since the Bakufu authorities were well aware of the issue certainly as early as 1660, they should have been able to force a solution long before 1671.

7. Foreign Affairs

Perhaps the most important decision made by Ietsuna's advisers during his minority concerned foreign rather than domestic affairs. In South China there was a strong movement against the so-called Tartar

---

[4] See Kawatake Shigetoshi, *Chikamatsu Monzaemon* (Tokyo, 1959). The first play dealing with the Daté affair was performed in Yedo in 1713. Donald Keene's *Major Plays of Chikamatsu* (New York, 1961) contains excellent translations and valuable commentary.

(Manchu) dynasty which had displaced the Ming. It was led by a southern Chinese known as Coxinga, who commanded a great fleet and was master of all the coastal regions. But he had no land force, and therefore in 1658 he appealed to Japan for military aid, being himself half Japanese (he was born in Nagasaki in 1624). One party in the Japanese government favoured responding to this appeal on the grounds that such an enterprise would keep the military class happy, many of its members, from daimyo and hatamoto down to the indigent rōnin, being restless and dissatisfied. These men would readily exchange their dull existence in a peaceful society for the possibilities of fame, promotion, and booty that foreign adventure would offer.

When the question was debated by the Shōgun's advisers, it was decided not to intervene. To send an army abroad would be a reversal of the national policy of seclusion. It would be costly and might end in disaster. Those who voted against the proposed invasion must have recalled the failure of Hideyoshi's great enterprise in Korea, and they no doubt had taken into account the fact that Japan had no naval strength and would have to depend entirely upon Coxinga for safe transport.

8. *Ietsuna's Last Years*

There is not much of political interest to record on the period from 1663 to 1680, when Ietsuna died. There were troubles in some of the important fiefs of the kind that had visited Sendai, and in dealing with one of these Tadakiyo came into collision with a Rōjū who would not tolerate his methods. This was Hotta Masatoshi (a son of the Hotta who had followed Iemitsu in death) who was appointed Rōjū in 1679. At that time Ietsuna was very ill, and in the early summer of 1680 he died. Tadakiyo then proposed that the next Shōgun should be a prince of the blood royal, according to the precedent of Kamakura in 1252, when Munetaka, son of the Emperor Go-Saga, was appointed.

Tadakiyo obviously saw himself in the position held by the Hōjō Regents; but Hotta was infuriated by his presumption and raised such violent objection that Tadakiyo hurriedly withdrew. That was the end of Tadakiyo's career. Within a few hours Tsunayoshi, Iemitsu's fourth son, was named Shōgun, to be installed the following day.

CHAPTER VII

LEARNING AND THE ARTS

1. *Confucian Philosophy*

OUR PURPOSE here is not to enquire into metaphysics, but to examine the trends of philosophy during the seventeenth century mainly in their bearing upon the political and social history of Tokugawa Japan.

By the middle of the century there was no scope for military adventure, and since the government was a closed bureaucracy, there were few openings for talented men in the sphere of national politics. The hereditary principle, tending to an increasing rigidity, was an obstacle to ambitious youth in most careers, whereas in the past, throughout the Middle Ages, warriors had risen in the world, while the Buddhist Church had offered opportunities to poor young men and a high place to the gifted few.

In the seventeenth century, however, the influence of Buddhism declined, except for the popular Amidist (Jōdo, or Pure Land) sects. This trend was due partly to the attacks of Nobunaga and Hideyoshi upon the great monastic foundations, but also to a lapse in the quality of the clergy in general. The mass of the population, both citizens and peasants, were practising Buddhists in so far as they followed Buddhist ritual at funerals and other family ceremonies, and in all classes the recital of the Nembutsu was common. Ieyasu himself was brought up in a Jōdo family and repeated the Nembutsu regularly. But if Buddhism was still the established church, it cannot be said that it exercised any spiritual leadership. Nor were the ruling military class entirely guided by Buddhist doctrine, since their standards of behaviour, including suicide and the vendetta, were in conflict with the gentle teaching of the Buddha.

Some of the ancient monasteries, notably those of the Zen sect, continued in the mediaeval tradition as homes of high learning, secular as well as sacred, and there came a curious sequel to their wide-ranging studies; for in pursuing the history of religion in Japan, we discover that it was students in Buddhist monasteries who called attention to a secular philosophy that was to govern Japanese thought in one or other of its manifestations for a century or more.

This was a form of Confucianism described as the Chu Hsi system after one of its most celebrated exponents in China. It was developed during the Sung dynasty (1130–1200), and it was well-known and discussed in Japan in the fourteenth century, for we learn of arguments by the young noblemen at Go-Daigo's court soon after 1333, arguments for and against the adoption of Chu Hsi teaching as a basis for the policy of the new government. But the new government was ephemeral, and except in erudite circles the new Confucianism seems to have been paid no further attention until a revival of interest came about soon after the establishment of the Tokugawa Bakufu by Ieyasu.[1] Ieyasu's 1614 proclamation against Christianity, drafted by the monk Sūden, states that Japan is the Land of the Gods. It goes on to identify those gods, the national deities of the Shintō creed, with the Buddhas, and by ingenious argument contrives to introduce into the principles of government which it is announcing a strong flavour of Confucian thought. This proclamation of 1614 seems confused, but in fact its meaning is clear. Its purpose was to secure the acceptance of an ethical code consistent with the aims of the Bakufu, namely absolute rule over a disciplined society.

Among the leaders of this new movement were several scholars who had first studied in Buddhist establishments, where it was usual to acquire some knowledge of Confucian teaching, not because of any link between Buddhism and Confucianism, but simply because the leading monasteries were seats of learning and had good libraries. In Japan Confucian studies held a place not unlike that of classical studies in Europe.

First in order of time among such scholars was Fujiwara Seika (1561–1617), a former Zen monk of the Rinzai sect who took employment in his native province of Harima as adviser to the daimyo on administrative questions. There he found time for deep study and turned away from Buddhism towards the new Confucianism. He had attracted the notice of Ieyasu during Hideyoshi's war on Korea, and in 1593 was invited to Yedo. He did not stay, but was invited again after the battle of Sekigahara; this time he gave some lectures before Ieyasu, but would not accept an official post. He was not fully persuaded of the truth of Chu Hsi's system, and wished to remain independent.

Before leaving he recommended to Ieyasu as his successor a scholar

---

[1] An exception must be made for the printing (in 1481) of one of Chu Hsi's commentaries in Satsuma, where a Zen doctor named Keian had taken refuge from the Ōnin war and was welcomed by Shimazu. Other warlords at this time were also inclined to favour Confucian studies, the Mōri clan, in particular, treating scholars and artists with respect. In studying the national history, events in the provinces should not be overlooked. Indeed, in some matters the provinces were in advance of the metropolis, where nonconformity was frowned upon.

Hayashi Razan

named Hayashi Razan (1583–1657), who had been his disciple. As a youth Razan had studied in the Kenninji, a leading Zen monastery in Kyoto. He had met Ieyasu in 1605, and in 1607 he became an adviser to the Bakufu in its early phase. He was responsible for most of the secretarial work required by Ieyasu, his colleagues being Sūden, Warden of the Konchi-In, Supervisor of all Zen establishments, and Tenkai, an Abbot of the Tendai sect.

According to some conventional histories of Japan, Ieyasu felt that he needed a philosophical principle to explain and buttress the authoritarian system of government which he intended to impose on the country. What could be better than that which Chu Hsi described when he stated that the fixed principle of the universe was the law of obedience by the son to the father, the subject to the ruler? With very little elaboration, it seemed, this could become the fundamental law of the land. But it is doubtful whether the general trend of government in any country follows a theory, still less a moral law, and we should be careful not to assume a direct relationship between systematic philosophy and political action.

In looking at the history of government in Japan, one cannot but be struck by the fact that, despite the respect paid to Confucian teaching from the eighth century onwards, it is hard to detect any deliberate application of a Confucian canon to the solution of political problems. From early times and well into the middle ages the prevailing world view, when not Buddhist, was Chinese, and all the complexities of astrology and divination (which had a great, but not always benign, influence upon the life of the ruling class) came under this rubric. Certain features of the social order were also affected by early Confucian ideas, and some of the names and functions of institutions were copied from Chinese originals. Yet it would be difficult to show that outside the institutional field Confucian thought had any creative or decisive influence on the actual conduct of government in Japan after the eighth century until the seventeenth. The directive moral force throughout that long period was Buddhism rather than any secular practice or belief.

Regarding the position of Confucianism in seventeenth-century Japan, there is a tendency to ascribe to Hayashi Razan an important share in the political decisions of Ieyasu. Razan certainly took a leading part in the promotion of Confucian studies, and perhaps also in the planning of details of governmental institutions, but there is no evidence to show that he was consulted on the initiation of policy. In considering the influence of scholars upon the practical decisions of statesmen, one should exercise some scepticism. The biographies of distinguished men of letters or great churchmen often give the impression that they were the authors of policy which the rulers put into practice; but biographers tend to forget that great men make their own political decisions without awaiting the approval of theorists.

Thus when we are told that men like the Buddhist dignitary Musō Kokushi influenced the policy of the Ashikaga Shōguns and gave it a certain Zen quality, we ought to accept such statements with caution. Coming to the early days of the Yedo Bakufu, we find nothing to show that Ieyasu consulted Razan on matters of policy, or even that he regarded Razan's doctrine as the official Confucianism. Ieyasu, though not learned, had a lively intellectual curiosity and a great liking for history, but his sympathies were with Buddhism, and (though it is true that he ordered new editions of Chinese and Japanese classical works) he is unlikely to have taken an interest in the subtleties of Chinese philosophical reasoning. It is significant that he ordered Razan to shave his head and wear a monastic robe, the conventional dress of a teacher.

We cannot undertake here a close study of the Neo-Confucian philosophy by which Razan was guided, but we must take note at least of its main features before discussing the growth of Confucianism in general during this period. The most striking quality of the Chu Hsi system is its rationalism. It resembles in some ways the positivism of Comte, in that it deals with ascertained facts and observable phenomena. It may be that these features made it attractive to Japanese thinkers. Apart from its simplicity, which is perhaps more apparent than real, the reasons for its adoption in Japan could not be more lucidly stated than in the following passage, quoted from the chapter entitled "Neo-Confucian Orthodoxy" in Sources of the Japanese Tradition (edited by William Theodore de Bary):

"Another important feature of Chu Hsi's philosophy is its essential humanism, which like his rationalism derives from the earlier Confucian tradition. The moral doctrines of this school focus directly upon man and his closest human relationships, not upon any supernatural or divine law. These are expressed most concretely in the Five Human Relations and their attendant obligations (between father and son, ruler and subject, husband and wife, older and younger brother, and between friends). Such an emphasis upon human loyalties was obviously congenial to the feudal society of Japan in this period and provided a uniform, secular code by which the Tokugawa could maintain social order in all their domains."

These are obviously principles of value to the state, though it is doubtful whether they were understood outside of learned circles, and they are unlikely to have attracted the attention of the practical men who were building the administrative system from its foundations in the two busy decades before 1650; for, we must remember, it was soon after 1630 that the principal organs of Bakufu government were established and put to work by Ieyasu's old comrades-in-arms. The main lines of the central administration had already been settled some years before that, soon after the fall of Ōsaka. There can be no doubt as to its character. It was a military government conducted by the leaders of a feudal autocracy, and its policy was conservative, being directed chiefly to upholding its authority over the vassals. Its treatment of domestic problems was of an almost negative character, being in general confined to the maintenance of order. But if Confucianism, of the Chu Hsi school or any other, cannot be regarded as the inspiration of the system of government developed in the first decades of the seventeenth century, there can be no doubt that Confucian thought, in one form or another, soon began to dominate the intellectual life of the ruling class in Japan.

The progress of Neo-Confucianism as accredited doctrine in Japan, almost as an official creed, can be best traced by studying the activities of Hayashi Razan, since he was its chief agent. Born in 1587 he belonged to the generation after Seika. He was a man of demonic energy, a voracious reader, and an indefatigable writer, firmly committed to Chu Hsi's Neo-Confucianism and violently opposed to Buddhism. His antagonism to Buddhism made little headway during the lifetime of Ieyasu, for he was no match in debate with men like Tenkai, or Sūden, both subtle and accomplished scholars. In fact Razan was distinguished by the breadth rather than the depth of his learning, and his method of argument was loose; but he could overcome most adversaries by sheer weight of knowledge.

His capacity for work was amazing. He wrote extensive treatises on history and literature, as well as expounding at length both Confucian philosophy and the national creed called Shintō. He was just the man to introduce a new gospel, a propagandist of the first rank. Among his major works was *Honchō Hennen-Roku*, a chronology of the national history, followed by *Honchō Tsugan*, a historical survey which was completed by his son. The purpose of these works was to legitimize the position of the Shōgun as the Emperor's deputy.

His house on the hill called Shinobugaoka in the Ueno district of Yedo became a Confucian college, with a great library. Thus he founded a long line of official Confucianists. His son Gahō (1618–80) was an able man, but from the time of his grandson Hōkō (1644–1732) the standard of scholarship of the Hayashi family declined. Their leadership was nominal, officially approved but exercised only in matters of ceremonial.

Antagonism to the Hayashi school came from several quarters. It first arose in important fiefs, where scholars in residence took issue with Confucianists in the capital. Their attack was directed not against the Chu Hsi philosophy which Razan and his sons professed, but against them as individuals, who were given to compromise and avoided vital issues. Prominent among these dissenters were Nakae Tōju (1608–48) and Yamazaki Ansai (1618–82).

Tōju questioned Razan's sincerity, arguing that his school of thought was proud of its learning but showed no zeal for the pursuit of the Way— that it to say, for the practice of the rules of conduct which it proclaimed. Hayashi was like a parrot, he said, thus suggesting that Razan repeated the words of the master but did not follow his ethical teaching.

Tōju is one of the most engaging characters in the somewhat peppery company of philosophers. Serving in a small fief in Iyo, he performed his military duty by day and devoted the night to a secret study of the Confucian Four Books. It was at the age of twenty-two that he started to speak out against the Hayashi school. He remained in the fief for a few years longer, and then (1634), evidently irked by the unfriendly attitude of his colleagues, left without permission and went to his birthplace in Ōmi on the shore of Lake Biwa, to live with his aged mother in poor circumstances. He worked hard at his Confucian studies, reaching a point at which he abandoned the Chu Hsi position and turned to a rival school of Confucian thought, that of Wang Yang-ming (known in Japan as Ō Yōmei), who flourished from 1472 to 1529. Wang's teaching was subjective and idealist as opposed to the objective and realist official Confucianism of Razan.

At the age of thirty-three Tōju wrote a dialogue called *Okina Mondō* explaining his views in simple language. His principal line of argument was that (contrary to the postulates of Chu Hsi, which require the operation of a principle and a force) in every man there is an inner moral sense, and it is this intuitive knowledge which results in right action. Reduced to simple terms this is a philosophy of deeds not words. It is anti-scholastic and forthright, thus likely to appeal to earnest members of the military class, and Tōju's own life was an expression of his unselfish nature. He was beloved of the poor among whom he lived and was widely known as Ōmi Seijin, the Sage of Ōmi.

Yamazaki Ansai was another important critic of the Hayashi family. He was born in Kyoto and as a youth entered holy orders in Tosa, where he studied in a Zen monastery. In that province a number of officials were interested in Chu Hsi's system, and Ansai, learning something of it from them, decided to leave the Church and set up as a philosopher. He returned to Kyoto in 1648 and opened with a violent attack upon Buddhism. He described the Hayashi family as failing to practise the Chu Hsi doctrine which they preached, called Razan a common Confucianist drudge, and began to lecture on Confucianism himself.

There were many more figures of interest among the Confucianists of this period. We must consider some of them later, in a slightly different context, but for the present we should return to the general question of the influence of Neo-Confucianism upon government. Some interesting evidence is furnished in the decrees issued by the Bakufu under the first three Shōguns, approximately from 1615 to 1650.

The first fundamental document is that which embodies the Rules for the Military Houses (Buke Sho-Hatto). It was issued in 1615, and its first article says: "The study of literature and the practice of the military arts must be pursued side by side." The revised version of 1635 contains no very marked change in this or the remaining articles, but both versions might be argued to have a slight Confucian flavour in certain clauses enjoining correct behaviour. It is true that the similar Shoshi Sho-Hatto of the same date (1635), addressed to samurai of all ranks (Shoshi) but particularly to hatamoto and go-kenin, opens with a clause calling for loyalty, filial piety, and decorum, and these are Confucian terms. But they were already in common use, and there is no reason to suppose that they were due to any new teaching. This was not a new thing. Some of the House Laws of the great families contain an article insisting upon learning as well as military exercises—e.g., *Shingen Kahō* and *Chōsokabe Hyakkajō*.

After the fall of Ōsaka, when the prospect of peace was assured, it was natural for those faced with new problems of government to ask themselves how best to deal with the warrior class. The most pressing need was to provide them with some occupation other than the practice of arms, and the most obvious course was to encourage them in the pursuit of some field of learning which might fit them for a new profession. A study of other decrees does not reveal any direct Confucian influence, unless it can be assumed that edicts controlling monasteries and monks are related in some way to the animus of Confucians against Buddhists. We must therefore conclude that the Neo-Confucianism of Chu Hsi, as expounded by the Hayashi family, did not sensibly influence legislation from 1600 to about 1650 or even later. But it did begin to influence the country's intellectual life, and it also served to stabilize the social order in a remarkable way, for it provided ethical principles well suited to the maintenance of an authoritarian state.

The feudal system of Japan had at length reached its maturity under the rule of Ieyasu after centuries of strife during which the country had suffered from almost continuous warfare and the breakdown of ancient institutions. Now an urgent need for peace was felt, not only by the Shōgun and his government, but also by a majority of the barons whom he had enfeoffed and who wished to develop their own domains without listening for a call to battle. Reason dictated that the system over which Ieyasu presided must be supported and that its permanence must be ensured by some kind of moral sanction. For such purposes Buddhism in Japan no longer possessed the necessary authority, and the Shintō cult was in a weak position. It was therefore felt necessary to adopt or devise some system of thought, some ethical principles, which would justify the absolute government of the country by a supreme overlord and a social structure in which a small privileged military class enjoyed rights denied to the remainder of the population. It would seem difficult to find a school of philosophy which could be depended upon to support so manifestly unjust a division, but in practice it was easy. It was there to hand in the Confucian system in general, and in the Chu Hsi system in particular. It was a question of emphasis on selected principles.

We have already noticed that an emphasis upon loyalty is one of the central features of Chu Hsi's philosophy. In its practical application the theory of the Five Human Relations can be made to justify the essential obligations of all members of the feudal society. It can be read as providing an ethical basis for the social hierarchy already existing in a loose form, namely the gradation of classes from the ruler to the samurai, the farmer, the artisan, and the trader, with their several responsibilities. The question of rights receives little attention, but otherwise we have here the elements of a secular ethos, narrow to be sure, but comprehensive in its scope.

Whether the supply of Confucian teachers followed a demand is difficult to say; but in general it appears that the decline of Buddhism gave a natural impetus to Confucian studies in Japan and thus increased the number of scholars available for service in Yedo or the baronial domains. That the study of Confucianism responded to no special demand from political leaders in Yedo is clear from the fact that in the first half of the seventeenth century the chief centre of Confucian studies was not in Yedo, which was still a new city, but in Kyoto, a home of learning since antiquity. Nevertheless, the energy with which Razan and his successors propagated Chu Hsi doctrine soon raised the number of scholars in Yedo, so that by the end of the century the Hayashi college was the headquarters of official Confucianism.

Although the Confucianists in Yedo could furnish an intellectual warrant for Tokugawa policy, it need not be supposed that a process of rationalization or, we might say, justification was deliberately undertaken for political ends. Official adoption of the philosophy was a natural outcome of contemporary circumstances, for Confucianism, irrespective of purposes and doctrinal splits, already dominated the intellectual scene. But this does not mean that Confucian scholars as such exercised political authority in any important degree. There were Confucian scholars in official service both in Yedo and the provinces. They gave advice when it was asked for, and they were of course consulted on questions of education, which was their chief concern; but it is clear from their official grades that save in exceptional cases they were not at the level of policy-makers. From their salaries they would appear to have ranked not higher than the hatamoto in Tokugawa service and well below the senior retainers (kashin) in a fief.

They presumably had some influence throughout the country in the aggregate, but in such matters influence is easier to allege than to prove. Looking at the political history of the period from, say, 1650 to 1700, one finds little indication of an orthodox ideology approved by the Tokugawa government; and if that is a correct view, it cannot be said that the government depended upon an "official" Confucianism for the support of its actions. The approved teaching in Yedo was that of the Hayashi college, but its leadership, as we have seen, had dwindled by about 1670. By that time a number of nonconformist voices could be heard throughout the country. The two young men, Nakae Tōju and Yamazaki Ansai, who attacked Razan in the 1640's were followed by stronger objectors, Yamaga Sokō (1622–85), Kumazawa Banzan (1619–

91), and others, who went so far as to denounce the orthodox versions of Chu Hsi's system without incurring much more than a sharp official rebuke, coupled with a warning.

We may take it, therefore, that the Tokugawa government did not seriously object to criticism of its philosophy. Indeed it may even be that the government was unable to define its own orthodoxy. The high officials of the Bakufu at the mid-century were the heads of military houses, such practised leaders as Sakai Tadakatsu and Hotta Masamori, who were certainly not skilled in philosophic argument, while Razan himself, the leader of official Confucianism, was from the point of view of a strict follower of Chu Hsi somewhat shaky in doctrine. Perhaps it is here that we should look for an explanation of the seeming leniency of the government in its treatment of dissident thinkers. What the Bakufu disliked was disagreement not with its ideas but with its policies.

A brief survey of the government's attitude to some of the leading nonconformists may help to make the situation clearer. The first of them to attract the attention of the Bakufu was Yamaga Sokō, a native of Aizu, a brilliant student of Hayashi Razan. While acquiring a deep understanding of both Buddhism and Neo-Confucianism he paid close attention to military affairs, because he was concerned to find a solution to the most serious contemporary problem, the anomalous position of the warrior class in a time of peace. His lectures were attended by large numbers, including daimyos and men of hatamoto rank. In 1652 he was invited to the castle of Asano, the daimyo of Akō, where he served as military instructor. Returning to Yedo in 1661, he wrote a work called *Seikyō Yōroku* ("The Essentials of Confucianism"), in which he called for a return to the pure doctrine and a repudiation of the versions of later dynasties. This was in effect a contradiction of the Neo-Confucianism which was the official creed, and the government could not but take offence. Sokō was sent back to Akō, where he remained in exile and continued his studies.

All his writings display an interest in military science and in the welfare of the military class. His work entitled *Shidō*, or "The Way of the Warrior," written under strong Confucian influence, contained his views on the place which the warrior class was to occupy in the new society. It described their duties and the moral purpose by which they should be inspired. This and his other works in the same series are the precursors of the teaching later to be known as Bushidō. He was alive to the difficulty of combining martial discipline and the civil arts, but felt strongly that if the samurai as a class were not to decline into uselessness they must take a lead in service to the state according to its needs.

It will be remembered that it was already before 1650 that Iemitsu's government began to be seriously concerned by the problem of the rōnin. It was in 1651 that the great rōnin conspiracy was revealed, though it had been brewing for several years; and it is clear that its ringleader, Yui Shōsetsu, though not a samurai by birth, was able to find support in many quarters because his rising was a demonstration on behalf of unemployed samurai, the class which caused anxiety to Yamaga Sokō. Yamaga Sokō, Kumazawa Banzan (next in importance to Sokō as a supporter of the samurai cause), and Yui Shōsetsu were known as the Three Great Rōnin—a description which shows the prominence of the rōnin problem in their time.

Kumazawa Banzan started his career in the service of the daimyo of Okayama, Ikeda Mitsumasa. Following this, he sat at the feet of Nakae Tōju, and in 1647, after some years of study, returned to the domain of Ikeda in Bizen province. His administrative reforms there attracted the attention of persons of high rank in the Shōgun's capital, and for a time he was in high favour. But his rivals in the Ikeda fief undermined him, and he was at length obliged to resign.

An interesting aspect of Banzan's term of office in the Bizen fief is the nature of the work to which he devoted his efforts. He gave advice on economic policy and was successful in such enterprises as controlling water supply by riparian works and in forestry development. He also organized education in the fief, and founded the Okayama Clan School, the first of its kind. He was promoted in rank by Ikeda Mitsumasa and was enjoying his success on a visit to Yedo when he came under the suspicion of Sakai Tadakatsu, the Tairō at that time, because his name was coupled with reform. It became clear that he must withdraw. He resigned his post in 1656 and went to Kyoto, but coming under suspicion again (owing to his close relations with some of the Court nobles to whom he lectured), he was obliged to leave and move to one remote country retreat after another. He remained suspect and was virtually banished for the rest of his life. He died in Shimōsa in 1691, in the fief of a friendly daimyo, Matsudaira Nobuyuki.

It is clear that Tadakatsu did not coerce Banzan because of his unorthodox philosophy. What moved the Tairō to action was the fact that Banzan in his writings (the best known is *Daigaku Wakumon*[2]) had criticized the policy of the Bakufu. He had urged a relaxation of the

---

[2] This work is a dialogue on the Confucian classic *The Great Learning* (one of the Four Books), which Banzan uses as a medium for expressing his views on current problems, political and economic.

system of alternate attendance, so as to relieve the daimyos of expense; he had proposed that the money thus saved should be devoted to the relief of rōnin; and he had recommended certain land reforms which were successfully introduced in the Ikeda fief. Although Banzan had not openly attacked the official Chu Hsi doctrine, he was openly ostracized by Hayashi Razan and his son, who proclaimed him a heretic. They seem to have forgotten the moral lesson of their own school.

Seeing that the official philosophy was under attack from so many men of high character and intellectual power, it is clear that it had some serious weakness. The truth is that the new Confucianism was intolerant and unpractical. It made no allowance for change. It gave a theoretical support to the Tokugawa system of government, but could not defend itself against shock, though of course the Five Human Relations remained unchallenged. It might therefore be said that its only success lay in offering an acceptable ethical standard for the individual.

Following upon the dissensions which we have traced there came a new trend, away from Neo-Confucian complexities to the original Confucianism of the Analects, free from metaphysical lumber. The leader of this movement, which was a natural reaction against learned squabbles, was a remarkable scholar named Itō Jinsai (1627–1705). He was a Kyoto man, a member of the merchant class, who was devoted to teaching. He opened a school for the study of the major classics, and attracted a great number of pupils. With Yamaga Sokō he formed what was called the Kogaku-Ha, the branch of Ancient Learning, which was opposed to Neo-Confucianism and indeed to all departures from the original doctrine.

The development of new schools or versions of Shintō is an interesting phase in the history of religion in Japan, which must be considered later; but for the present we may conclude this survey of Confucianism in Japan by some general observations on its practical effect, in both political and social spheres.

Its direct effect upon Bakufu policy is scarcely discernible. If we examine the main political events after Ieyasu's death, we find the development of an anti-Christian movement, following a series of seclusion orders culminating in 1639; the land survey order of 1649; and the order known as Keian no Furegaki of the same year, which was principally concerned with agrarian problems and laid down some severe rules for the treatment of peasants. In 1651 came the rōnin conspiracy of Yui Shōsetsu. In 1658 six hundred Christians were killed in Omura, and in 1683 two hundred in Owari—events which can scarcely be examples of "Jinsei," or Humane Government, which was a Confucian ideal. From 1638 to 1656 Sakai Tadakatsu was Tairō, followed by Tadakiyo, who was finally driven out of office in 1680. Neither of these men was of a kind to be sympathetic to current philosophical issues; both were conservative, and Tadakatsu, as we have seen, persecuted a scholar for venturing to suggest changes in Bakufu policy; but it is only fair to add that Tadakatsu was an upright man, interested in learning, in whom Iemitsu had great confidence.

The idealism of Chu Hsi's system was not adapted to solving current political problems; for—to paraphrase the view of a modern Japanese historian, Kitajima Masamoto—its optimistic view of human nature and its quietist attitude made it helpless when confronted with disturbances of order. But there can be no doubt of the value of Neo-Confucian studies in strengthening the social structure of Tokugawa Japan, and at the same time providing an ethical basis for the organized society which was to replace the ill-regulated condition of a country enjoying only intervals of peace. The doctrine of the Five Human Relations, while supporting a system which made for harmony and order in the state, furnished each individual with a rule of conduct suited to his own position. The practical and the ethical were thus combined, for the samurai as well as the peasant. The keynote to this system is of course Duty, but it is to be noted that it includes the duty of the governing class as well as the duty of the lower orders.

It was fortunate for Japan at this juncture that so many young men of samurai origin took to study, for the administration of the whole country and the management of fiefs both great and small required educated men brought up with a sense of loyalty. Thus it may be said that Neo-Confucianism furnished Tokugawa Japan with a civil service following a strict code of behaviour. It may be objected that an acquaintance with metaphysics is not a good preparation for official life, but it should be remembered that in Western countries a good classical education is still thought to be a qualification for responsible posts in government. To quote the Chinese sages is like quoting Plato or Lucretius.

The number of Confucian scholars who served in the fiefs as advisers or teachers was considerable, especially from about 1651, when the country had settled down after the seclusion orders and the discovery of the rōnin conspiracy. By that time the daimyos, having carried out certain reforms and made progress in the administration of their several fiefs, were finding a need for competent officials.

The student essaying a general view of the growth of Confucianism in seventeenth-century Japan is faced with two interesting questions of cause and effect. In the first place, how was it that at a time when Japan stood in need of a new system of government, a new system of thought was ready at hand for its rationalization? In the second place, how was it that the time for the adoption of such a system coincided with a phase of intense intellectual activity among students of religion and philosophy in Japan?

On reflection the answers are simple. It is obvious that we must look for an explanation which does not assume a sudden conversion of scholars to Confucian learning. That would be to deny a natural continuity to scholarship in Japan and to suppose that students suddenly sniffed in the air a new wind of doctrine; but we know that Neo-Confucian philosophy had been studied in Japan on its own merits long before its official adoption. It will be remembered that Fujiwara Seika, who inspired the official school of Hayashi Razan, was himself a student in a Zen monastery. He was born forty years before Sekigahara. As for the second question, it is easy to answer, since it was to be expected that once the prospect of peace became clear, the minds of men, especially young men, would turn in general to ideas of public and private morality and in particular to their own future employment. Such a ferment would naturally begin as soon as Ieyasu became Shōgun and started to fashion a new government.

It is difficult to devise a schematic treatment of the growth in Japan of Neo-Confucian moral principles as distinct from institutions, since so many issues are involved. For one thing there is a temptation to ascribe all changes to the strength of the doctrine itself, although other important influences were at work. There were, for example, vestiges of the warrior code of obedience and self-sacrifice going back to Minamoto times; but perhaps the commonest error is to suppose that Buddhism declined as Confucianism prospered. It is true that Buddhism had lost spiritual authority, but it still had a role of importance. It had charge of all household registration, of burials, and of memorial services for the dead; and many men in their late years turned from Confucius to the Buddha. The great monasteries were still centres of learning, and a new Zen sect (Ōbaku) was imported from China in 1655. Moreover, despite an edict of 1631 prohibiting the erection of new monasteries, chapels, and shrines, the total number of Buddhist buildings increased, partly because of the growth of new sects and partly because of the growth of towns and villages. Such buildings were generally small, but they were spread widely over the country. It might therefore be said that under Ieyasu Buddhism recovered some of the ground that it had lost under Nobunaga and Hideyoshi.

Confucianism was stern and just, but it could not offer the consolations of religion, although it adopted some practices of a religious character. Such were the ceremonies, seasonal or annual, by which Confucius was worshipped in temples built for that purpose, not only in Yedo but in the capitals of the leading feudal domains.[3] Thus the lord of Owari, Ieyasu's ninth son, Yoshinao, employed a number of Confucian scholars and built a hall (seidō) for the worship of Confucius in his castle at Nagoya. He also provided a similar edifice at Ueno, an adjunct to the Hayashi school, in 1632. It was used for ritual purposes. In this connexion it should be noted that members of the Tokugawa family in general did much to promote the worship of Confucius, such great lords as Mitsukuni of Mito and Hoshina of Aizu, as well as Yoshinao, playing a leading part. In Mito the Ming refugee Chu Shun-shui presided over the ceremonies in 1672.

These ceremonies in honour of Confucius—they may be called the worship of Confucius—were concentrated in Ueno, where they were regularly performed until 1690, when, upon the order of Tsunayoshi, the fifth Shōgun, a great hall (Taiseiden) was built upon an eminence in Kanda called the Shōhei Hill.[4] It was styled the Shōheikō (Shōhei Academy), and it became the centre of Confucian ritual for the whole country, its Spring and Autumn ceremonies being attended by the Shōgun and his great vassals.

It will be seen that Confucianism as an official cult was firmly established, but after Tsunayoshi's death it declined in importance. It should be remembered, however, that the Shōhei Academy survived. It grew in influence and efficiency as the leading educational institution in the whole country, the centre of classical studies. It was the University for all members of the Tokugawa family and all Fudai daimyos, as well as the Hatamoto class.

Something should be said here about the attitude of the Imperial Court to Confucian studies. Traditionally the Court had always promoted learning, and Emperors regarded this as part of their mission. The three Emperors Go-Yōzei, Go-Mizunoo, and Go-Kōmyō, whose reigns covered the years from 1584 to 1654, paid special attention to Chinese studies. Go-Yōzei ordered fine new editions[5] of the Four Books as well as a copy of the "Classic of Filial Piety"; and Go-Kōmyō, an

[3] The shrines in the feudal domains were erected either as separate buildings or as part of the domain school.

[4] Shōhei was the name of the birthplace of Confucius.

[5] They were known as Keichō-bon, having been produced in the Keichō era, 1596–1614.

earnest student of Chu Hsi, wrote a preface to the works of Seika, who besides being a fine scholar belonged to the Reizei line of poets.

Reverting to the ideals of private and public morality that were offered to the members of the most numerous category in the upper class, the samurai, it is important to note that duties arising from the Five Human Relations presented no difficulty to men born in a tradition of loyalty and obedience. They needed no instruction in those human obligations, for it was on such a basis that the warrior society had been founded. It could even be argued that the ethical standard, the ideal way of life, of the samurai was closer to truth, more rooted in history, than the precise dogma of a philosopher. This and other aspects of Neo-Confucianism as it was brought to Tokugawa Japan seem to be ill-suited to the native Japanese temperament, which was emotional and empiric rather than strictly rational. It may be for such reasons that in some respects the influence of Neo-Confucianism in Japan began to diminish in the eighteenth century, because it could not be applied to contemporary problems, which needed pragmatic treatment. As we have seen, nonconformist opinion had begun to find expression in 1630 by Nakae Tōju, and in different forms was continuously spread thereafter, sometimes incurring official punishment upon the dissidents.

A glance at the list of dissidents will show that the official teaching came under heavy fire:

Nakae Tōju	1608–1648	Wang Yang-ming school
Yamazaki Ansai	1618–1682	Refashioned Chu Hsi
Kumazawa Banzan	1619–1691	Followed Tōju
Yamaga Sokō	1622–1685	Repudiated Neo-Confucianism
Itō Jinsai	1627–1705	Against Neo-Confucianism
Kaibara Ekken	1630–1714	Qualified Chu Hsi

Among the defenders of Chu Hsi was a sturdy philosopher named Muro Kyūsō (1658–1734), who in his "Conversations" (*Shundai Zatsuwa*) explained how he came to his views after many years of study and reflection. Men who venture to criticize the founders of Neo-Confucianism, he says, are like the caterpillar who presumed to measure the ocean, or like a man who sits at the bottom of a well and looking up at the sky pronounces it small. He is also perturbed by the contemporary condition of Japan, for he feels that the samurai are gradually being corrupted by avarice. What he says on this score is of historical interest, since it shows how moral standards had been affected by the growth of commerce. He holds that the ideal warrior is a man who thinks first of his duty, which comes before his life and his possessions. Consequently,

Kyūsō argues, until recent times the samurai knew nothing of money matters and lived a frugal life. "As I remember my youth," he continues, "young men of that time never mentioned prices, and there were some who blushed when they heard lewd stories. Thus have social standards changed in fifty years or so."

There is no doubt that this kind of sentiment was genuine in the samurai of the best type. The same rigid code governed the behaviour of Arai Hakuseki, who, writing in his old age, described his own rigorous upbringing and the almost inhuman self-control of his father, who died in 1679. Such stoic standards continued to govern the conduct of conservative samurai until recent times. On their contempt for money we have the testimony of Fukuzawa Yūkichi, who, writing in the mid-nineteenth century, described the wrath of his father when he learned that his son Yūkichi was being taught arithmetic at school. Numbers were the tools of shopkeepers.

Kyūsō can offer no remedy for the evils attending commerce. He takes the classical view that countrymen if well treated are simple and honest, while townspeople are greedy and profligate. He thinks that severe laws should be promulgated forbidding extravagance and rebuking dissolute conduct; yet as a philosopher he ought to have known that sumptuary legislation never works.

It is remarkable that the Japanese people should have adopted a foreign doctrine which a priori one would suppose to be ill-suited to their character; but it is no less remarkable that they borrowed and discarded as seemed fit to them, performing eclectic feats which bear witness to the toughness of their native tradition. Thus, in the promotion of their own views, as we have seen, men like Fujiwara Seika, Hayashi Razan, and Nakae Tōju found no difficulty in reconciling Shintō beliefs with atheistic Confucian principles.

2. Shintō and Confucianism

In the galaxy of philosophers that illumined the Yedo firmament, no star shone with such a lively radiance as Yamazaki Ansai (1618–1682). The outlines of his life have already been given in connexion with his criticism of the Hayashi family, but these may be recapitulated and filled in here. Son of a rōnin born in Kyoto, Ansai became a Zen monk as a youth. Later he studied Confucianism with a group of young men in Tosa. In 1648, at the age of twenty-nine, he returned to lay life in Kyoto. There he began with a deep study of Chu Hsi metaphysics, and later developed a vocabulary of his own for the description of essentials of belief. He then turned to an interest in education, and towards the end of his life he took up Shintō studies.

He figures in several anecdotes as a strong-minded eccentric. One favourite story records that he asked his pupils what the Japanese disciples of Confucius and Mencius should do if those sages came in command of a great army to invade Japan, and when the pupils were silent, he said that, for his part, he would have no fear, but would put on his armour and with his spear would capture them alive. This, he said, was in accordance with the teaching of Confucius and Mencius themselves. Another comment on the wide range of his interests is attributed to Itō Jinsai, who said in jest that Ansai's enthusiasms went from one subject to another so frequently that if he had lived longer he would no doubt have become a Christian missionary.

Ansai was not alone in his enthusiasm for the national Shintō cult, which in the Middle Ages had come to terms with Buddhism. Hayashi Razan used Shintō as an ally of Confucianism against Buddhism, and this was a general trend. It also became common to give a Confucian colour to the native creed. Seika had already proclaimed a unity between the two schools of thought, and Hayashi followed him, or indeed went beyond him, saying in effect that they were identical. Tokugawa Yoshinao was an ardent Shintōist.

Among the scholars of the Ō Yōmei school of Confucianism, Nakae Tōju had written his *Shintō Taii* (The Meaning of Shintō), in which he identified Shintō principles with those of certain concepts in the Confucian doctrine of the Mean. Kumazawa Banzan went even farther, saying that Confucianism was not suited to the climate of Japan. His laudatory language is startling, for he said that the Buddha, if he came to Japan, would abandon his own view of an endless succession of worlds and follow the teaching of Shintō. Similarly, the great sages of China, and the very name of Confucianism, would be forgotten and Shintō would take their place. But apart from mere words it was Yamazaki Ansai rather than Kumazawa Banzan who carried the Shintō movement to greater lengths in practice.

Ansai's enthusiasm for the principles of Chu Hsi was of an emotional nature, and from a complex metaphysical system he selected a single principle, that of "devotion," which he made the foundation of a worship, religious rather than secular. He thought that Confucian principles in general could be combined with Shintō beliefs. He received the idea of an amalgam from a Shintō teacher and pursued it impetuously. He is said to have preached with great vigour to his disciples, who described his demeanour as alarming. His voice was vibrant like a bell, his face inflamed as with anger.[6] Satō Naokata, one of his hearers, recorded that when they entered his doorway, they felt as if they were going to prison, and that when they left, it was as if they had escaped a tiger's jaw.

There is not much to be said for Ansai's reasoning, and the further development of Shintō in combination with Confucianism was accomplished by more rational arguments than his. One of the strongest features of the movement to amalgamate the native tradition with a borrowed philosophy from China is its element of nationalism. Ansai's attitude to a hypothetical invasion of Japan by Chinese sages is an expression of this sentiment.

It is not easy to detect the early stages of this patriotic feeling. It had of course existed from ancient times, but not in an active way; and during the Middle Ages it was masked by internal strife. But with national unification there came a strengthening of national consciousness, hastened perhaps by the Korean campaign. The motives of the seclusion policy are not entirely clear, but a desire to protect the national culture against foreign influence was doubtless one of them.

3. The Neo-Confucian Ethic

The last critique of Neo-Confucianism in the seventeenth century was not an attack but a successful endeavour to make its essence intelligible to ordinary people. It was the work of Kaibara Ekken (1630–1714), a native of Kyūshū, who was trained as a physician. His study of medicinal herbs led him to a general interest in natural science, which coloured his philosophy. He believed in a single, benevolent creative force, thus differing from the dualism of Chu Hsi. His simplification of orthodox Neo-Confucianism reflected his own direct and single-minded character. His writings set forth in easy script and in simple language principles easily understood by people of all classes. He brought the Confucian ethic to women and children. A later scholar—a man notoriously sparing of praise, Dazai Shundai—said of Ekken that he was the most learned man in Japan.

A work called *Onna Daigaku* (The Greater Learning for Women), which may have been written by Ekken, sets forth the rule of subservience and obedience to parents, parents-in-law, husband, and (when

---

[6] A startling contrast to oratory in the West, where it could be said by an actor (Garrick) that the preacher Whitefield could reduce a congregation to tears by the one word Mesopotamia.

widowed) to a son. But Ekken's own wife (Tōken) was treated by
him as an equal, and it is said that she wrote the book. She was a very
gifted woman, and perhaps she and Ekken were jointly responsible.[7]

Ekken himself ranked high, perhaps the highest, among the Confucianists of his day, since he combined great analytic power with practical wisdom. In other words he was able to apply the rationalizing
principle of Chu Hsi to the formulation of a simple code of everyday
morals. Probably no Japanese thinker had so great an effect upon standards of behaviour in Tokugawa society, especially in its middle classes.

The Tokugawa social order of four classes, shi, nō, kō, shō (warrior,
farmer, artisan, trader), fitted well enough into a Confucian pattern—
in fact it was of Confucian origin. But the Confucian teaching was not
essentially concerned with such public matters, its stress being laid upon
morals within a family system. It should be understood that the moral
principles in question are not primarily concerned with the character
of the individual, but are directed to the welfare of the family, its
strengthening and its continuity. All members of the family must subordinate their thoughts and their acts to those purposes. The virtue
upon which the family depends is filial piety, the duty of a son to the
head of his family rather than the allegiance of a vassal to his lord.
Filial piety is indeed the foundation of the feudal ethic, for it is by extension of this virtue that submission and obedience to a superior come
to be regarded as an aspect of the pietas which the Chu Hsi system and
its variants require.

To understand the nature of filial piety, said Nakae Tōju in his
Okina Mondō, we must consider the debt of gratitude owed to parents
for their affection—this is true at all times and in all places, for the natural love binding parent and child is universally recognized. But the development of this theme in feudal Japan was carried to extremes by
treating filial gratitude not as a natural feeling but as a rule of conduct
imposed from outside, thus obliging the child to submit blindly to the
parent. It is somewhat surprising to find this doctrine propounded by
Kaibara Ekken, who (in his Dōji-Kun, or Instructions for Children)
warns the parent that he must not be governed by instinct and must
guard against being soft and affectionate, for that, he argues, is contrary to the teaching of the sages, because it means that the child does
not fear his parent. Therefore such affection must be repressed. In
Ekken's words: "The child must accept in silence the censure of his
elders. He must listen respectfully to what they say, whether it is right

[7] B. H. Chamberlain's Things Japanese (London, 1927) has a translation of
Onna Daigaku.

or wrong. However violent and insulting their language may be, he must not show the slightest trace of anger or resentment."

This absolute submission to the will of the head of the family relates to all aspects of daily life. It is the duty of the head of the family to preserve its good name, and for that purpose he may punish any member of the family. In order to free the family relatives from joint responsibility for an offence he may divorce or disown (or even in some cases kill) an offender.

The relationship between brothers is equally governed by age. The younger brothers and sisters are distinguished from the eldest son. They receive from their parents inferior treatment in food, clothing, lodging, and their upbringing in general. This is a great change from the custom of the Kamakura and Muromachi eras, when the heir was chosen for his capacity and not by primogeniture. It illustrates a retrograde aspect of Tokugawa conservatism, and compares ill with the ideal of filial piety that had been familiar in Japan throughout the Middle Ages.

This severe code bore with great hardship upon the younger sons of poor samurai. In all fiefs where the daimyo's income was fixed it was obviously not possible for samurai of the lower grades to be granted stipends sufficient to keep both the eldest son and his brothers on the same standard of living. The younger sons, however able, were obliged to seek adoption in another family, or to live a life of poverty, or to make their way to a city, where they could either find employment (thereby losing their samurai status) or join the ranks of the rōnin.

But the worst treatment of all was that to which a woman had to submit. During her life she had to devote herself to what were called the "three obediences" (sanjū): to her parents when a child, to her husband when married, to her children when she grew old. Too much learning was thought to spoil a girl's character, but in the middle and upper classes some education was approved, in literature, music, versifying, and handwriting. These arts were supposed to be exercised in private, for the separation of the sexes was strict. There was even an absurd rule, of Confucian origin, saying that after the age of seven boys and girls could not sit together, even for meals.

Marriages were arranged by parents in the interest of the families concerned, and a husband could divorce his wife on one of seven grounds, barrenness, loose behaviour, and disease being the commonest. It was permissible for the husband to declare as a proper ground for divorce that his wife was out of harmony with his family's customs. No legal proceedings were necessary beyond handing to a wife or her parents a short notice of divorce—so short that it was known as mikudari-han, "three lines and a half." The private relationship between husband and wife is a matter of secondary consideration, if it is considered at all. The wife's function is to give birth to children, or as it was crudely put, "the womb is a borrowed thing" (hara wa karimono).

Such rules as these, if strictly applied, inflicted hardship to the point of cruelty upon women and children, and there is no doubt that the life of married women was often full of suffering. But it is clear that except perhaps in the strict households of upper-class samurai, the rules were only partially followed, so that affection and common sense could soften their harsher aspects and make for a happy family life. The tyrant most feared by a wife was usually not her husband but her widowed mother-in-law, who after a lifetime of submission could at last give orders.

It should also be remembered that since family pride was strong, a wife's parents or brothers might take revenge upon a husband who wantonly ill-treated and disgraced her. The vendetta was a feature of life in the warrior society. It might be supposed that during an era of peace the warrior's mind would turn away from such violent practices, but in fact the adjustment of the warrior society to peaceful conditions was one of the most difficult problems facing the Bakufu during the seventeenth century. It was easy enough to find some theoretical justification of a class which produced nothing and had no occupation. The practical difficulty was to find useful employment for men who had been trained only for war.

As the organization of the central government and the fiefs progressed after the foundation of the Bakufu, the position of the bushi (warriors) in the lower ranks deteriorated. They began to look back with regret to the old life of the camp and the battlefield, for they were not at home in the new conditions. They were left behind by new men, often men brought in from the other clans or rōnin ready to serve a new master. The new bushi was of a very different character. He lived in a castle town, where, if he showed special ability, he worked as an official in the government of the fief. Officials familiar with accounts who could plan revenue and expenditure or perform important administrative duties were regarded by the old-fashioned bushi as cowardly evaders of military service. Yet these were the men who rose in importance, while a loyal retainer with no special ability could look forward to little promotion.[8]

As the new bushi replaced the old in new circumstances, standards

---

[8] According to Fukuzawa Yūkichi, whose father was a samurai of the lower rank in the Okudaira fief, during the whole 200 years of the history of the fief only 35 samurai of the lower rank were promoted to the lowest grade in the upper rank.

of conduct of necessity changed; and it was for that reason that the intellectual leaders (if we may so label the Confucianist scholars) sought to develop a logical system of ethics which should apply to the life of the military class, from the daimyo down to the samurai of the lowest degree.

The first serious effort to lay down principles of this nature was made by Yamaga Sokō, whose work called *Shidō*, or "The Way of the Warrior" (ca. 1665), has already been touched on. In this he opens his argument by saying with great truth that the samurai is one who does no work, whether as farmer or artisan or trader. What then, he asks, is the samurai's function? The answer is that the samurai is a leader, showing the path by his own example in fulfilling the moral obligations of loyalty and family piety. According to Sokō's argument, the samurai is a teacher who thinks of his function in terms not of reward but only of duty. The special interest of this and related treatises of Sokō lies in the fact that they propose a new concept of the place of the samurai in society. He is no longer a military, but a civil, officer, charged with the intellectual and moral guidance of the people at large. Sokō further postulates of the relation between the warrior and his lord that it is something divinely decreed, absolute and inviolable, superior to all considerations of gratitude or reward.

This is a neatly constructed abstract system, but it will not stand up to close examination. Sokō himself, though ruling that the samurai should not think in terms of reward, wrote when he was in exile that he would not take employment for less than ten thousand koku. The truth is that what was wanted from the samurai was not high-sounding professions of loyalty and service but practical contributions to the government by which they were employed. For this purpose obedience and assiduity were required, and there was no need for a philosophical support for such virtues. They were the traditional virtues of the samurai, and they were still practised, imperfectly no doubt, but commonly enough to exert influence as ideals.

Other Confucianists as well as Sokō attempted to rationalize a situation in which a class comprising rather less than one-tenth of the population produced nothing and lived as parasites on the more numerous element consisting of farmers, artisans, and traders. In this sphere the proposals of the philosophers were ineffectual if not positively harmful; but they were right to oppose certain features of the older tradition of the samurai.

The durability of the older code in some of its aspects is exhibited in certain survivals which were in flat contradiction to the ethical teaching of the Confucianists. Among them was the practice of "junshi," or self-immolation, in order to follow a warlord to the grave. It belonged to an age when the bond between the leader and his liegeman who fought by his side in battle was very close and personal, so close that when the leader was killed the liegeman would at once seek death to keep him company. It was perpetuated in the Yedo period by the suicide of several men on the death of a Shōgun or a great Daimyo. From any rational point of view this was regarded as wrong-doing, and it was opposed by Ieyasu on general grounds and by most of the daimyos who were influenced by Confucian teaching.

Early examples of junshi in the Yedo period were the suicide in 1607 of four pages on the death of Matsudaira Tadayoshi and of four retainers on the death of Matsudaira Hideyasu. After this, cases were frequent for some time, and there were even examples of junshi in the second degree, that is to say of junshi to follow a superior who had already committed junshi.

The argument in support of this practice was that a warrior cannot serve two masters, and therefore when his lord dies he must end his own life. When the Shōgun Hidetada died, one of the Rōjū followed him, and when the Shōgun Iemitsu died thirteen persons committed junshi, among them being the two distinguished Rōjū Hotta Masamori and Abe Shigetsugu. This ghastly habit was at last forbidden by enlightened daimyos, such as Hoshina, Ii, Ikeda, and Kuroda, and finally by the Bakufu in a decree of 1663. The ban was strictly enforced, and when a certain vassal of Okudaira Tadamasa killed himself on Tadamasa's death in 1668, the vassal's two children were executed, other relatives were banished, and Okudaira's heir was transferred to a less important fief. This brought the practice of junshi to an end. The intervention of the Bakufu here may be regarded as an instance where Confucian sentiment influenced government policy.

A more common and less unnatural practice was the vendetta (kataki-uchi), which was of ancient origin. The first recorded case of kataki-uchi in the Yedo period was the Igagoe ("crossing Iga") encounter of 1634, between one Watanabe Kazuma and Kawai Matagorō, who had murdered Kazuma's father. Kazuma, accompanied by a brother-in-law and two young samurai, pursued Matagorō and more than a score of his kinsmen into a lonely upland in the province of Iga. Kazuma's small party overcame their enemies, and Matagorō was killed. In this quarrel there was a homosexual element. It was the theme of many stage plays.

Better known is the celebrated story of the Forty-Seven Rōnin (1702), where the motive was loyalty to a feudal lord. Theatrical versions of this act of vengeance have been the most popular plays ever since it was committed, and there can be no doubt of its influence upon the mind of all classes. It is a curious fact that whereas in the first half of the Yedo period among the recorded cases of kataki-uchi most were the work of bushi, in the second half (except in cases of single combat) farmers and merchants were in a majority. It would thus appear that in the beginning the militant spirit of the bushi had survived from the age of the wars, but that with the lapse of time warriors became adjusted to civilian life, while the middle and lower classes gradually came under the influence of the Confucian pattern of behaviour; or perhaps the theatre put ideas into their heads.

The attitude of the Bakufu towards the vendetta was not unfavourable. Since a question of moral duty was involved, the government could not forbid acts of vengeance inspired by Confucian ideals of loyalty and piety. On the contrary, persons intending to execute vengeance had to apply to the Bakufu for permission, which was usually granted.

There is specific authority for this action in the Code of One Hundred Articles (sometimes called the Legacy of Ieyasu, though it belongs to a later period, probably about 1650). This document is a kind of Constitution of the warrior society. Regarding the vendetta it is quite clear. It says that a man "must not live under the same sky as one who has injured his lord or his father" (Article 51). It goes on to state that notice must be given to the authorities of the intention to kill an offender, and that permission will be granted so long as there is no delay and so long as no rioting is involved. The same document contains an article stating that a samurai may kill a member of the lower class "who has behaved offensively to him." In this case, the authorities do not require notification, the samurai being given "kirisute gomen," or permission to cut down and leave without further to-do (Article 44).

4. Historical Studies

When Ieyasu displayed an interest in the printing of new editions of classical Chinese works on government, military science, and history, and when Hayashi Razan and other scholars began to go deep into Confucian studies, they were not introducing a new kind of learning. They were restoring their country's intellectual tradition after a lapse due to the wars of the Middle Ages. Indeed they were leaders in an important renaissance movement which encouraged not so much the fine arts as the study of philosophy in general and of history in particular.

There had been no historical study of importance since the *Gukan-shō* of 1223 (one of the great historical works of Japan and the first to attempt a reasoned interpretation of the past), and it was to be expected that at the beginning of a new dynasty—the Tokugawa—scholars would wish to review the history of their country in the light of ideas then current in Japan.[9] A leader in this movement, most appropriately, was a Tokugawa of distinction, Mitsukuni (1628–1700), the daimyo of the Mito fief and a grandson of Ieyasu. As a youth he is said to have been a turbulent character, much given to dissipation; but from the age of eighteen he appears to have reformed, and he was chosen to succeed his father as daimyo of Mito. He thus became the head of one of the Go-Sanke, the Three Great Families collateral to the main line of Ieyasu.

He plunged into classical studies and developed a strong feeling for history. At the age of thirty (in 1657) he began the compilation of a national history. His purpose was to displace the *Honchō Tsugan,* the official history written for the Bakufu by Hayashi Razan, to which he objected as a mere calendar of events. His own plan was to produce a comprehensive work on the lines of the great Chinese histories. It was to cover Japanese history from antiquity to the end of the Namboku-chō period. It was to be entitled *Dai Nihon Shi.* The compilation made good progress during Mitsukuni's lifetime, but stopped in 1715 and was not resumed until late in the nineteenth century. It is the only Japanese work which resembles in form and quality the great Chinese histories, since it includes their standard features and is extremely accurate.

Mitsukuni's purpose was didactic. He hoped that a study of history would improve the minds of the samurai in the fiefs, and show them the importance of national unity. He was a firm follower of the school of Chu Hsi, which holds that the purpose of the study of history is to obtain moral guidance. The recorded actions of historical figures must be examined in the light of the essence or true nature (li) of virtue.

The early drafts of the portions relating to the conflict between the Northern and Southern Courts contain a close enquiry into the true nature of *taigi meibun,* the moral law in the relations of ruler and subject. These sections reach the conclusion that the Ashikaga Shōguns, by their support of the Northern Court, were traitors. As the work proceeded and new scholars were brought in—such men as Asaka Tampaku (1656–1737) and Miyake Kanran (1674–1718)—the language used became

---

[9] The *Jinnō Shōtōki* (1339) of Kitabatake Chikafusa is a polemic treatise rather than a history. It was written in difficult circumstances, without access to written sources, and its truly historical value lies in the description of events within Chikafusa's own direct knowledge, such as political and military incidents during Go-Daigo's reign. Its general attitude reveals influence of the *Gukanshō.*

more objective and temperate. Among the compilers of the *Dai Nihon Shi* was the Chinese scholar Chu Shun-shui, who was living in Nagasaki and whom Mitsukuni invited to take part.

Although the main purpose of this great undertaking was to relate the history of the country in terms of the acts and policies of the legitimate sovereigns of the Imperial dynasty, the writers "did not condemn the Shōgunate as an institution, for it was an arm of Imperial rule. They insisted that Shōguns were subjects, but they did not presume to deny an emperor the right to delegate his authority to any officer of his choice."[10]

[10] From "What Is the Dai Nihon Shi?," an essay by Dr. Herschel Webb in *Journal of Asian Studies*, Vol. XIX, No. 2 (1960).

CHAPTER VIII

RURAL LIFE

1. Farms and Farmers

BEFORE entering upon a survey of rural life in the seventeenth century, it is useful to gain some general acquaintance with its character and its environment. The most remarkable feature of Japanese agriculture is the small size of the holdings, their great area in aggregate, and the intensive cultivation to which the land is subjected. The chief crop is rice, grown in wet fields (paddy), and next in importance are the grains and vegetables from the dry fields (hatake). The fields are small. The measures of superficies are

1 chō = 10 tan = approximately 2½ acres

and the product of one chō of first-class paddy is of the order of ten koku, a koku being the equivalent of about five bushels dry measure in England or the United States.

In all discussion of the amount and quality of the crop, the ruling fact is that one koku of rice is the average annual consumption of one person, so that since there is no import of food, the total production in koku gives approximately the total population of the country.

To cultivate one chō of mixed (wet and dry) arable land required the full-time labour of four or five men.[1] In practice most of the holdings were small, and it might be said that the frequency of holdings was in inverse proportion to their size. Thus a single village of twenty holdings might have the following distribution:

12 holdings under 5 koku
5 holdings from 5 to 10 koku
2 holdings from 10 to 20 koku
1 holding of 20 or more koku

This is a hypothetical distribution, but it gives a fair picture of the elements of a rural community. An important point which these figures

---

[1] This figure is conjectural, since the amount of labour required depended upon the nature of the soil, the proportion of dry to wet fields, and other variables. A sixteenth-century work (Seiryōki) gives 800 man-days and 200 woman-days for an area of one chō, of which one-fourth is dry. Allowances being made for seasonal changes, this would give about four men for one chō, but an exact figure is not possible; and changes in farming methods, with better implements, would tend to reduce the number of workers per chō but to increase the acreage tilled.

do not reveal is the high proportion of very small holdings, for in most parts of the country many of the holdings of less than five koku would be in dimensions of two or three tan, producing as little as two koku and therefore of marginal utility.

A holding with a yield of twenty koku (an area of two chō) would require the labour of from five to eight men, a number which the holder's family could scarcely furnish. He would therefore be obliged to depend upon collateral relatives, or upon persons not related but generally treated as members of his family circle. Where further labour was required, the family would call upon a class of workers of whom some were hereditary servants (called *fudai*) and others were bound by contract. These servants (generally styled *genin* or "underlings") were part of the household of the landholder, living with him or in adjacent dwelling places furnished by him. It is estimated that the genin formed about 10 per cent of the peasant population of the country in the seventeenth century. Where still further labour was required, it would be furnished by persons known as *nago* or *hikan* (or equivalent local names). These were men who held small plots and dwellings allotted to them by the landholder in return for labour supplied as rent.

It will be clear from the foregoing summary that the large holdings of arable land in the seventeenth century were farmed by families composed of several elements brought together not only by kinship but also by economic need; but there can be no doubt that family feeling was strong and comprehensive, and that the "underlings" were treated as relatives, however humble.

2. *The Village*

To understand the agrarian society of Tokugawa Japan it is necessary to look back to the land policy of the sixteenth century, before the great cadastral survey of Hideyoshi was accomplished.[2]

During the Middle Ages the farming population of Japan was heterogeneous, since it included men of different classes who enjoyed freedom of movement in the social scale. In other words the division of classes was not the fixed partition it became when Hideyoshi's policy brought about the separation of the farmer from the soldier. The farmer-soldier of the Middle Ages had considerable freedom for the reason that in the aggregate the farm population had formidable military strength. Indeed it was to destroy this potential danger that Hide-

---

[2] This great survey, known as Taikō no Kenchi, was ordered by Hideyoshi in 1582 and continued until 1598.

yoshi's policy was intended. During the land survey which he inaugurated, every plot of farmland was inspected and registered. The survey recorded the area, the class of land, the quantity of rice or other crop which it was called upon to produce, and the name of the person responsible for its cultivation.[3]

The result of Hideyoshi's policy was to deprive the farming population of social mobility, to fix each man's status, and thus to bind him to the soil. During this process the lowest grade of farm worker gained his independence in that he could not be deprived of the plot registered in his name. But his freedom was only nominal, for the holdings of such men were small and usually insufficient for their subsistence. Most of them had plots of only one or two tan (the tan being .245 acres), which would produce under five koku, an amount less (after tax) than the consumption of a small family at the normal rate of one koku per head per annum. Consequently such smallholders were obliged to work for families owning much greater areas, usually by sending a son or daughter or other relative out to service.

The owners of large holdings were generally families descended from members of the rural gentry who, after Hideyoshi's survey and the announcement of his attention to disarm all but members of the military class, decided to abandon their military status and devote themselves to agriculture. By comparison with the smallholders these rich farmers—gōnō as they were called—were not numerous. As we have seen, small and medium holdings made up a very large proportion of the total of the country's arable land.

The condition and organization of the workers on the land is a matter of great complexity which is not suited to treatment here, since it requires highly specialized knowledge. For our purpose a broad perspective is appropriate, and it is sufficient to examine the village rather than the single farm, premising that the principal mode of farming in the seventeenth century was the working of a large holding by the owner and his family and dependents. This was called "tedzukuri," or hand-cultivation, because it meant real digging by the owner's men as contrasted with "kosaku," which was cultivation by tenants. The village was the administrative unit with which the feudal officials dealt.

Before treating of the village, it is useful to consider briefly the attitude of the ruling class towards the peasantry. In theory the farmer ranked next to the samurai and above the artisan and the trader. But

---

[3] For an account of farm labour before Hideyoshi's survey, see the section "Rural Life" in Volume II of this work, pages 333–35.

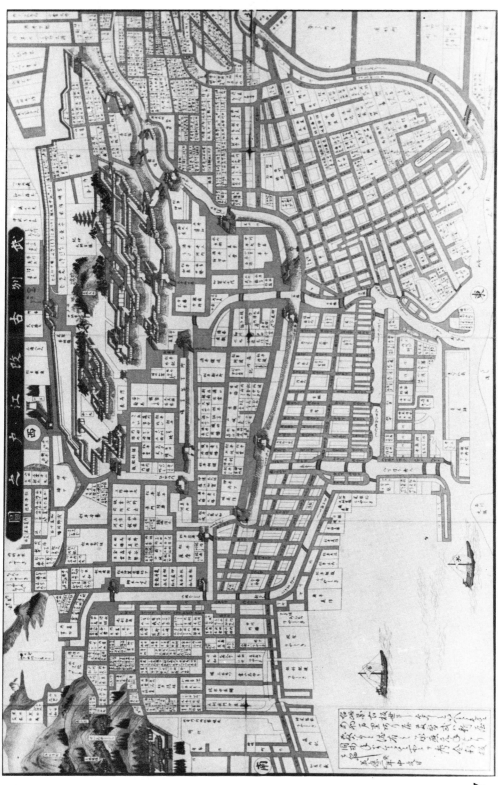

8

9

10

11

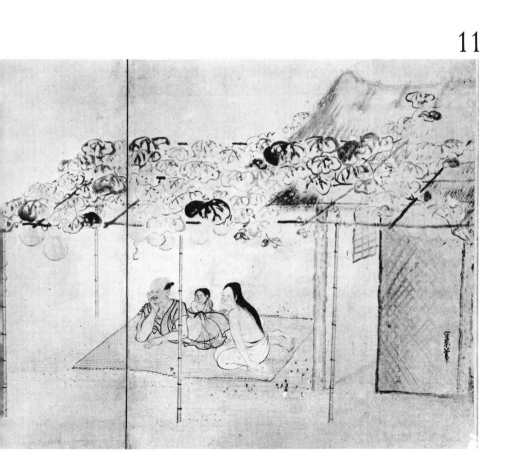

in practice the men who tilled the soil were heavily oppressed, and their life was often wretched. It was the policy of the Bakufu and of most daimyos to tax them to the point of exhaustion. Honda Masanobu, Ieyasu's trusted adviser, wrote that the peasant was the foundation of the state and must be governed with care. He must be allowed neither too much nor too little, but just enough rice to live on and to keep for seed in the following year. The remainder must be taken from him as tax.

This unhappy situation is amply described in many official documents, notably in the order known from its date as Keian no Furegaki, which was issued to all villages in 1649, following a shorter notice of 1642. The general purpose of these injunctions was to impress upon the peasants the importance of unremitting toil and frugal living. The following extracts will give a fair impression of the nature of the legislation as a whole:

—Farm work must be done with the greatest diligence. Planting must be neat, all weeds must be removed, and on the borders of both wet and dry fields beans or similar foodstuffs are to be grown, however small the space.

—Peasants must rise early and cut grass before cultivating the fields. In the evening they are to make straw rope or straw bags, all such work to be done with great care.

—They must not buy tea or saké to drink, nor must their wives.

—Men must plant bamboo or trees round the farmhouse and must use the fallen leaves for fuel so as to save expense.

—Peasants are people without sense or forethought. Therefore they must not give rice to their wives and children at harvest time, but must save food for the future. They should eat millet, vegetables, and other coarse food instead of rice. Even the fallen leaves of plants should be saved as food against famine. . . . During the seasons of planting and harvesting, however, when the labour is arduous, the food taken may be a little better than usual.

—The husband must work in the fields, the wife must work at the loom. Both must do night work. However good-looking a wife may be, if she neglects her household duties by drinking tea or sightseeing or rambling on the hillsides, she must be divorced.

—Peasants must wear only cotton or hemp—no silk. They may not smoke tobacco. It is harmful to health, it takes up time, and costs money. It also creates a risk of fire.

The peasants were heavily taxed, and in addition to payments in cash or in kind they were called upon to do work on the roads and embankments, to supply post horses, and to render other services without pay. Under what was known as the "sukegō" (corvée), men and horses were requisitioned from villages along the main highways sometimes for days on end. These practices interfered with farming to such an extent that a number of peasants were impoverished and deserted their plots. Those who suffered most were the labourers dependent upon small pieces of land.

The Bakufu and the several fiefs announced strong measures against absconders. Thus in 1642 Ikeda, daimyo of the firmly governed Okayama fief, issued an order laying the responsibility for absconsions upon the Five-Man Groups (Gonin-gumi) in each village. Persons contributing in any way to the escape of peasants or other offenders were to be punished by fines levied upon individuals or upon a whole village. The whole village, or the gonin-gumi, was obliged to cultivate the deserted plots for a year or until a suitable cultivator could be found. Here also the cost (including the tax assessed upon the plots) must be borne by the village. The village as a whole was stronger and more influential than its individual members, so that to a point it could resist pressure from local authorities or at worst could negotiate with some modest hope of success.

The village of the seventeenth century developed in a natural way from the mediaeval village, which was of various origins. Its social classes included the old settlements developed by rural gentry (myōshu, dogō, or jizamurai) and later groups of farmers formed by warriors taking refuge in remote country places after defeat in the civil wars. But the commonest class was the group of farmers engaged in opening up new farm land. This kind of enterprise was much encouraged by the Bakufu and the leading daimyos. It was furthered by an increasing supply of capital as the mercantile economy expanded, and by improvements in the techniques of civil engineering needed for surveying and for constructing dykes and embankments.

In size the average village was a group of about fifty homesteads, and towards the end of the sixteenth century its chief habitants were independent farmers of the class called hon-byakushō (landholders with full membership in the village), some of whom were former well-to-do soldier-farmers, who after Hideyoshi's Sword Hunt of 1588 had surrendered their arms and become civilians, and might be described as country squires. To this class should be added the small cultivators (ko-sakunin), whom, as we have seen, the Sword Hunt had released from their ties to the gentry and turned into independent landowners chiefly of minimal areas of wet and dry fields.

This period of relative freedom for the village did not last long, for by the cadastral surveys of the years between 1574 and 1600,[4] and particularly the great survey ordered by Hideyoshi, which lasted for some fifteen years, the village became the administrative unit to which the feudal authority (central or provincial) applied its measures of control, including the levy of land-tax assessed upon each separate field and the determination of agricultural policy in general. The village for its part was a corporation which acted for the cultivators in all matters such as petitions, contracts, leases, and the management of common lands. It was even at times held responsible for the wrongful acts of individual villagers.

Local official agents (daikan and gundai) supervised the affairs of the villages, but there were no officials resident in any village. The village headman, of whom there were three kinds (nanushi or shōya,[5] kumigashira, and hyakushō-dai), conducted village government in accordance with instructions from the official agents. The holders of these three kinds of posts were nominally appointed by election or by the decision of a committee, but in practice most of the appointments were hereditary in the long-established influential families of the small rural gentry.

In addition to these appointments there was usually selected a subordinate, a kind of go-between, who assisted the headman particularly in arranging the payment of taxes but generally in all matters pertaining to the production of crops and the maintenance of order. Under the nanushi or shōya, there were three or four assistants called kumigashira. The hyakushō-dai was a village officer chosen to represent the interests of the majority of the peasants, particularly in regard to liability for tax or the sharing out of duties. It was customary in most parts of the country for a number of villages to form a larger unity, the "gō" or rural district, over which a senior headman, the Ō-Shōya, presided. This was a post of great honour.[6]

(a) The Five-Man Group (Gonin-gumi)

The Gonin-gumi were groups of five householders who were jointly responsible for the actions of each member. Their functions were nu-

---

[4] It should be remembered that surveys of agricultural land were ordered by individual warlords long before this, as for example by the Hōjō and Imagawa families early in the sixteenth century. Nobunaga ordered surveys of single provinces from 1568.

[5] The appellation nanushi means "name-master" and recalls the term myōshu, which has the same meaning and was the title of mediaeval landowners of myōden, or name-fields. In the Home Provinces the term shōya was in common use.

[6] For further details on the organization of village and family life, see the Appendix, pp. 245–47.

merous. They had to certify marriages, successions, testaments, and contracts for sale, purchase, or loan. When tax payments of a member were in arrear, they had had to give security for the amount due; and when an offence was committed they had to accept responsibility for the act. In general their obligations included mutual aid and mutual surveillance of all public and private actiivties within the group.

The Gonin-gumi was thus an agency of self-government not arising from popular initiative but imposed upon communities by the governing class. Its chief purpose was to preserve order and to keep the authorities informed of conditions in both town and village. It was in fact a police organ for spying and delation, characteristic of the official attitude towards problems of administration.

Its duties were laid down in a preface (Zensho) to the register (called Goningumi-chō) which every village possessed. This register was signed by the headman and contained, for observance by members of the groups, a list of positive duties and prohibited acts. Some of these documents are simple and brief, others recite rules at considerable length and in great detail. An early and comparatively brief example (1658) contains fifteen articles, the chief of which may be summarized as follows:

—Instructions for receiving visiting officials; for clearing roads; and for tying up dogs and cats.

—All wells, ditches, and streams are to be cleaned and embankments repaired early in the New Year.

—All arable land is to be cultivated, no empty spaces left.

—Trees and bamboo are not to be cut without permission. When wood or bamboo is required for building, application must be made to the authorities.

—No rōnin, merchants, or beggars are to be allowed to spend a night in the village if they come from another fief and are unknown.

—All bridges, roads, and paths must be kept in order by daily attention.

—Rules for the sale of horses and oxen.

—Gambling and bribery are forbidden.

—Persons in a rural district who do not qualify as farmers, traders, or members of other recognized occupations must be closely questioned and the result reported to the authorities. They must be expelled if the authorities so require.

—In a rural district not a single Christian priest or brother or other member of a forbidden sect may be allowed entry. Care must be taken to prevent such entry.

—In case of fire or robbery in a village, help must at once be given by another village if requested.

—No person must be bought or sold in breach of the law fixing the lowest age at ten.

These regulations were read aloud to the villagers by the village headman or other official several times a year.[7] The Gonin-gumi as an institution continued until as late as 1888, when it was replaced by a new system of local government. But the principle of group responsibility survived, and the neighbourhood group (Tonarigumi), a larger and unofficial body, was used by the government in the 1930's as a unit in the organization of civil defence, food rationing, and other wartime functions imposed upon local associations in town and country.[8]

Despite the elaborate nature of the regulations drawn up by the villages, it is doubtful whether they were in practice observed by the members of the Gonin-gumi except in a general way. They were devised to make a good impression upon the authorities rather than for the guidance of the peasants, who had their ways of dealing with offenders in their midst.

(b) Class Distinctions in the Village

In the early land surveys the name registered was that of the actual farmer (sakunin), that is to say the landholder or, as he was called, the hon-byakushō. But actually there were in addition to him a number of men, ranging from smallholders to serf-like labourers, whose names did not appear in the register. These were common in backward areas, and were known as hikan or nago or by similar names denoting their dependent position. They were servants, not subject to tax and having no say in village government. The only persons who could take part in village meetings or belong to Five-Man Groups, or who could claim preferential rights in the use of common land or in water supply were the hon-byakushō.

Thus the village in the seventeenth century was by no means a simple Arcadian settlement but a small community in which there were very marked social gradations and a growing conflict of interest between rich and poor. These class distinctions differed from place to place. In the Home Provinces and central Japan in general, the scale of farms was

[7] A very full account of the Goningumi-chō, with texts, is in *Goningumi Hōki-shū* (3 vols.), edited by Hozumi Nobushige (Tokyo, 1930).

[8] For the modern Tonarigumi, see R. P. Dore, *City Life in Japan* (Berkeley, Calif., 1958).

small and there were many non-cultivating landowners. In the East and North there were many large holdings belonging to men of the landlord-moneylender class and farmed by hikan, nago, or other subordinates, who, in addition to working on their own small plots, were obliged to furnish as rent not only payment in kind but also free labour for a specified number of days each year.

The strict class divisions in the rural society are a remarkable feature of village life. They depended not upon the amount of land held by a family but upon the family's pedigree. The farming community was very conscious of distinctions of birth and rank. Most of the members of the old and respected families were descendants of landowners who in late mediaeval times had been active leaders of rural settlements which cohered into villages. Their position was so firm that it was not affected by variations in their incomes. Thus the heads of most old families occupied the important posts in the village government. They exercised the strongest influence upon its decisions, as well as enjoying preference in the use of common lands and irrigation works. Their superior social position is well illustrated by their authority in the "miyaza," which were bodies of parishioners of the Shintō shrines in the locality. In their meetings the old families took precedence over all other members. They occupied so many ritual posts that there was little room for the ordinary villager.

Since the peasant population provided the staple food of the whole country it was essential for the government to keep control of agriculture. This control was best exercised by supervising the activity of the village rather than of any greater or smaller unit, and the most effective method was to make use of the procedure laid down in the cadastral surveys by which the product of the farms was measured and assessed for tax. This procedure involved a close examination of the land and its yield by inspecting officers who were on the look-out for lazy farming. Their treatment of the peasants was oppressive, but it must be remembered that the government was properly anxious to conserve and increase the food supply which was dangerously low in a country where agricultural techniques were old-fashioned even towards the end of the seventeenth century. A rising population called for rising production.

The basic tax was an annual levy upon the crop of wet fields (paddy) and dry fields (hatake), as assessed in the register (kenchichō) of the survey. The rate of tax varied from 40 to 60 per cent of the crop, payable usually in kind on rice, and partly in cash on the product of dry fields; but allowance was made for deficits due to bad weather or other natural causes. The fields were tested for quality of the crop by "tsubo gari," that is by reaping and examining the grain from selected squares of one tsubo (six feet square).

A specimen calculation of the tax would be as follows:

	Area
Class 1 fields (paddy)	5 tan
Class 1 fields (dry)	5 tan
Homestead	1 tan
	Crop
Crop from paddy, 1.8 koku per tan	9 koku
Crop from dry fields, 1 koku per tan	5 koku
Homestead, assessed at	1 koku

In this example, on the total of 15 koku the farmer would pay, say, a 50 per cent tax, amounting to 7.5 koku of rice, or the equivalent in grain and cash. This leaves him little rice for his own consumption, but fair supplies of other grain or vegetables. In addition to this tax there was a miscellaneous levy to provide funds for post-stations and for the transport of tax goods to official storehouses. There were also taxes upon profits from the sale of articles made by the peasants or of special local products such as fruit or fish; and there were occasional obligations to contribute to the cost of riparian works. These additional imposts were less onerous in Bakufu domains than in the fiefs of independent daimyos, but the collection of the basic tax was uniform throughout the country.

In order to perfect their system of taxation the daimyos in some fiefs imposed further limits upon the freedom of the peasants. Thus in 1643 the sale or mortgage of arable land was forbidden in order to prevent peasants not only from selling their rights and migrating to the towns, but also from creating minimal holdings. A later order, of 1673, prohibited the subdivision of lands by ruling that a holder must retain from one to two chō, or an area providing from ten to twenty koku. At current rates of production to split a holding of less than one chō would be to involve both parties in trouble.

Peasants were subjected to burdensome restrictions. They could not change their occupation. They could not travel outside their own district, in search of employment or to attend a wedding, until they had obtained a certificate from their parish shrine. Peasants who failed to furnish the required amount of tax goods were sometimes very harshly treated, and it was not uncommon for the village headman to be deemed responsible and detained as a hostage. His property might be confiscated and his person subjected to torture.[9] Kumazawa Banzan wrote

[9] One of Chikamatsu's plays (*Keisei Shuten-dōji*) refers to a wooden horse (mokuba), astride of which the victim was obliged to sit with heavy weights on his legs.

in one of his memoranda to the daimyo of Bizen: "Naturally the peasants hide their rice, knowing that they will in any event be cruelly treated." He meant that cruelty only served to create a desperate reaction; and it is true that as the administration of the fiefs improved (perhaps under the influence of Confucian teaching), these methods of violence were abandoned. But they were replaced by other forms of pressure.

One of the victims of oppression was the village headman (nanushi or shōya). The classic case is that of Sakura Sōgorō, a village headman who presented a direct appeal to the Shōgun, protesting against the ill-treatment of peasants by the daimyo Hotta Masanobu. The appeal was granted, but the offence of approaching the Shōgun's palanquin was punished by the execution of Sōgorō, his wife, and their children. There is probably more legend than exact truth in this tale, which was made into a rousing stage play; but there are many authentic examples of revolt against heavy tax and other impositions.

These protests usually took the form of mass demonstrations, sometimes accompanied by violence. An early example was a protest against the survey of 1641, in which wealthy farmers led by village officials took a part. For the offence of resistance in the fief (Uwajima) seven headmen were executed. There were also numerous risings by peasants of the lower grades, but these were usually rather modest affairs, settled without much difficulty. The most effective form of resistance was not a threat of force but the planned desertion of villages. Here the farm labourers of two or three or more villages would leave their fields and scatter. They would then send a petition to the daimyo, adding that if their requests were not granted they would all abscond. As a rule such demonstrations were not punished so long as they were made through proper channels. A good example is the case of the Obama fief (in Wakasa), where in 1652 the headman (shōya) Matsumoto Chōsō stubbornly appealed for a reduction of the tax claimed from his village. This was granted, but the headman was executed.

Protests of this kind were often unavailing because they had no strong and unanimous support from the villages; but by the end of the seventeenth century the peasantry were more conscious of their strength and, as we shall see, at times made demonstrations in such force that their daimyos were rebuked by the Bakufu for misgovernment.

3. *Progress in Agronomy*

The advances made by agriculture in the seventeenth century are striking. The area cultivated grew from about 1,600,000 chōbu to about 2,900,000 chōbu, and the crop increased from about 18 million koku to 25 million.

The change was most rapid in the latter half of the century. It was made possible by the organization of the farms under the hon-byakushō, and the tireless, intensive cultivation of farmlands which was encouraged, and indeed exacted, by the Bakufu and the daimyos. The opening up of new land was facilitated by newly acquired techniques which were applied to such works as the completion of irrigation channels from the upper waters of the Tamagawa (1655) and from Lake Hakone (1670) to newly developed farmlands in the great Kantō plain.[10] This notable increase of the area under cultivation was accompanied by important advances in husbandry, such as widespread double-cropping, improved implements, more and better fertilizers, and deeper cultivation. Treadmills for the raising of water from ditches, and mechanical devices to save time and labour in threshing and other operations, added to the efficiency of most farms.

In addition to these primary increases the peasants made profits from the sale of products other than grain and vegetables. They grew cotton, tobacco, oil seeds, vegetable wax, indigo, and mulberry for silk-worms. Such extra earnings had at one time been discouraged by the authorities, who were intent upon the production of food; but presently new enterprises came to be looked upon with favour as the daimyos began to compete with one another in trade.

Evidence of a rising standard of living is the regular supply of delicacies to the towns from the country, such as oranges from Kishū, grapes from Kōshū, sweet corn, melons, and other fruit and vegetables from warm provinces. As we have noted, the total production of rice may be taken as a crude index of population, since one koku of rice or rice-equivalent is the average annual consumption per capita. Reliable census figures are not available for the seventeenth century, but about 26 million is thought to be a reasonably accurate figure for 1721 (though it excludes certain categories—the samurai and the classless persons). We may therefore conclude that 25 million is a reasonable estimate for the population in 1700. As to the proximate causes of this rapid population growth we can only speculate. The country was at peace after 1615, and both the Bakufu and the daimyos turned their attention to improving their economic condition. Throughout the country the growth of agriculture was matched by a great increase of mercantile

---

[10] In 1631, in Shinshū, water was carried for miles through channels dug in solid rock, and in part by underground channels pierced through rock for about 800 yards, by a technique borrowed from copper-mining. In consequence of such irrigation systems the yield of rice in Musashi province rose from 667,000 koku to 1,167,000 koku during the seventeenth century.

activity in the towns, especially the already populous cities of Ōsaka and Kyoto and the growing capital of the Shōgun at Yedo. No doubt a rising standard of living—more and better food and security of employment—contributed to a rising birth-rate.

But it is extremely difficult to distinguish here between cause and effect or demand and supply. The increase in production cannot be ascribed solely to new methods. It was due in part at least to an expansion of travel and trade throughout the country which could not but influence backward regions by bringing them into a national system. Some explanation can be found in a book called *Nōgyō Zensho* ("The Farmer's Compendium") written in 1696. This was the first really important practical treatise on agriculture, although there were several theoretical works tracing its foundation to Gods and Sages, as the invention of horticulture might be traced to Adam and Eve. *Nōgyō Zensho* was a serious work, written by a remarkable man named Miyazaki Antei, who had spent forty years in practical farming and forty years in travel and study of the work of others.

He wrote the preface to this classic after consultation with Kaibara Ekken on points of style and content. In it he said that hitherto there had been no practical handbooks, because peasants were illiterate. Lack of knowledge had not mattered so much in earlier times because the demand was not so great. "But now," he goes on, "there is no surplus. The demand is tenfold, and it is essential to produce more. Hard work and tenacity are not enough. The truth is that peasants are not aware of the real art of farming [sono jutsu kuwashikarazu]. The result is frequent shortages, which are not due to poor soil or to lack of effort. Knowledge and effort must go together. Japan has good soil and a climate favourable to growth. A Chinese poet praising the Japanese sword once said that we are blessed with a bountiful land; but if we do not make full use of those gifts of nature, there will not be enough food, shelter, and money for the people. If we do make full use of them, we shall not have to depend upon foreign countries."

Antei's work was widely read. There is no way of measuring its influence, but it was regarded as important by his contemporaries, in particular by Kaibara Ekken, a wise man who contributed a long appendix to the edition of 1697.

By the end of the century the character of the rural communities had undergone a great change. Not only had the production of foodstuffs increased, but also the range and quantity of other farm products had steadily expanded. As subsistence farming developed into commercial farming throughout the country (and particularly in the Home

Provinces), the small quantities of local specialties such as lacquer and paper grew into large amounts and greater variety of local products. Cash crops of cotton and tobacco, for instance, together with cash receipts for a diversity of articles manufactured in the villages from local materials, changed the character of the rural economy in many respects and improved the position of the landholder. It may be said that by 1700 the peasants were more self-confident and less yielding than before. They were no longer under the thumb of the warriors. Government was more regular and predictable; the villages were better off. The market for their commodities extended throughout the country, from the centre to the remotest corners, as travel by land and sea became easier, and backward areas were drawn into the national economy as sellers and buyers.

In the foregoing pages the life of the peasant has been described as poor and wretched, and it is true that he was oppressed by the governing class, sometimes to the point of sheer cruelty. But there is another side to this picture. The wisest rulers were sensible enough to know that harsh treatment did not produce good results, and some of them took measures to alleviate distress in the villages; moreover, the villagers themselves were often able to devise methods by which their own hardships were reduced, and in this way they were helped by the incompetence or the laziness or the dishonesty of the inspecting officers.

In theory the surveys were repeated every ten years, but in practice this duty was often neglected, and additions to the cultivated area easily escaped the officials' notice, especially if they were offered bribes. Moreover the registers used were soon out of date. They did not show the increased yields resulting from improved methods or from putting new land under the plough. According to the rules laid down by the government, the yield was to be assessed annually for the purpose of tax, but in practice the annual tax was usually fixed for several years ahead, so that the farmer profited by any increase in production achieved during that period. In general, therefore, the tax burden was far less than the nominal 40 or 50 per cent of the crop, and a large proportion escaped taxation altogether.

There can be little doubt that a farmer and his family cultivating a modest holding of five acres lived a fairly agreeable life with no great hardship, especially as production increased in quantity and variety towards the turn of the century. It was the poor labourer and his patient wife, toiling from dawn to dusk, of whom it may be truly said that they carried an oppressive burden.

It may be asked how it came about that accounts of the misery of

the peasants have been contradicted or qualified by recent studies of
the rural society. Japanese historians in the 1920's were under the influence of a somewhat fugitive post-war liberalism, and inclined to take
the side of the peasant against the capitalist. There was good material
to support this line of argument; but subsequent research has not borne
it out in all respects.[11]

[11] Some scholars, writing after the war of 1941–45, have argued on Marxist
lines to show the "place of the Meiji Revolution in the agrarian history of Japan."
See for example an important essay, thus entitled, by K. Takahashi in the *Revue
Historique*, Vol. CCX (1953). Its argument is not flawless.

CHAPTER IX

URBAN LIFE

1. *The Growth of Towns*

PARALLELING the growth of rural communities, there was a remarkable increase in the number and size of towns during the seventeenth century, especially in its latter half. Until the foundation of the Yedo Bakufu, Japan had been a country of incessant movement. Great armies were always on the march over the length and breadth of the land. Then, as peace came with the fall of Ōsaka Castle, life took on a more sedentary character. Small townships were strung along the highways, now trodden by pedlars with their packs or by officers on tours of inspection, and only rarely by armed men as a daimyo's procession passed on the way up to Yedo.

Now the Bakufu and the daimyos turned to the arts of peace. They were filled with a desire, indeed a determination to increase their strength by encouraging profitable enterprises within their respective domains, and thus the castle town (*jōka-machi*) tended to become a commercial as well as a political centre.

The population figure of the castle towns was a function of the revenue of the fiefs. Yedo, of course, was the castle town par excellence, and it was followed in size by the capitals of a few great baronies—Nagoya, Sendai, Fukushima, Kumamoto, Wakayama, Shizuoka (Sumpu), Kagoshima, Fukuoka, and Kanazawa—all of which had a revenue of 500,000 koku or more towards the end of the seventeenth century. Next in order of amount of revenue was a group of fiefs with from 200,000 koku to 500,000, whose capitals were: Tsu, Fukui, Kōchi, Hiroshima, Hikone, Okayama, Kurume, Mito, Kōfu, Tokushima, and Saga. Finally came about one hundred castle towns in fiefs of from 50,000 to 200,000 koku.

The population figure of Nagoya at the close of the century was 63,000, or about one-tenth of the revenue figure of 620,000 koku. The same ratio applied roughly to most castle towns. Thus Himeji in a fief of 150,000 koku had a population which fluctuated round 15,000 after the year 1700. Ogaki, capital of a fief of 100,000 koku, had fallen to below 6,000 by the year 1700.

Of the fiefs in general it may be said that their administration was of a conservative character and tended to place restrictions upon commerce and industry which prevented the full growth of castle towns and thus encouraged the development of other urban centres. Consequently, in most castle towns, population was stationary or declining in the last years of the century. The castle towns in fiefs of under 50,000 koku were unable to support a large population. To take an extreme case, Ueda in Shinshū had a population of only 2,600 in the year 1665, and this tended to decrease. It must be remembered that the position of many daimyos was dictated by strategic needs, and was not necessarily favourable to commerce. Where castle towns were suitably situated, they might attract wholesale and retail merchants, who were granted monopolies or other privileges by the daimyos and found the jōka-machi a convenient centre for trade, both in the town and in its vicinity; but small fiefs could not support a large population unless they controlled some especially valuable product. If they depended upon agriculture alone, they were likely to be financially weak. A fief assessed at 10,000 koku would supply to the daimyo and his vassals a tax revenue (at 50 per cent) of only 5,000 koku, an amount which would leave very little after the payment of the stipendiaries and the expense of maintaining the household of the daimyo and the upkeep of the castle, unless the fief as a whole could profit by the sale of commercial crops. In such domains the lower rank of samurai would receive a very small stipend.

Consequently, as growing centres of population, the castle towns were less important than, for instance, the expanded villages in the environs of Ōsaka. These ancient rural settlements were spread over a large area in the provinces of Settsu, Kawachi, and Izumi; and, being separated by only short distances from one another, they tended to coalesce and form urban conglomerations. Another striking example of the growth of a town is a place called Tondabayashi, which already in the fourteenth century was of some importance owing to its position on a road through Kawachi from Yamato.[1] It was a convenient place of residence for well-to-do merchants and for workmen whom they employed in the cotton industry, which flourished in that neighbourhood from about 1640. Similar country towns, such as Hirano, Tennōji, Sumiyoshi, and Sakai, developed close relations, and towards the end of the century had coalesced to form the great national market of which Ōsaka was the axis.

Although the economic importance of castle towns tended to diminish, their political development was of value to the nation as a whole. They were first of all military bases, but they were also administrative

[1] Tondabayashi was at a junction on the road from the Chihaya Pass (defended by Kusunoki in 1333) through Kawachi. See map in Volume II, page 124.

capitals in which able members of the warrior class held important posts and thus contributed to the spread of law and order through a country only lately freed from civil war and vestiges of anarchy. Without sacrificing their local characters these provincial centres contributed to a certain cultural unity which had been lacking, or at best imperfect, in mediaeval Japan; and no doubt this trend was amply reinforced by the experiences of the daimyos and their advisers during their periods of attendance in Yedo. In most fiefs, as we have seen, there were Confucian scholars serving as advisers or as teachers, who kept the inhabitants of the castle towns aware of the intellectual movements of the day.

2. The Great Cities

At the end of the seventeenth century the population of the leading cities (excluding the military) was approximately as follows:

		Date
Kyoto	400,000	1700+
Yedo	500,000	1700+
Ōsaka	350,000	1700
Kanazawa	65,000	1697
Nagasaki	64,000	1696
Nagoya	63,000	1692

The castle towns have already been described, but the character of the three greatest cities calls for further attention.

Kyoto was the principal and largest city in Japan throughout the Middle Ages, having been not only the capital of the empire and the seat of the sovereign but also the centre of the most populous region—the Home Provinces. From 1338 for more than two centuries it was the seat of the military government of the Ashikaga Shōguns. It had long been the home of learning and the arts, and of great Buddhist establishments.

Yedo was a political centre, and its population consisted of the members of the Bakufu government, with a multitude of officials and servants; a small garrison; the daimyos in alternate attendance with their numerous following of samurai and servants; and a great number of craftsmen, artisans, shopkeepers, labourers, and persons engaged in retail trade to meet the requirements of the city. Yedo was not an industrial city or a commercial entrepôt. It was a congregation not of producers but of consumers. It depended for supplies of food, building materials, and other necessary articles upon sources in distant parts of

Japan, notably the tax rice and local products from Tokugawa domains in northern Japan, and rice stored in Yedo by daimyos in attendance. Much was shipped from the city of Ōsaka, which was known as the Kitchen of Japan (Tenka no Daidokoro).

Yedo began to increase in extent and population as the daimyos established residences from about 1643, but its growth was checked in 1657 by the great Meireki fire, which destroyed more than half of the city and part of the castle. It was not until well into the eighteenth century that, fully restored and enlarged, it reached a population figure of half a million—or, if the military families were included, close upon one million.

Of its nature it was a centre of wholesale and retail trade on a grand scale, and among its first new residents following the warrior families and their dependents were merchants from Mikawa and Tōtōmi, provinces which had once been ruled by Ieyasu. After them came men from Ōmi, Ise, and Ōsaka, who opened markets for their own special products. Thus trade began to flourish, assisted by the freight brought by the annual voyages or in the "tarubune."[2] The articles most in demand were rice, miso, charcoal, salt, saké, soy, oil, cotton goods, and haberdashery. The busy wholesale and retail markets required much capital, so that moneylenders and exchange brokers drove a thriving trade. One lucrative business was the advance of cash by rice brokers to daimyos, and also to hatamoto and go-kenin, against their rice stipends. The leading merchants in Yedo were such men as Naraya Mozaemon and Kinokuniya Banzaemon, speculative dealers in building materials, which were in frequent demand in a growing city plagued by fires.[3] They made great fortunes, partly through their close connexion with government undertakings but also by their skill in seizing opportunities for profit.

The true native of Yedo was not of this kind. He was (in the words of Saikaku, the novelist) a gullible fellow, without any forethought and thus liable to make bad bargains. It was common for the Ōsaka merchants to say that Yedo people were like children, and did not understand how to use money. Certainly they were not given to saving.

---

[2] The "tarubune" were vessels which carried goods packed in barrels (taru). They sailed regularly from Ōsaka to Yedo.

[3] Naraya was in Ieyasu's service in Mikawa and followed him to Yedo. A merchant named Taruya was respected because his ancestor had fought well in Nagashino (1575). Both these men played an important part in the early stages of the development of Yedo and founded their fortunes there. Kitamura Bungorō was another pioneer who made money by seizing opportunities, especially after the Meireki fire.

Yedo indeed was a free-spending city, where shopkeepers could make handsome profits. The Mitsui family, which had founded its fortunes in Ise, added to its wealth by opening large and imposing drapery shops, such as the celebrated Echigoya, where they sold cotton goods in great variety at fixed prices for cash, a departure from the common practice of chaffering. They aimed at attracting customers in great numbers, they advertised freely, and they were ready to sell small quantities to poor purchasers. They were thus forerunners of the modern department store. Competing with the Echigoya was the Iseya, which opened branches in every ward of the city.

That these great establishments prospered is evidence of a growing population. The daimyos in residence were no doubt among the most lavish customers, followed by their household staffs and by all the samurai who came in their retinues to Yedo. Even more numerous were the servants, indoor and outdoor workers, employed in the city, not only by the hatamoto and go-kenin but by the officials great and small of the central and municipal government offices. Peasants and labourers from the countryside, attracted by good wages, poured constantly into the city, and there was no doubt a considerable floating population of travellers from all provinces, as is evident from the list of inns and restaurants catering for such visitors.

Yet the growth of population in a city without important industries is not easy to explain, though it is evident that it exercised a great attraction. No doubt most young men in the eastern and northern provinces wanted to find work in the capital, and of the thousands who streamed along the Tōkaidō (the eastern coast road) on errands from the merchant houses in the Home Provinces or as workmen in search of well-paid jobs, many must have decided to stay in Yedo.

The great increase in agricultural production which took place after about 1700 would at first sight seem to have required an increased number of farm workers, and it is true that the working farm population increased in some areas despite the introduction of labour-saving devices; but the ratio of increase was not such as to absorb all the new population. The flow of surplus labour to the towns was great and continuous. Another result of increased production on the farms was to develop a direct relationship between the village and the town. Since the tax assessment remained unchanged, there was a surplus of rice which the farmer could sell direct to merchants.

Ōsaka, the greatest commercial city in Japan, was originally a small market ancillary to the Ishiyama Honganji, the headquarters of the Ikkō sect of Buddhism. This fortified cathedral, thanks to its strategic position in the midst of swamps and waterways, held out against attack by Nobunaga year after year until 1580.

Hideyoshi saw the value of its position as the site of a fortified military base, and he built his great castle there to command the approaches to Kyoto from the west. He regarded it as his capital and encouraged its growth as a trading centre. Besieged and reduced by Ieyasu in 1615, it lost its political importance, but the topographical features that had made it a great stronghold were equally favourable to its further growth as a commercial metropolis. It had easy access to the sea, and was close to the productive Home Provinces. Because the transport of heavy goods by land was difficult and slow,[4] it was ideally placed as the great national entrepôt for the collection and distribution of supplies by sea, and consequently as a financial centre of national importance. Its position was more central than that of Yedo, since it had the Inland Sea to the west and the Tōkaidō to the east.

Apart from the three principal cities, a few others deserve mention. Nagasaki did not come into the category of great cities, but it was of special importance after the seclusion edicts, since it was the only port of entry for foreign ships and cargoes. It was here also that the Dutch merchants were allowed to reside under strict surveillance on the reclaimed ground—an artificial island—called Deshima. It was through the Dutch settlement that Japan learned about the outside world, and that the outside world gained some knowledge of Japan. Nagasaki was under direct Tokugawa rule, governed by two Commissioners in accordance with instructions from Yedo.

Chinese merchant ships called frequently at Nagasaki and through their passengers the Japanese authorities got news of events in China, from the decline of the Ming to the rise of the Manchu dynasty.

Nagoya and Kanazawa have already been mentioned as the greatest castle towns. Nagoya was of importance as the capital of the great Owari fief, held by one of the three Tokugawa collaterals (Go-Sanke). It stood overlooking the vast and fertile plain of Owari and Mino. Its position on the Tōkaidō gave it great commercial importance. Kanazawa was the castle town of the head of the Maeda family, the richest daimyo in Japan, with a revenue of over one million koku.

3. The Townspeople

Some attention has already been paid (in Chapter IV) to the character of the populace in Yedo and the difficulty of controlling its lively

---

[4] The main roads were improved under Tokugawa rule, but much of the country was too rough for wheeled traffic. A packhorse could not carry more than two bales of rice. There were high passes to surmount and torrents to cross.

and undisciplined members. Their behaviour was largely determined by their surroundings, which were favourable to street-fighting and robbery with violence, since Yedo was a new city with no tradition of order, where the unemployed members of the warrior class and its dependents were always on the lookout for excitement. The Bakufu was at length able to deal with these trouble-makers by drastic measures after the rōnin conspiracy of 1651, but they were not thoroughly suppressed until a generation or more later. Quarrelsome elements were to be expected in a city populated principally by men-at-arms and their servants, the more so since most of them had no important duties to perform.

But it should not be supposed that the ordinary citizen was a man of this rowdy habit. The chōnin—so called because he dwelt in a city ward (chō) and not under the shadow of the Castle—in general was a respectable artisan or tradesman anxious to bring up his family in peace. Because Yedo was a new city its population included a number of enterprising migrants from all parts of the country, but chiefly from the eastern provinces, which bred a tough and quarrelsome type of man. There was also an admixture of enterprising traders from Mikawa, Tō-tōmi, Ōmi, and Ise, those from the last two in particular being so numerous and successful that they were called by their envious rivals Ōmi Robbers and Ise Beggars. They were prominent in retail trade throughout the city, and contributed much to the mores of the chōnin. Compounded of such elements, the Yedokko (the cockney, we might say) was apt to be a self-reliant, outspoken man, not easy to get on with. This was perhaps especially true of men of warrior origin, but the ordinary townsmen shared those qualities in some measure.

Since much that was written about the bourgeois society of Yedo in the seventeenth and eighteenth centuries, and much of its popular art, portrayed the places of entertainment, the theatres, the restaurants, and the gay quarters, a student is apt to gain the impression that these were scenes of normal Yedo life. But because the quiet existence of the ordinary man goes unrecorded, we ought not to suppose that the average citizen was an indefatigable pleasure-hunter.

Yedo being the seat of government, a large proportion of its inhabitants were servants of the state, from the high officers of the Bakufu down to the police, and these we may presume, whatever their private lives, maintained a public decorum. Further, Yedo tended to replace Kyoto as the intellectual centre of Japan, or at any rate the home of philosophy as Kyoto had been the home of religion. Perhaps the most interesting aspect of the life of the chōnin is the influence of the Neo-Confucian ethical standards which had come to govern the conduct of the warrior class. The Confucian virtues of filial piety and loyalty were those which guided the serious members of the merchant class; and even the dissolute recognized the power of the moral law, of giri or duty, which was a concept of Confucian pedigree. It was the conflict of duty and passion that thrilled the theatre-going citizens of Yedo and Ōsaka, whether the hero was a samurai or an apprentice.

The population of Ōsaka was in many respects of a different character from that of Yedo. Ōsaka had a longer history than Yedo. It was

a commercial and not a political or military centre; its citizens were nearly all engaged in trade and grew in numbers while it developed from simple beginnings as a local market to become the national emporium, attracting goods to its warehouses from most parts of the country and distributing them widely by land and sea. The earliest great merchants in Ōsaka were those who (in competition with merchants in Sakai) made fortunes as war contractors for Hideyoshi, among them being Yodoya Keian, who founded a great family of purveyors, which after 1600 supplied the needs of daimyos by storing their rice and selling it on commission. Before Ōsaka reached the summit of its importance it was the centre of a network of small towns or seaports which served as intermediaries between distant provinces and the rice storehouses along the waterfront of the

A rich merchant, allowed to wear one sword

growing city.

But there was a limit to the growth of Ōsaka because of the difficulty of overland transport of rice and other heavy goods. It was not until this difficulty had been overcome that the great period of expansion began. In considering the character of the people of Ōsaka, therefore, we have to distinguish between the early and the late members of the mercantile community. In the first period the prominent Ōsaka merchants were prosperous members of respectable families who filled positions as City Elders (Toshiyori) with dignity. But as the city developed, thanks to certain improved methods of transport which we shall examine later, a change took place in the character of its citizens. A new class of trader appeared, described by Saikaku in his *Eitaigura* (1688) as follows: "In general prominent people in Ōsaka are no longer the members of old families, but for the most part newcomers, Kichizō and Sansuke [*videlicet* Tom, Dick, and Harry], who have risen in the world." These were lads from the farms of Yamato, Kawachi, Izumi, and Tsu, determined to become rich by their own exertions. "The successful merchants of today came here thirty years ago," he adds, giving as examples the names of Kōnoike and Sumitomo.

Engelbert Kaempfer, the scientist in Dutch employment who visited Ōsaka in 1690, described the city as he saw it: the great traffic of boats on the Yodo river, the teeming population, the crowded streets, the rich supply of victuals, and all that which "tends to promote luxury and to gratify all sensual pleasures." There is no doubt that the citizens of Ōsaka composed a pleasure-loving society, fond of good food and sentimental plays, more epicurean than their Yedo counterparts. But as a class the Ōsaka merchants were serious, hard-working men, and Ōsaka life in all classes was penetrated by an urgent desire for profit. In this last respect it differed from the dominant warrior society of Yedo, in which money-making was despised.

CHAPTER X

THE EXPANDING ECONOMY

1. *Agriculture*

PERHAPS the most remarkable feature of the early modern history of Japan is the rapid growth of farm production in both quantity and range which began with the improvement of farming methods late in the seventeenth century. Production does not usually increase where there is no rising demand, and there is some interest in enquiring what set in motion this new activity. Probably the gradual improvement in the condition of the farmers, their growing self-confidence, and their relative freedom from interference by officials encouraged them to meet demands from an obviously widening market.

Commercial farming had for long been the practice in the rich farmlands serving consumers in the city of Kyoto, who required not only rice but also such produce as vegetables and fruit. The farms were in fact kitchen gardens. There followed demands for other crops, such as tea, tobacco, hemp, mulberry leaves (for silkworms), indigo, and (especially in the provinces of Settsu, Kawachi, Izumi, and Yamato) cotton. Cotton, indeed, was the principal item to increase at a great speed. In those provinces, it is said, about one-fifth of the irrigated land was under cotton by the first decades of the eighteenth century.

Cotton was more profitable than rice, and there was also profit to be had from subsidiary crops of tobacco or tea. Thus a change of temper in the villages becomes apparent, for the peasant is now impelled not by anxiety to appease the tax collector but by a desire for profit. Agriculture now becomes a business, a trade rather than an occupation. Much farm work is done by hired men holding no land themselves; and soon they or their relatives begin to leave for the city—for Sakai or Ōsaka—in large numbers, hearing good news of prospects of employment.

This change in the character of the village was noted by a Bakufu official (a Daikan) named Tanaka Kyūgu in his *Minkan Shōyō*, a description of social conditions at the beginning of the eighteenth century. He observed that the old style of farm was uncommon. In most villages, if there were prosperous farmers, they did not depend upon their rice fields alone, but were engaged in buying and selling.

2. Handicrafts

Although the great increase in agricultural production was directly due to the efforts of the villages, it was encouraged by the enterprise of merchants who sought new markets and stimulated output of any commodity that might bring a profit. Here manufacturing industry played a part in the expansion of the national economy. There was little that could be called machinery apart from the rudimentary apparatus of the farm, and even there the water pump was unknown until it was introduced by the Dutch; but an important exception must be made for the craft of weaving, which had been practised since antiquity. Substantial advances had been made since the Middle Ages in the manufacture of looms and the production of fine weaves of silk (such as the celebrated Nishijinori) and of cotton in a seductive variety of colour and pattern. Apart from these lovely fabrics, often matchless in design, highly skilled artisans led the way to the manufacture of porcelain and paper on a commercial scale. Brewing may be included as an industry, and brands of saké from western centres (Nada, for example) were much relished by the convivial citizens of Ōsaka and Yedo.

Most of these products of craftsmen were easy to transport, or were made in no larger quantities than met local needs. It was the harvest of the farms that raised a difficult problem of transport. The conveyance of heavy merchandise from Ōsaka to Yedo presented no great difficulty; but a really serious problem was how to carry bulk supplies of heavy goods, rice in particular, from distant parts of Japan to Ōsaka.

3. The Problem of Transport

We have seen (in Chapter IX) that there was a limit to the efficacy of Ōsaka as a collecting centre so long as it depended upon supplies carried overland. The great landlords at a long distance from Ōsaka needed to dispose of their surpluses, but carriage by land was always difficult, sometimes impossible, because the country was rough, the roads poor, and rivers often in spate. A packhorse could carry only two bales of rice.

Therefore the carriage of goods had to follow an indirect route determined by the accidents of topography. They were taken to the nearest point where merchants were established, generally a small seaport town. Such were Ōtsu on Lake Biwa; Hyōgo, Onomichi, and Sakai on the Inland Sea; Obama, Tsuruga, and Mikuni on the Japan Sea coast; Kuwana, Yokkaichi, and Ōminato on the Pacific coast; and Hakata in Kyūshū. In the Middle Ages these had been important points where prosperous merchants were usually established, and where freight-carrying vessels were available. Such merchants were sure to be in touch or in communication with regional landlords who had rice or other produce to dispose of—a good example being a Tsuruga merchant named Takashimaya Denzaemon, who was an agent for Maeda, the daimyo of Kaga, in selling his rice or in procuring supplies from other provinces. This connexion was of long standing, for a Takashimaya had bought and transported arms and provisions when a Maeda contingent was due to take part in the invasion of Korea. Similar services were performed in other baronies by agents: for example, Suminokura in Saga, Sumiyoshi in Hirano, Kamiya in Hakata. There were few harbour towns in which a wealthy merchant did not perform such functions or arrange their performance.

Rice from the province of Kaga or from Echizen had first to be sent to Tsuruga, thence some twenty miles by land to the northern shore of Lake Biwa, then by boat on the lake as far as Ōtsu, and finally down the Yodo river to Ōsaka.[1] An even more complicated journey was required to bring to Yedo the Bakufu tax rice from northern Japan (Mutsu). It was first carried by sea to Chōshi (in modern Chiba Prefecture), where it was transferred to river craft and taken upstream on the Tonegawa for shipment on the Yedogawa, and thence by connecting waterways to Yedo itself.

Such slow and cumbrous transport was obviously inadequate to supply the growing needs of Ōsaka and Yedo, and it has been described here in detail only in order to show how urgent it was to find a way to ensure safe and regular delivery of great quantities of rice and other produce from distant points. An increase in production of food would be of little value otherwise. The obvious answer was to improve and develop transport by sea.

As early as 1619 a Sakai merchant had chartered a vessel of 250 koku to carry a mixed cargo (cotton, rape-seed oil, saké, vinegar) from Kishū to Yedo. Soon after that a group of Ōsaka merchants combined to furnish a regular freight service to Yedo by specially designed craft. By the end of the century they had a fleet of vessels of from 200 to 400 koku capacity. This business proved lucrative, and severe competition from rivals followed. The shipowners' position was very strong, since

---

[1] The first direct shipment from Kaga to Ōsaka was a test cargo of 100 koku in 1638.

Ihara Saikaku

as the population of Yedo increased a steady flow of food from Ōsaka became more than ever essential. But it still remained to ensure that supplies, of rice in particular, should reach Ōsaka regularly.

The problem was solved by an elaborate organization of two annual circuits of the main island of Japan, from two different ports on the Japan Sea coast. One (called Higashimawari, or the Eastern Circuit) was a voyage north-east along the coast of Dewa, through the Tsugaru Straits, and thence south to Yedo. The other (called Nishimawari, or the Western Circuit) was a voyage south-west along the Japan Sea coastal route, then through the Straits of Shimonoseki, and on by the Inland Sea to Ōsaka. Each of these voyages out and home, together with the time spent in harbour during stormy seasons, occupied a full year.

Thus the main problems of sea transport had been solved. Kaempfer, visiting Japan in 1690, observed that the ports were full of ships, that there were multitudes of people along the coasts, and such a noise of oars and sails that one might suppose the inland parts of the country to be deserted. Saikaku, in a more picturesque description of the scene on the estuary of the Yodo river, writes of the small craft gliding on the current "like willow leaves on autumn streams."

4. *Growing Markets*

Once the problem of transport was solved, however awkwardly, there was nothing to check an all-round increase in production except a saturated market. This was far ahead at the end of the seventeenth century, since populations were increasing and the standard of living was rising, in urban centres particularly but generally throughout the country.

One incentive to increased production was the demand of daimyos for commodities which their own domains could not produce. Each barony strove to increase its wealth by developing its resources and becoming as far as possible self-supporting. Thus Fukushima in Iwashiro was a centre of sericulture and sent to the market a large supply of raw silk—a valuable product; but this was an exceptional case. In general the principal product was rice, and it was sent, usually to Ōsaka, for sale on the central rice market there. In default of a freely circulating and reliable currency, rice acted as a medium of exchange, and it was in handling the amounts which flowed regularly onto the market that the Ōsaka brokers made great fortunes.

The policy of most daimyos was backward in so far as they aimed at economic independence by erecting barriers both physical and political against intrusion from other domains. They did, however, on balance contribute to an all-round increase of production; and in the administration of their fiefs they paid special attention to economic matters. It is significant of the trend of the times that the most enlightened daimyos employed as advisers scholars with a reputation for political wisdom, and most of these scholars can be described as economists. Indeed it may be said that of the eminent Neo-Confucianists of the mid-century many were interested as much in commerce and agriculture as in political issues. Kumazawa Banzan is perhaps the best example of this school, and he did a great deal to organize the resources of the Okayama fief.

The physical barriers between fiefs (the "seki," or octroi stations) were a hindrance to trade, and most of them had been abolished by 1600; but a number of daimyos still restricted passage through their domains, thus slowing down commercial traffic. In general, however, there was a growth of commercial activity throughout the country, and Bakufu territory in particular was free from burdensome regulations except where watch was kept for political suspects. Moreover, all the important towns (other than the castle towns) were under direct Bakufu jurisdiction and were governed with an eye for profit as well as for peace.

Consequently the increase of production continued at a good pace, and Ōsaka as a market for both collection and distribution spread in size and grew in importance. The foundation of its prosperity was the rice market, which was in constant activity. A daimyo needing money or merchandise would send his surplus rice to his agent in Ōsaka, usually a merchant in good standing who would store it in a warehouse in the daimyo's name. Such an agent was in charge of the property in storage and kept custody of money or goods received from the sale of rice at a price which was fixed by the wholesale rice merchants or (later) by the Rice Exchange, which dealt in futures.

The function of this agent (known as a kuramoto) was one which required a knowledge of the market and good relations with other Ōsaka merchants. The warehouse did not belong to the daimyo, but to the merchants who were licensed by the Bakufu to build and own property in the city. This is an important point to be borne in mind when considering the nature of the mercantile community. It is sometimes said that administration of the city and control of the activities of trade associations were in the hands of a council composed of leading merchants. In normal circumstances this was true, but in all matters the last word was with the two governors (machi-bugyō) appointed by Yedo. The simple view that the Yedo government was unable to enforce its decisions upon the rich merchants, and that therefore the feudal power declined, is not based upon facts. We have only to look at one or two examples of the attitude of the Bakufu towards offenders.

In 1642 certain officials and merchants conspired to corner a market, in disregard of the Bakufu's known antagonism to monopolies. The punishment was cruel. The conspirators' children were executed, the merchants exiled, and their wealth confiscated. This and similar cases were expressions of the general dislike felt by members of the warrior class for combinations of merchants for the sake of profit. This feeling was expressed in several edicts, notably one of 1657 setting forth a long list of trades in which price agreements are forbidden.

Exception could not be taken to the requirements of the merchants who had to deal with the property of a daimyo when it was shipped to Ōsaka. A daimyo or his representative had to rely for a warehouse upon a merchant from whom it was rented. He depended also upon the purchasers in Ōsaka of his rice or other produce for payment, either in specie or preferably (because the freight on specie was prohibitive) by bills of exchange which could be cashed in Yedo when he was in residence there for attendance on the Shōgun.

It may well be supposed that Ōsaka merchants, holding a virtual monopoly as rice brokers or exchange brokers, made very great profits and were among the leaders of the mercantile community. Rice, of course, was the most important commodity, but once the position of Ōsaka as a collecting centre was established, merchandise in the greatest variety poured into the city. There were, for example, among agricultural products, cotton, dyestuffs, vegetable oil, and tea; manufactured goods such as textiles; and bulky cargoes such as timber and minerals. All these commodities were handled by wholesale merchants known as *toiya*.[2] They usually had specialized functions, as shippers at the point of origin, or as handlers at the point of arrival, and finally as holders of quantities to be stored in warehouses if they were not to be reshipped to another market.

It will be seen that the collection and distribution of goods required a great number of merchants and intermediaries, known as *nakagai* (middlemen), especially since in many cases they dealt only in one article, or shipped to or from one particular market. This may seem an excessive multiplication of functions, which indeed it was; but conditions were difficult, since the normal channels of trade proved inadequate to meet the rapid expansion of the national economy. There was, as we have observed, a great increase in the number of places—seaport towns and castle towns—from which goods converged upon Ōsaka or to which goods had to be sent in exchange. Distances were great, and transport, though much improved, required careful planning. Moreover questions of price constantly arose and were not easily settled until exchanges were established where sellers and buyers could meet to make their bargains.

The most important of these was the Rice Exchange at Dojima,[3] where prices were fixed not only for the Home Provinces but also indirectly for the Yedo market, which was influenced by Ōsaka quotations. There were in addition to this most important market a number of speculative exchanges in other commodities which could be kept in storage and therefore admitted dealing in futures.

The handling of this great flow of merchandise required the services of special organs controlled by experienced men. It was therefore natural that such organs should be developed from an already existing system. The characteristic method of control of commerce and industry under feudal rule was the formation of approved trade associations or guilds. Such combinations already existed in a rudimentary form in mediaeval Japan, and were known as "za"; but they lost their influence with the formation (under Nobunaga) of the so-called "free" markets

---

[2] In Yedo pronounced *tonya*. They were lineal descendants of the mediaeval toiya, the agent of a manor.

[3] The Dojima Exchange began as a licensed rice market in 1697. It dealt in actual rice until about 1710, when it began to issue and accept warehouse notes, and to deal in futures ("nobemai"). Ths kind of transaction was officially sanctioned in 1733, when the Bakufu established its own rice storehouse in Ōsaka. There had been riots early in 1733 owing to famine.

and guilds, called "rakuichi" and "rakuza." After the seclusion edicts, with the growth of domestic trade and industry, the need for direction was felt, and associations called "nakama" (which may be translated as "guilds") were formed, and exercised a growing control over the activities of their members, while protecting their interests.

For artisans the nakama was a craft guild. For merchants it was a trade association, known as "kabunakama" when it was approved by the Bakufu. The word "kabu" means a share, but the share was not transmissible. The Bakufu at first opposed such associations, since it was against monopolies, but later approved wider associations, for example a kabunakama of exchange brokers that was recognized on payment of a fee. The authorities saw that the kabunakama was formed not in restraint of trade but to promote cooperation rather than competition among its members. Some Japanese scholars regard these merchant guilds as social organizations, almost religious in character. No doubt they expressed certain ethical principles which a merchant should observe, for the leading merchants agreed that honesty was the best policy; but their motive was profit—an end with which regulated activity is not incompatible.

The number of guilds grew rapidly towards the end of the century. In Ōsaka there were at least twenty-four wholesale shippers of freight to Yedo, and there were numerous guilds of dealers in separate commodities, such as cotton, sugar, and paper, as well as guilds of merchants dealing in the produce of special areas, usually regions at a distance from Ōsaka, such as Satsuma Tonya and Matsumae Tonya. The Ōsaka merchants in particular were organized on a large scale. In the aggregate they were exceedingly rich, and therefore powerful. But the Bakufu kept a watchful eye upon them.

5. Capital Growth

It is clear that in the first decades of the eighteenth century the activities of the Ōsaka merchants had so increased in scope that they must have accumulated immense capital funds. There is no exact evidence of the amount of this accumulation, but there are some conjectures which may be accepted as fair approximations of its order of magnitude.

It is estimated that merchandise to the value of 286,000 kan of silver arrived in Ōsaka in 1714.[4] The greater part of this amount was the value of the annual arrival in Ōsaka of 4,000,000 bales of rice. Much of the

---

[4] One kan is equivalent to 1,000 momme of 2.12 drachms.

profit arising from this trade, whether from actual transactions of sale and purchase or from speculation in futures, was available for investment. Thus in 1704 the exchange broker Kōnoike had put money into the purchase of farmland in Kawachi province and had extended this operation by reclaiming new land along the Yamato river.

Kōneike's is an interesting case. He was agent (kuramoto) for over a score of daimyos and was also the financial agent for the Bakufu in Ōsaka. He was a samurai by birth, but became a commoner when he started as a saké-brewer. He then saw the benefit which would accrue to him if he could be of service to daimyos who needed funds in Yedo during their period of attendance, and accordingly he put himself at the disposal of western daimyos by advancing funds or shipping goods on credit.

In the Shōtoku era (1711–15) the commercial community in Ōsaka is said to have been composed as follows:

Tonya 5,655
Nakagai 8,765
Independents 2,343
Purveyors to the Castle 481
Agents for daimyos 483

Of these the tonya, the nakagai, and the exchange brokers were the most suitably placed to make loans at high interest, since they drew great profit from financing the flow of merchandise throughout the country.

It is clear that this accumulated wealth put much power into the hands of the great Ōsaka merchants and (in a less degree) their Yedo counterparts. Most of the daimyos were in their debt, partly because they were ignorant of financial matters and partly because prices continued to rise while feudal revenues were fixed. Nor were the daimyos the only debtors. With the rapidly increasing supply of consumption goods there came inevitably a rise in the standard of living at every social level, and the samurai who could not make ends meet on his fixed stipend contracted debts to moneylenders or to retail traders. The feeling of antagonism between the samurai and the merchant class tended to spread, and there was little the Bakufu could do to remove it.

Thus the power of the great merchants remained unchallenged, and they continued to thrive; but they knew that if they went too far they would have to meet pressure from the Shōgun's government. They had indeed been warned in 1705, when the Bakufu confiscated the entire fortune of the house of Yodoya, one of the wealthiest and most respected merchant families in Ōsaka. The ground for this punishment was ostentatious conduct unbecoming to a member of the trading class. It is true that Yodoya had great possessions and lived in a grand style, but the true reason for the severity of the Bakufu was no doubt the fact that a number of important feudatories were deeply in debt to him and had thereby lost the power of independent action.

Apart from such individual disasters the merchants continued to flourish, and it was in conditions of prosperity that the first two decades of the eighteenth century peacefully ebbed away. Production was still rising, the chōnin society was gay and extravagant, and it seemed as if the life of Genroku (the era name for the years 1688 to 1704) would continue its pleasant course. This phase of bourgeois culture calls for some description, but first we must return to the study of political developments following the installation of the fifth Shōgun, Tsunayoshi, in 1680.

CHAPTER XI

THE SHŌGUNATE, 1680–1716

1. *Tsunayoshi, 1680–1709*

SINCE Tsunayoshi was much under the influence of his mother, it may help to an understanding of some of his remarkable actions to preface this chapter by an account of that remarkable lady. It is a fascinating study, and it has the advantage of revealing some of the more intimate aspects of an apparently rigid aristocratic society in which persons of humble origin could rise to the highest places.

In contemporary documents she was described as the daughter of one Honjō, a domestic servant of the Kampaku (Regent) Nijō; but in fact she was the daughter of a greengrocer in Kyoto. When her father died her mother took service in the Honjō family, where she gave birth to a son by her employer. As a result of this connexion she was taken into the Honjō family with her elder sister, who had married a servant in the Ichijō household. The head of the Honjō family, Honjō Munemasa, was an assistant cook in the Nijō household, and was familiar with the servants of other great Kyoto families. His father was a rōnin, at a time when the Bakufu was treating the rōnin with severity, and he had thought it prudent to set up in business as a maker of straw mats (tatami). Being impoverished, he depended upon his children; and fortunately for him, since the Nijō were closely related to the Rokujō (another great Kyoto family), and the two young women became acquainted with a daughter of the Rokujō family, who was disposed to help them. This daughter became first a priestess at Ise, and then the concubine of Iemitsu, with the name of O-Man. When she went to Yedo she took with her Honjō's adopted daughter, who soon attracted Iemitsu's attention and at the age of twenty gave birth to the child who was to become the Shōgun Tsunayoshi.

After Iemitsu's death Honjō's daughter was granted the appellation Keishōin, and when Tsunayoshi entered the castle at Yedo, she moved into the inner palace apartments with him. In 1702 she was appointed to the lower grade of the first Court rank—the highest possible for all but members of the Imperial family—and lavish presents were given to the Honjō family, Honjō himself receiving a fief of 50,000 koku.

Her influence upon Tsunayoshi was most powerful. Most of his social policies were adopted upon her advice. The encouragement of

Shōguns, 1623–1716

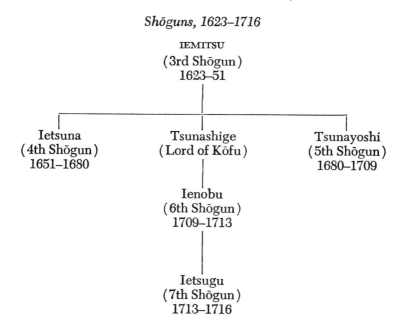

IEMITSU
(3rd Shōgun)
1623–51

Ietsuna
(4th Shōgun)
1651–1680

Tsunashige
(Lord of Kōfu)

Tsunayoshi
(5th Shōgun)
1680–1709

Ienobu
(6th Shōgun)
1709–1713

Ietsugu
(7th Shōgun)
1713–1716

Chinese studies, the promotion of Buddhist worship, the laws protecting animals, all were her work.

Upon Ietsuna's death in 1680 the choice of his successor was (after some disagreements) decided by Mitsukuni, the lord of Owari, and Hotta Masatoshi, the Rōjū, in favour of Ietsuna's younger half-brother, Tsunayoshi. Tsunayoshi at once asserted his authority and made Hotta Masatoshi the Tairō. He next showed his own quality by solving a difficult problem of feudal discipline. He ordered an insubordinate vassal of the daimyo of Takata in Echigo to commit suicide, and confiscated the fief (of 250,000 koku) on the ground of misgovernment. This was in 1681. His subsequent actions were no less firm and arbitrary, but they tended to excesses which bear out the view that his character was abnormal.

During his term of rule he confiscated the estates of more than twenty daimyo and one hundred hatamoto, worth in all some 1,400,000 koku. He was determined to be an absolute ruler, and for this purpose he decided to destroy the influence of a number of Fudai vassals who had a virtual monopoly of important posts in the Bakufu. In the Palace he rearranged offices so as to reduce the authority of the Rōjū and to increase that of the Chamberlains (Soba-yōnin). These changes were made easy by the death of the Tairō (Masatoshi), who was murdered in 1684 by an envious cousin. During Masatoshi's lifetime, administration had been sound and beneficent, but no successor to the office of Tairō was appointed, and Tsunayoshi thereafter exercised absolute power.

But he had no taste and little capacity for those practical tasks of government which involve considerations of finance and the preservation of order in the realm by lawful and just measures. It was in the domain of theory that he supposed himself to excel, though it must be granted that it was his government which in 1683 revised the Buke Sho-Hatto by adding an article ordering private disputes and farmers' grievances to be referred to law officers, and in 1686 put an end to the riotous kabukimono who had for long disturbed the peace of the capital.

He was a devoted follower of the school of Chu Hsi, and it was to him that Neo-Confucian studies in Japan owed the foundation in 1680 of the Seidō and other contributions to the official status of Confucianism which have been described in Chapter VII. He himself was an earnest student and even tried to inculcate Confucian principles by notices posted up throughout the country announcing rewards for virtuous behaviour. Indeed soon after his installation in 1680 he called upon Hayashi Nobuatsu, the head of the Confucian college, to give three lectures a month on the new Confucianism; and on New Year's Day of 1682 an assembly of daimyos and officials was given an exposition of *The Great Learning*. This became an annual practice at the Shōgun's court on the first day of the New Year. Tsunayoshi's classical fervour increased to such a point that in 1690 he himself addressed an audience composed of the Rōjū and Bakufu officers on the same work; and after that he lectured each month on the Four Books to daimyos, hatamoto, Buddhist monks, and Shintō ritualists, to say nothing of visitors to Yedo from the Court in Kyoto. His own lectures were delivered between 1692 and 1700, six times a month, their total reaching two hundred and forty-four, according to his favourite Yanagisawa Yoshiyasu.

In addition to this he would, when visiting his vassals in their own residences, first deliver an address himself and then listen to lectures by his hosts or their retainers. His favourite works were *The Great Learning (Ta Hsueh)* and *The Classic of Filial Piety (Hsiao Ching)*.

Tsunayoshi's own claim to classical learning was by no means unfounded. He was genuinely interested in literature and the fine arts. He employed as a teacher the eminent poet Kitamura Kigin (1618–1705), an authority on the arcana of the Imperial Court, and he patronized the leading painters of the Kyoto schools. One artist, Hanabusa Itchō (1652–1724), offended him by a satirical picture and was sent into exile.

Tsunayoshi is often supposed to have been under the influence of his favourite Yanagisawa Yoshiyasu, but there is little to support this view. Yoshiyasu was the son of a small Bakufu officer, and being a gifted youth he was taken into service by Tsunayoshi on his accession in 1680. He was soon promoted and before long became a Chamberlain with a lavish allowance of 10,000 koku. He grew so intimate with Tsunayoshi and his mother that they visited him very frequently. He was rapidly promoted in rank and given new honours and emoluments.

He is alleged to have procured good-looking girls and boys and Nō actors for the Shōgun, and this may well be true; but though as a companion he was very close to Tsunayoshi, he did not suggest lines of policy, nor was Tsunayoshi a man to accept suggestions from subordinates. Tsunayoshi's lavish treatment of Yoshiyasu was characteristic of his mania, but Yoshiyasu was not a mere flatterer. He genuinely shared Tsunayoshi's literary taste, his interest in classical learning, and even his religious beliefs.

Tsunayoshi seems to have entered upon his term of office in an optimistic mood, for in 1682 he ordered his Commissioners and Censors to take steps (apart from normal judicial measures) to raise the standard of morality among the people. The specific measures which he recommended were sumptuary rules. They included a ban upon prostitution, upon the employment of waitresses in teahouses, and similar practices. In the following year he ordered the Governors of Nagasaki to prohibit the importation of articles of luxury and to put a limit upon the cost of embroideries containing gold thread and in general of rare and expensive fabrics. There is little evidence to show that these embargoes were successful and good reason to suppose that they encouraged smuggling.

Although Tsunayoshi's policies were on the whole well-intentioned, he went at times to such extremes of cruelty and sentimentality that he must be regarded as a mentally unbalanced man. Under the influence of his mother, who appears to have been afflicted with religious mania, he spent great sums on building or enlarging sacred edifices of the Shingon sect of Buddhism to please her and her spiritual advisers. His own passion for learning grew year after year. He also endeavoured to practise, and to oblige others to practise, the virtues recommended by the sages of Buddhism and Confucianism, his most noteworthy action in this field being the issue of charitable ordinances for the protection of abandoned children and travellers overcome by sickness.

A Shingon monk having suggested that Tsunayoshi had no male heir because he had taken life in a previous existence, he (or his mother) decided that he must now devote himself to the protection of living things. He had been born in the Year of the Dog. Therefore, his advisers said, he should pay special attention to the welfare of those creatures. Accordingly, in 1687, orders protecting living things in general, but especially dogs, were issued day after day to the dismay of the citizens. No doubt there were too many wild and hungry dogs roving in the city and fouling its streets, and no doubt people were too ready to dispose of them; but it was excessive if not insane to order the execution of an apprentice for wounding a dog, and it was ludicrous folly to insist that dogs should be addressed in honorific terms, such as Mr. or Mrs. Dog (O Inu Sama). The city government was helpless. Unable to solve the problem, at length it decided in 1695 to move the source of trouble to a distance, by building shelters in the suburbs, where (it is said) in the next two years no less than 50,000 dogs were kept and fed on rice and dried fish at the expense of taxpayers.

Despite Tsunayoshi's obvious weaknesses and the distress they caused to Yedo citizens, the nation at large does not seem to have suffered any serious harm from his erratic conduct of affairs. He interfered from time to time, but his chief interest was in literature and the arts. He liked to produce Nō plays in his palace apartments, and took leading roles himself. For the latter part of his life as Shōgun there is little of political interest to record, probably because the executive officers of the government performed their tasks competently and in an unobtrusive manner. The only striking event of a political character was the affair of the Forty-Seven Rōnin, which the Bakufu handled well enough.

In finance the most important action was a "revision"—it may be called a debasement—of the gold and silver currency in 1695.[1] This gave a profit to the Bakufu treasury and seems to have had no marked ill effect upon the economy. That Tsunayoshi's misgovernment cannot have caused serious harm to the country is clear from the ample evidence of prosperity in both urban and rural life during the era named Genroku —from 1688 to 1704. The great capital sums accumulated by the first three Shōguns had not been entirely spent, commerce was flourishing, and capital funds were available for investment in the development of farmland or in other productive enterprises.

The economy was still expanding, though at a slackening speed, and the financial condition of the government was not unfavourable. Indeed

---

[1] Arai Hakuseki, who endeavoured to reform the currency and to cut down expenditure in 1709, wrote in his memoirs that the "revision" of 1695 gave the Bakufu a profit of five million ryō. *Oritaku Shiba no Ki*, Vol. II, Section 1.

it was even improving until the end of the year 1703, when Yedo suffered a disaster, an earthquake that wrecked a great part of the city and caused much loss of life. In the countryside there was also loss of life and serious damage from the action of tidal waves along the Tōkaidō littoral. Then, a few days after the earthquake, a fire beginning from the Mito mansion in the Yotsuya ward of Yedo was spread by a hurricane and did further damage.

These were unhappy times for the country, particularly the eastern provinces, since there were more earthquakes and conflagrations at the end of 1707, when Fuji erupted, and much of the surrounding region was deep in ashes from volcanic action which continued for several days. There was little loss of life, but much arable land was devastated, and great efforts were needed before it could be restored to cultivation. A sum of 400,000 ryō was allotted for the removal of ashes. Not long after these disasters there was trouble in Kyoto, where a fire destroyed a wide area in the city; and this misfortune was followed in April 1708 by storm and flood which ruined the growing crops of the fertile Kinai.

Tsunayoshi had gone into retirement, leaving the conduct of affairs to Yanagisawa. In the summer of 1708 he announced that he would resign in favour of the Shōgun-designate, his nephew Ienobu, the lord of Kōfu, who had been recommended by Mitsukuni of Mito. Tsunayoshi had not long to live. He was ill when the New Year's reception was held by Ienobu as his deputy, and he died a few days later.

It so happens that we have good evidence of conditions in Japan under Tsunayoshi in Engelbert Kaempfer's description of his experiences in 1691 and 1692, when he visited the capital as a member of the annual Dutch embassy from the trading settlement of Nagasaki.

Kaempfer gives a picture—he was a trained observer—of the towns and villages through which he and his companions passed on the long journey from Nagasaki to Ōsaka, thence to Kyoto, and along the Tōkaidō to Yedo. They went by road first to Kokura, and crossed over in small boats to Shimonoseki, there to transfer to a barge which with a fair wind would reach Ōsaka in eight days. Travel by ship was somewhat hazardous, because owing to the seclusion edicts no large seagoing craft might be built; but by taking frequent shelter the voyage was safely accomplished. From Ōsaka the journey was continued by land, along the Tōkaidō after Kyoto.

Travel along the highways he describes as agreeable, the roads being broad, well drained, and kept in good repair by villagers. His company went on horseback or in palanquins. The villages along the highways, he thought, were only thinly inhabited, but in the towns and cities he was surprised by the great number of shops and the variety of their wares. Of the life of the peasants he says: "Of household goods they have but few, while it is generally their lot to have many children and great poverty; yet with some small provision of rice, plants, and roots they are content and happy." He observes at the crossroads in each town or large village notice boards used for publishing the orders and edicts of the central government or of the feudal lord of the region.

He is vastly impressed by the great number ("scarce credible") of people who daily travel on the roads. The Tōkaidō, the chief and most frequented of the highways in Japan, "is on some days more crowded than the public streets in any of the most populous towns of Europe." Of course the great barons passing to and from Yedo were escorted by trains of hundreds, even thousands, of men, but apart from these the roads were always thronged by ordinary citizens, mostly on business but many on pilgrimages at certain seasons, making their way to some sacred place like Ise, but always with an eye to enjoyment. Kaempfer has much to say about the inns and eating houses along the roads, and dwells at length upon the "numberless wenches" offering their services to wayfarers. Altogether the picture he paints is one of bustling activity and a great measure of prosperity. This is borne out by contemporary Japanese descriptions of the years at the turn of the century, coinciding with the rule of Tsunayoshi. These were still years of expanding trade and production.

Kaempfer's account of the reception of the Dutch embassy by Tsunayoshi is entertaining and throws some light on life in high military society. On the visit of 1691 the party reached Odawara on March 11, finding it a handsome town with an imposing castle. The inhabitants were well dressed and of polite behaviour, except for small boys who shouted insults at the strangers. They continued along the Tōkaidō and, passing by the execution ground at Shinagawa ("a very shocking sight"), they rode into Yedo in the afternoon of March 13. They met, as they rode along, the numerous trains of princes and great men at Court, and ladies richly dressed. On both sides of the streets were multitudes of well-furnished shops kept by merchants and tradesmen of all kinds. Their own little train attracted no attention in a city accustomed to imposing cavalcades.

They were treated hospitably while waiting for an audience with the Shōgun, saw a fire that destroyed six hundred houses, and experienced a slight earthquake. The audience was fixed for March 29, the official in charge of the arrangements being none other than Makino,

Bungo no Kami, one of Tsunayoshi's favourites and formerly his tutor. Passing through several gateways and observing numerous guards posted along their route evidently for display and not for protection, they entered the innermost Palace enclosure and were conducted up stairways to a spacious waiting room, where they remained for some time while the head of their mission was received in audience by the "Emperor," that is to say by the Shōgun.

The audience was very brief, and Kaempfer was disappointed because he had no opportunity to examine his surroundings closely. But on its next visit, in 1692, the Dutch party saw a great deal. After the formalities of obeisance paid to the Shōgun by the Dutch ambassador, all members of the mission entered the spacious hall of audience, where Tsunayoshi and some of the ladies of the Court sat concealed behind reed screens, through slits in which they could see the Hollanders clearly. The great Councillors of State (Rōjū) were present, and also "gentlemen in attendance" (Soba-yōnin, or Chamberlains).

After making their obeisance, the members of the mission were welcomed in the Shōgun's name by Makino, who then asked them to stand, to dance and sing, to converse with one another, and generally to show how Westerners behaved. Kaempfer himself danced and sang, much to the pleasure of the ladies, who cleverly enlarged the slits in their screens so as to get a better view. This incident is drily recorded in the official record, which gives a list of the presents brought by the Dutch and says: "The Dutchmen sang and danced, and wrote some words in their own language for the Shōgun to see." The same journal tells us that a day or two later Tsunayoshi took part in a Nō performance in his palace, dancing a role in "Yashima" and other plays.

It is clear that at this time there was no marked decline in Tsunayoshi's health, for it is not a sign of disease to prefer plays to politics; but he seems to have tired from about 1698, when Yanagisawa was made equal to Tairō, and to have gradually withdrawn from official life in order to devote himself to his studies and his Nō performances. According to some accounts he was given to debauchery, but the evidence on this point is scanty. It is best to assume simply that in the last ten years of his life he suffered a slow deterioration of mind and body. He died at the age of sixty-four, so that it can scarcely be said that he ruined his health by dissipation.

Some writers say that under Tsunayoshi the Bakufu was weak and incompetent, but there is little evidence to support this view. It is true that the Shōgun was no longer a military dictator like Iemitsu; but Tsunayoshi's government kept the feudatories in order by very drastic methods; its financial policy was on the whole successful despite the great strain of natural disasters, and it did not hesitate to deal firmly with the great merchants in Yedo and Ōsaka. It approved, if it did not initiate, important riparian works and great advances in the transport of passengers and goods. Under Tsunayoshi's guidance, relations between the Bakufu and the Imperial Court were much improved. He revived and furnished funds for the major Court ceremonies and several other observances that had lapsed for a century or more, including the annual festival of the Kamo shrine, which was almost as old as the city, and had an historical connexion with the Court.

The fear inspired by Tsunayoshi's methods is clearly shown in contemporary records. The slightest mistake of a vassal was severely punished. Officials tried to avoid accepting appointments for fear of making a mistake which would end their careers. There was an active secret police, watching the movements of visitors to the houses of daimyos or of Rōjū. Tsunayoshi's major political achievement was to strengthen the authority of the central government, and his work for that purpose is described by some historians as the Reforms of the eras Tenna (1681–84) and Jōkyō (1684–88).

2. Ienobu, 1709–13

The reign of Ienobu, the former lord of Kōfu, was brief and uneventful, but it witnessed a reaction against the license of the society over which Tsunayoshi had presided. Ienobu's task was to complete the transition (begun under Ietsuna) from a predominantly militaristic to a civil form of government. It was now more than a hundred years since Sekigahara. The echoes of war had died away, and political theory of a Confucian character had already gained much influence in the ruling class, that is to say among Bakufu officials and the administrators of the fiefs.

Ienobu was a scholarly man of high character, anxious to govern wisely, but his experience as a ruler of a fief did not fully qualify him for his new task. It was natural that he should at times consult a man of great learning and acknowledged loyalty, who had been his tutor for many years. This was the scholar Arai Hakuseki, whom he employed as an adviser. Opinions differ about the part played by Hakuseki in the formation of policy, but owing to his previous employment by Ienobu he was in a good position to watch, if not to influence, the course of events, and his memoirs furnish a valuable picture of life in official circles as well as showing the ideals of members of the samurai class in his youth.[2]

Hakuseki (1656–1725), a rōnin through no fault of his own, was the son of a samurai of modest rank but good repute in a small daimyo's domain. An infant prodigy, he studied hard and, as a young samurai of good judgment ready if need be to use his sword, earned the respect of his comrades. His early life was a hard one (the details are given in Section 5 of this chapter), and it was not until 1694 that he rose to any prominence. In that year he succeeded in obtaining an appointment as tutor to the daimyo of Kōfu, an important fief held by a Tokugawa collateral, at that time Ienobu, who was to become the sixth Shōgun.

Ienobu was a studious man, and he must have had great powers of endurance, for according to Hakuseki's account he listened patiently to 1,299 lectures on the Chinese classics over a period of nineteen years. Hakuseki obtained this valuable appointment in a curious way. He was earning a precarious livelihood in Yedo by teaching, when, thanks partly to the recommendation of the philosopher Kinoshita Junan (who employed him temporarily), he was summoned to the lord of Kōfu's Yedo residence and within a day or so was lecturing to Ienobu on *The Great Learning*. At that time he was in his thirty-seventh year. He was given an adequate stipend, and was now well established. Not long before that he and his wife had only thirty cents in cash, a few quarts of rice, and a manservant and a maid who refused to leave them.

Kōfu listened to the lectures regularly. They lasted for two hours each, and during that time Kōfu and all others present sat motionless. In addition to his lectures, Hakuseki wrote historical treatises for his pupil's instruction, the first being a history of the fiefs of over 10,000 koku. It was called *Hankampu*, and covered the years 1600–1680.

Shortly after his accession in 1709 Ienobu began to introduce reforms. It was easy to make sure that the blunders of Tsunayoshi were corrected, his ludicrous edicts withdrawn, and his wicked companions dismissed; and since Tsunayoshi in his wiser decisions had promoted the liberal movement begun under Ietsuna, Ienobu could here with confidence follow his lead. In 1710 he issued a revised order to the military houses (Buke Sho-Hatto), in which the style of language used was improved and some new material was included. There were new

---

[2] These memoirs were published under the title *Oritaku Shiba no Ki*. A translation by G. W. Knox contains some errors but is on the whole reliable. See *Transactions of the Asiatic Society of Japan*, Vol. XXX. Students who read the original will be impressed by its clear style.

articles against bribery and corruption, aimed chiefly at the private influence of the Chamberlains. There were also clauses stating that popular feeling must be allowed expression and officials must not prevent complaints from reaching the proper quarter.

Ienobu also introduced reforms in the judicial system, abolishing certain cruel punishments, increasing the efficiency of the law courts, and insisting upon prompt decisions. On most of these points he was furnished with written opinions by Hakuseki, who was able and willing to lecture copiously on problems of government in accordance with Neo-Confucian principles. Doubtless his opinions influenced the practical decisions of the Bakufu officers, but he was not a policy-maker.

The main lines of policy were decided by the Shōgun's chief officers —the Chamberlains (Soba-yōnin), in particular a very able and experienced man, Manabe Akifusa (formerly a Nō actor), who had served in important posts in Ienobu's Kōfu domain. Hakuseki was on good terms with Manabe, and was sensible enough not to disagree with him, but to devote himself to the study of specific problems, and to offering advice on their solution.

One of Hakuseki's contributions was in the practical field of economic reform. This was the first question upon which he was consulted. There had been a disconcerting rise in prices, which he attributed to a fall in the standard of the metallic currency coupled with a rise in its quantity. He urged prompt action to put this right in a memorandum to the government, and a new gold coin was issued, the amount in circulation being reduced by half. He also recommended steps to reduce the outflow of silver, which was being shipped in quantity from Nagasaki in order to balance the import of foreign goods. For this purpose he proposed to limit the total volume of foreign trade, though a more rational solution would have been to increase exports other than silver. But this would have been contrary to the Chinese principles of self-containment.

Other official tasks entrusted to Hakuseki were the redrafting of the Buke Sho-Hatto and—of more significance—discussions with the ex-Kampaku Konoe Motohiro, who came from Kyoto to Yedo to reach an agreement on relations between the Imperial Court and the Bakufu, which were already improving under Tsunayoshi. Hakuseki's account of the conversations with Konoe gives the impression that he took the lead; but he was not free from vanity, and no doubt his actual role was to listen and report, not to argue. It was agreed that younger sons of an Emperor should be allowed to found new families (instead of entering the Church), and that future imperial princesses should be allowed to marry. The agreement was sealed, so to speak, by the betrothal of a princess to an infant son of the Shōgun. The Court also profited by new grants from the Shōgun. These arrangements seem to have been expressions of a wish on the part of the Bakufu to be regarded as the supreme organ of civil government rather than a despotic military headquarters.

It may be asked why an official of modest rank in an advisory position should concern himself with such issues when there were many political and financial questions that needed attention. But although Hakuseki's situation did not entitle him to make policy, for this was the function of the high officers of the Shōgun, it was his business to suggest ways of dealing with problems as they arose, always within limits laid down by the Bakufu. His position resembled that of a modern civil servant, who draws up documents on current questions for the consideration of his political superiors. It is in that capacity that Hakuseki dealt with such problems as currency reform.

Hakuseki was a remarkable man, of very strong character, high principles, and great learning, but he disclaimed any intention to make decisions for his superiors. At the end of his memoirs he states clearly: "Nowadays people talk as if everything was carried out on the sole decision of Manabe, even as if the government of the country was conducted by a person like me. But a person like me does not hold office permitting the exercise of authority. Moreover Akifusa, under the orders of the sixth Shōgun, acted as an intermediary between the Shōgun and the Rōjū, and after the sixth Shōgun's death Akifusa (in accordance with his testament) took part in discussion of affairs of state with the Rōjū.[3] When my opinion was asked it was at the suggestion of Akifusa, presumably in accordance with the same orders. If there had been any objection to this, surely the Rōjū could have put an end to it by dismissing Akifusa."

Hakuseki's statement is of course true in form, but in substance it needs some qualification, since once Tsunayoshi had passed over the Rōjū and leaned upon his Chamberlains, the full powers of the Rōjū were no longer exercised. It is true that Yanagisawa Yoshiyasu, who had the power but not the office of Tairō, lost his place as a Chamberlain upon Tsunayoshi's death; but after his fall the Rōjū did not resume their lost authority.[4] Nor did they recover it upon the accession of Ienobu, for he brought with him from his Kōfu fief a number of his most trusted officials, among them Manabe Akifusa himself.

[3] The Seventh Shōgun being an infant.
[4] Hakuseki says: "All the Rōjū did was to pass on his [Yoshiyasu's] instructions."

Hakuseki's contribution to the government was evident in the field of theory rather than practice. A Confucianist by training and temperament, he naturally approved of the adoption of classical Chinese principles, and he announced clearly that what the state needed was the benign influence of Ritual and Music (*Reigaku*, or in Chinese *Li* and *Yueh*.) So baldly stated, such a proposition is hard to accept, but it becomes intelligible when it is explained that *Li* means a code of behaviour or, in a broader sense, fixed principles of conduct, and *Yueh* stands for the elevating and refining influence of music (and the arts in general), in contrast to the hard realism of military rule. In pursuit of these ideals Hakuseki paid much attention to Court ceremonies and to such matters as the correct procedure for receiving embassies from Korea.

He was respected by Ienobu, who treated him well, gave him a stipend of 1,000 koku, and raised him to the rank of hatamoto in 1713. By then he was in his fifty-seventh year and had already been employed in the Bakufu for four years. He remained in employment after Ienobu was succeeded by Ietsugu, and until Ietsugu's death in 1716. Thus he was in office for only eight years, and although during that period he occupied no position of authority, he was trusted as an adviser and much admired as a scholar. His views on history may have had some influence on the mind of Ienobu, and he may have contributed to policy-making in a general way, as for example when he pointed out abuses which needed attention. In the government departments there were many serious shortcomings, carried over from the days of Ietsuna and Tsunayoshi, as is clear from a study of the *Tokugawa Jikki*, the official Tokugawa history. A purge was needed, and Hakuseki did not hesitate to say so.

3. *Ietsugu, 1713–16*

Ietsugu was an infant when he became Shōgun, and his life was short. No events of importance took place in those few years, except for a so-called "reform" of the coinage and some attempts to improve the regulation of foreign trade at Nagasaki.

The currency problem was difficult, and no satisfactory solution was found; but it needs some separate description, since it plagued the government incessantly.

4. *Currency Reform*

Hakuseki's account of the financial problems of the Bakufu sheds an interesting light upon the incompetence and the dishonesty of the officials of the Treasury. Deficits were so great that auditors were appointed, and their investigations laid bare peculation on a large scale, especially by one officer, the Finance Commissioner (Kanjō-Bugyō) Hagiwara Shigehide, who made great profits by secret arrangements with building contractors. By debasing the silver coinage he is said to have made a profit of more than a quarter of a million ryō. He was known to have been cheating for thirty years, but nobody denounced him until Hakuseki took his pen and wrote accusations which could not be disproved.

Some idea of the degradation of official morality towards the end of the seventeenth century may be gained from an outline of the currency problem as it developed from the early years of the Bakufu. The coinage in the Keichō era (ca. 1615) had consisted of gold pieces (called "koban") containing 85.69 per cent of pure gold and 14.25 per cent of pure silver, while the Keichō silver pieces contained over 80 per cent of pure silver. By 1695 (Genroku 8) this was changed so that the Genroku gold koban contained only 56.4 per cent of gold and 43.19 per cent of silver, while the silver pieces contained only 64.35 per cent of pure silver.

This process of debasement reflects a progressive failure in the financial policy of the Bakufu. In the days of Ieyasu and Hidetada there had been a vast accumulation of capital derived from taxation, from profits in foreign trade, from the yield of mines, and even from economies in administration.

Under Iemitsu about half of this capital sum had been spent; under the fourth Shōgun (Ietsuna) income and expenditure no longer balanced. The great fire of Meireki caused cruel losses, and the cost of relief and restoration was so heavy that the strain on the finances of the Bakufu was borne only with difficulty. Yet the extravagances which began in Iemitsu's time increased rather than diminished, and annual expenditure continued to rise—under Tsunayoshi in particular. Apart from these avoidable losses, the output of the silver mines diminished, and continued natural disasters, combined with embezzlement by dishonest officials, ended in a complete breakdown. It was at this point that in order to patch up the damage the first debasement of the coinage took place in 1695, as an emergency measure. The immediate cause of this action was an urgent need for funds to build the costly shrine and carry out the customary funeral rites for a deceased Shōgun—in this case Ietsuna. It was Hagiwara Shigehide who proposed the debasement to Tsunayoshi.

According to Hakuseki's calculation the Bakufu made a profit of more than five million ryō by this conversion. Meanwhile in 1695 the

Bakufu had called in the former gold and silver coins, but with little success. The edict was repeated in following years (1696 to 1702), but the response was poor. Hakuseki's opinion was that more than half the old issue was being secretly held. This was only an estimate, but there is no doubt that the public had little confidence in the Bakufu's coinage policy; and this attitude of mistrust was reflected in the growth of counterfeiting, for which there were over five hundred convictions a few years after 1695.

By 1713 prices were again rising. Various proposals were made to the Bakufu, among them plans for a new coinage submitted by Shigehide. These were rejected and Shigehide was removed from office, but no further action was taken until late in the year, after the death of Ienobu. Then a currency reform was proposed, which included withdrawal of the Genroku (1695) coins and a new issue.

It was urged that the people had no trust in the government's policy, by which the standard of purity of gold and silver had been lowered and the ratio of value between gold and silver had been changed; therefore there should be a return to the Keichō standards, which would restore confidence and reduce prices. A new metallic currency was accordingly introduced in 1714. It was of the same quality as the Keichō currency, and its effect was beneficial. The price of rice in silver, which had remained fairly stable from 1695 to 1710, rose rapidly from 1710 to 1713, and then as the new coins came into circulation, fell steeply to a minimum in 1718, when it stood at a point lower than the 1695 figure.

The currency problem was closely related to the regulation of foreign trade, since any adverse balance had to be met by the export of precious metal. After the enforcement of the seclusion policy, private foreign trade was forbidden and public foreign trade was limited to exchange of goods with China and Holland (or strictly speaking with Dutch merchant ships) through the settlement at Hirado ,or later at Nagasaki.

This trade had continued without restriction for some years, and as late as 1683–84 hundreds of junks from China arrived in Nagasaki, where there was a thriving Chinese settlement on shore. In 1685, however, the Bakufu placed a limit upon the total amount of foreign trade. The reason for this restriction was, according to Japanese statements, that the Ming policy of limiting foreign trade had been reversed by the Manchu rulers, and Chinese vessels now began to enter Japanese ports in increasing numbers, to the alarm of the Japanese government. But the embargoes of the Bakufu were not observed by the Chinese, and in 1688 a further ban on entries was issued, limiting the Chinese to seventy-three vessels a year, and allowing only a specified small number of Chinese traders to open premises on shore. But these measures did not solve the problem. They merely encouraged smuggling and other illicit transactions.

This was the situation which faced Ienobu's government and which the Bakufu hoped to rectify. But the Governors of Nagasaki complained that the loss of trade was already causing great distress to the Japanese population of Nagasaki, and they asked for relief in the shape of a plentiful supply of copper for export, so as to redress the adverse balance.

The position at the opening of the Shōtoku era (1711–16) can now be described in some detail, thanks to recent scrutiny of records kept at Nagasaki.[5] Full lists of cargoes are furnished, but for our purpose it suffices to summarize the situation in terms of a plain balance sheet. Trade in Nagasaki in 1711 was composed as follows: imports to the value of 4,193 kan of silver; exports to the value of 2,918 kan of silver—in other words, an adverse balance of 1,275 kan, which had to be redressed by a reduction in imports or by the shipment of silver or copper.

There were strong objections to any increase in the export of silver and copper, partly because the output of the Japanese mines had been falling off and partly because of currency needs. After much discussion and the proposal of several unworkable plans, a new ordinance was promulgated dealing with the question in all its aspects. It was an elaborate document, but its most important provisions may be easily summarized:

Two Commissioners of Foreign Trade to be appointed, to serve alternately for a year in Yedo and Nagasaki.

Thirty Chinese vessels and two Dutch vessels to be allowed entry each year.

The Chinese ships to take cargoes up to a total value of 6,000 kan of silver each year.

The Dutch ships to take cargo up to a total value of 3,000 kan of silver each year.

At the same time there was to be made available for export each year 3,000,000 kin of copper for the Chinese and 1,500,000 kin for the Dutch. (The actual amount exported in 1711 was 1,797,694 kin, approximately 1,000 tons.)

---

[5] These records incidentally show that Hakuseki's figures were unreliable, thus confirming an impression that the great man was not always accurate. The source is an article by T. Yamawaki, in *Tōhōgaku*, No. 19 (1959).

This trade was in quantity of no great importance, and at first sight it seems as if it were not worth the trouble which it gave to both national and local authorities. The earlier restrictions of about 1640 were part of the seclusion policy, but those imposed by Tsunayoshi in 1688 were of an economic character, designed to check the import of luxuries, and the consequent loss of gold and silver. This was, or appeared to be, a matter of some urgency in the light of shortages at home. The imports were of no vital importance to the Japanese economy, since they consisted chiefly of silk yarns and textiles, skins, sugar, medicines, and books and paintings. Of these only the last three items might be regarded as necessities. No doubt if a greater effort had been made the value of exports could have been increased, but the attitude of the Bakufu was still governed by prejudice against freedom of commerce. The regulations of 1715 were inspired not only by a desire to make economies but also by the isolationist ideas which were traditional in China and had affected Japanese thought.

Ienobu adopted the recommendations of Hakuseki, who made no effort to restore the balance of trade by increasing exports, because he believed that a country could be impoverished by sending its products abroad; and as for purchases of foreign goods, he approved only of the aforesaid medicines and books.

5. *Arai Hakuseki*

Hakuseki's autobiography, *Oritaku Shiba no Ki,* deserves some special attention, not only on account of its author's achievements as a scholar, but also because it illustrates very clearly the code of behaviour of the best type of samurai of the day. By the middle of the seventeenth century, town life and the lack of suitable employment had brought about a sad deterioration in the behaviour of many members of the lower ranks of the military class; but in the countryside remote from urban influences the old, rigid standards were preserved. They are well portrayed in the pages which Hakuseki devoted to the life of his parents and to his own early experience as a youthful samurai.

His father, born in 1602, a wanderer in his youth in the confused post-war society of Japan, was a rōnin until at the age of thirty he entered the service of Tsuchiya, a daimyo of 21,000 koku in the province of Kazusa. He had a fair position in Tsuchiya's household, being promoted for good conduct and courage. Hakuseki records his own youthful memories of his father in the following terms:

"Father's life followed a strict and uninterrupted routine. He awoke at four in the morning, bathed in cold water and dressed his own hair. In very cold weather Mother wished him to use warm water, but he would not give the servants trouble. When he was past seventy, fire was kept in the footwarmer at night, and he used hot water then for Mother's sake because it could be heated easily at that time.

"Father and Mother were both Buddhists, and after their bath put on their special clothes and worshipped. . . . When they awoke before dawn they sat up in bed and silently awaited the daybreak."

Hakuseki relates the story told by his father of a remarkable sword called the Dish-Cutter: "The sixteen-year-old son of an important officer named Katō was shouting from an upstairs room in a quarrel with a young samurai who was cleaning fish in the yard below. I had a room on the same floor, and when I saw Katō rushing down I picked up my sword and went down to see. Katō had struck the youth, but he was not badly hurt and turned on Katō with his fish knife. So I cut him down from the shoulder, my sword going right across his body and splitting the dish. As he fell I said to Katō 'Now finish him,' wiped the blood from my blade, and returned it to its scabbard and went home. So when others came rushing up they called Katō's sword the Dish-Cutter! My sword had belonged to a man named Gotō, who had it from his brother who had cut a man's head in two with it. He kept the skull as a memento."

Hakuseki described his father in simple language: "As I remember father . . . he was short, large-boned, strongly built. He showed no sign of emotion in his face. He did not laugh loudly or scold in an angry voice. His words were few and his movements dignified. I never saw him surprised or lacking in self-control. . . . When off duty he swept his room, hung up an old picture, arranged a few flowers, and sat silent all day, or painted, but in black and white, not in colour. . . . At home he wore only carefully washed clothes, and when he went out his dress was new and fine, but not extravagant or beyond his rank. When he was past seventy he wore only one sword, not over a foot long, and his servant followed bearing his long sword, because he thought that a man should not wear a weapon which he could not handle. He kept the short sword all his life, but put it away when he took the tonsure."

Some years after his father's death, Hakuseki was told by a monk that when his father was past eighty a drunken man came to the monastery flourishing a sword. The monks were afraid, but Hakuseki's father came out, caught him by the arm, tripped him, and threw his sword into the drain.

Hakuseki displayed great talent as a child and is said to have written ideographs with skill at the age of three. By ten he wrote his father's letters, and at eleven he had fencing lessons and did well in matches with other boys. He was a page in the Tsuchiya household, and there he continued his studies with the aid of a friendly scholar who took him through some Chinese classical works. Thereafter he was mostly self-taught and continued his studies alongside his duties as a young samurai. He was popular among his comrades, shared in their escapades, and was ready to use his sword when loyalty demanded.

He tells an interesting story of a youthful experience which illustrates the attitude of the samurai towards the lower classes. He had been placed under arrest for some minor offence, but planned to escape in order to take part in a fight between two rival groups of young samurai. He prepared by putting on chain armour under his dress and waited for a call. At length a member of his party came to tell him that the affair had been settled and asked Hakuseki how he had proposed to break out of confinement. Hakuseki replied that he was guarded only by an old man and woman, who had the key of the gate. If they had refused to open he would have cut off their heads and taken the key. He thought this a venial offence owing to the low rank of the victims.

On Tsuchiya's death his successor treated Hakuseki and his father so contemptuously that they were obliged to resign. Hakuseki's parents were supported by a relative, but he himself was at a loss. He continued his studies and refused to take employment, though short of funds. An old friend of the family proposed that Hakuseki should marry the daughter of a rich merchant who had social ambitions and would make over a fortune to the girl. But Hakuseki refused this and similar offers, telling his father (now a widower) that he could not forsake the samurai path which his ancestors had trodden.

In 1682, at the age of twenty-six, he went to Yedo in search of a post, which he found under Hotta Masatoshi, the Tairō. After Hotta's murder in 1684 he stayed in Yedo, looking for employment. But he found no suitable post and, still pursuing his studies, lived in penury with his wife and children. Fortunately he had attracted the attention of Kinoshita Junan, a prominent scholar who had been given office in Yedo as a Confucianist independent of the Hayashi family. Hakuseki became the chief of Junan's disciples, and this, as we have seen, led to Junan's recommending him as tutor for the young man who was to succeed to the office of Shōgun. This was Ienobu, the lord of Kōfu, an important Tokugawa domain. Hakuseki's service from that time under Ienobu and then under Ietsugu has already been described. From 1716 he was independent and could devote himself to his own pursuits as a scholar, a poet, a philosopher, and an historian. It was in this last capacity that he showed his truest gift.

6. Arai Hakuseki as an Historian

Hakuseki had a sense of the past and a rare analytic gift, qualities which made him one of the greatest historians of Japan, despite his inaccuracy in matters of detail.

Apart from the very full descriptive list of fiefs known as *Hankampu*, which is a compilation rather than an original treatise, his most important historical works were *Koshitsū* (1716) and his masterpiece, *Dokushi Yoron*, which was the basis of his lectures to Ienobu in 1712.

Koshitsū (meaning "A Survey of Ancient Historical Writings") is a critical study of the earliest documentary sources, such as the eighth-century *Kojiki* and *Nihongi*. In his preamble Hakuseki pays special attention to linguistic problems and shows an awareness of the importance of paleology in the interpretation of early texts. *Koshitsū*, though a careful review of the written traditions of the "Age of the Gods," is in fact more valuable as an exposition of Hakuseki's methods. In general he owes something to his precursor, the learned monk Jien (1155–1225), whose *Gukanshō* showed belief in an historical continuum; but Hakuseki's view of life was rationalistic rather than religious, as would be expected of a Confucian scholar. There can be no doubt that he introduced a new and advanced method of historical enquiry.

More immediately interesting than either *Hankampu* or *Koshitsū* is *Dokushi Yoron*, a title which might be translated as "A Reading of History." It is a study of the history of Japan from the ninth to the end of the sixteenth century, a survey in which Hakuseki relates the course of events principally for the purpose of stating his own view of the movement of history. He distinguishes phases—nine in which the Imperial rule gives way to a developing warrior class, and five in which at length the warrior class reaches its situation of supremacy under Tokugawa rule. As might be expected, the general tenor of Hakuseki's interpretation, though condemning individuals, favours the leaders of the feudal society. He traces the Throne's gradual loss of power from the days of the Fujiwara to the rise of the great captains, and implies that this was inevitable because of the incompetence of the Imperial rule. The point of interest here is less the correctness of Hakuseki's opinions—he distributes blame and praise in decided terms[6]—than the

---

[6] It is an interesting exercise to compare his account of Ashikaga Takauji with the *Baishōron* version.

picture of his attitude towards historical enquiry. He departed from the annalistic convention of Chinese historical writing because he saw history not as a series of discrete situations but as a continuous process which could be described and explained on rational grounds in clear language.

A word should be said here on Hakuseki's relations with other historians. His was not an amiable character, and he showed signs of jealousy. His relations with Hayashi Nobuatsu were strained, but he owed something to the work of the official Hayashi school, using their results freely. Late in life he was on friendly terms with the Mito historians, corresponding with Asaka Tampaku and Miyake Kanran (see articles by Miyazaki Michio in *Nihon Rekishi,* Nos. 148 and 158).

The merits of Hakuseki as an historian were of course due to his intense curiosity about the past, and in some measure to his speculation about the future. From all available sources—principally from the Dutch at Deshima and a Sicilian missionary named Sidotti, who was imprisoned for breaking the law by secretly entering Japan (1711)—he learned a number of facts about the geography and history of Western countries and the scientific knowledge which they possessed. He was impressed by their secular learning, but he thought that their Christian beliefs were so much nonsense and need not be regarded as a danger to the state. He was therefore prepared for some relaxation of the seclusion policy, and he may be regarded as the first member of the official class to see that Japan must enter into relations with the outside world. The stiff martinet in his character was overcome by the seeker after knowledge.

CHAPTER XII

GENROKU

STRICTLY speaking Genroku is the name of the era lasting from 1688 to 1704; but it is commonly used to denote a pattern of life which flourished in those years, when urban society in Japan had reached a peak of material prosperity and a blossoming of the arts was enjoyed by the citizens.

As we have seen in preceding chapters, there was a great increase of production during the seventeenth century, indeed an all-round expansion of the national economy; and in all the towns, but principally in Yedo and Ōsaka, there came into prominence a very prosperous bourgeoisie, so lavish in its expenditure that it called forth frequent rebukes and economy edicts from the government. But it need not be supposed that the citizens indulged only in disorderly pleasures, for they developed high standards of taste in literature and the arts. While departing from the ancient tradition of Court painting and of classical romances, which were in an elevated style and often the work of Buddhist monks, the writers of popular books and the painters of popular pictures were nevertheless men who followed a strict canon in portraying not the past but the decidedly contemporaneous life of the town.

These were the painters of "ukiyo-e," the writers of sketches called "ukiyo-zōshi," who depicted the leading figures in the "floating world," the fugitive society (ukiyo) composed of actors, dancers, singers, and fashionable beauties. In the Genroku era the most prominent figures were Chikamatsu Monzaemon, the great playwright (1653–1724); Ihara Saikaku, the most gifted novelist (d. 1693); Hishikawa Moronobu (d. 1714), a founder of the ukiyo-e school of painting; and perhaps here should be included the itinerant poet Matsuo Bashō (1644–94), a great master of the "haiku," or seventeen-syllable poetic epigram.

Not all these were members of the trading class. Saikaku was the son of an Ōsaka merchant, but Chikamatsu was the son of a provincial samurai of modest standing and was brought up in Kyoto. Some of the most successful painters belonged to the classical Kanō school. These included men like Morikage and Hanabusa Itchō, both of whom were pupils of the distinguished Tan'yū, but departed from the strict canon of Court painting and were expelled from the school for nonconformity.

It will be asked who were the patrons of these writers and artists, and the answer is practically all but the poorest citizens, for most of the work of novelists, painters, and playwrights was addressed to the ordinary man and woman, who crowded the theatres and bought for a few small coins pictures of actors and lovely ladies of a kind familiar to modern collectors in the work of Utamaro and other late masters of the colour print.

The growth of a numerous class of patrons of the arts in a society hitherto regarded as beneath the notice of even the lowest rank of samurai is a remarkable phenomenon in the social history of Japan. It would be a mistake to regard it as a sign of the decadence of the military class. It testifies rather to a widening of the horizon of the city-dwelling samurai, and in the economic sphere it discloses his poverty and the pressure upon him to find suitable employment to eke out his stipend.

The population of the two great cities, Kyoto and Yedo, was of the order of half a million about A.D. 1700, while Ōsaka had about 350,000, the figures in each case being exclusive of members of the military class. In these three great centres, the townspeople had reached a comparatively high degree of affluence and a definite standard of taste in judging a picture, a novel, or a play. Their code of behaviour was within certain limits strict, and lapses from it furnished the themes of the tragedies upon which the theatres thrived. It is a curious fact that the moral principles which the people sought to observe were of Confucian origin, and life was regarded as a conflict between duty and emotion.

On a smaller scale, of course, these conditions were common in urban life throughout the country. The Bakufu had to take note of them, for the power of money in the feudal society, and especially of great riches, had to be reduced or restrained if the military autocracy was to survive. In practice this did not prove easy. The usual stream of sumptuary rules was issued, but they were not easy to enforce. In some flagrant cases the authorities took a strong line, as when they confiscated the property of Yodoya, the great Ōsaka rice merchant, who was immensely rich and given to display. But in the Genroku era the growing wealth, and consequently the growing power of the townsmen caused frequent clashes between them and the samurai, whose incomes declined while they continued to assert their superior social position.

This proud attitude was not difficult to sustain in Yedo, but in Ōsaka, and even in Kyoto, there was little genuine respect for the military. It was an inevitable sequel of the expansion of the total economy that the importance of the warrior class should seem to diminish, for the process which enriched farmers and merchants raised the cost of living to the disadvantage, even the dismay, of men on a fixed stipend.

The brief Genroku era was marked by several notable events which included a great fire in Kyoto (1692); the debasement of metallic currency (1695); a great fire in Yedo (1698); a great earthquake in the Kantō in which 150,000 lives were lost (1703); and the first performance of Chikamatsu's tragedy *Love Suicide at Sonezaki* (1703).

Considered in retrospect the most attractive feature of this era is the gaiety of colour and pattern in clothing and decoration which reflected the mood of the times. It is an especially interesting aspect of the social history of Japan that the rise of a prosperous class of shopkeepers and craftsmen was accompanied by a lively creative phase in the arts. Perhaps at a later date an elderly Japanese gentleman in his reminiscences might have observed that this was the age when Japan savoured "la douceur de vivre."

CHAPTER XIII

A NEW REGIME

1. Yoshimune's Character

YOSHIMUNE, who became Shōgun in 1716, was the daimyo of Kii, one of the three rich fiefs of the three collateral Tokugawa houses, the Go-Sanke. In administering this domain of over 500,000 koku, he had learned a great deal by coping with difficulties, for it was in financial trouble owing to a succession of misfortunes, which included a debt to the Bakufu, great outlays on rebuilding after disastrous fires, costly entertaining of the Shōgun, and in 1707 serious damage to the southern shores of Kii by a tidal wave.

The experience which he gained by dealing with these problems was of great value when at the age of thirty-three he took office in Yedo to find similar trials awaiting him, though on a larger scale. He was well equipped for mastering such difficulties, for robust is an epithet which may properly be applied to his character, both physical and moral. Unlike Ienobu, he had been brought up to a hard and vigorous country life, and he had his own views on government. He was convinced that reforms were necessary. He had, however, little trust in the ability of Confucian scholars to solve practical questions, and one of his first steps was to do away with most of the reforms which Hakuseki had recommended to Ienobu, and to appoint Muro Kyūsō as a Confucian adviser in the place of Hakuseki. Kyūsō was known as a sensible, practical philosopher, and a strong supporter of the Shōgunate.

In official circles there was a not unnatural reaction against the principles laid down by Hakuseki. His stress upon ceremonial was displeasing to Yoshimune, who disliked punctilio; and his rival Hayashi Nobuatsu now restored the influence of the official Confucian college. But Yoshimune did not show any marked prejudice, and he made no attempt to revise the financial policy which Hakuseki had advised. The effect of the new coinage introduced in 1714 was obviously beneficial, and he was wise enough not to propose any change. He did, however, abolish most of the "reforms" which Hakuseki had recommended to Ienobu. It is not surprising, therefore, that Yoshimune was regarded with mixed feelings by members of the old regime. He entertained Ienobu's widow courteously in the Castle, and she wrote to her father, the Regent (Sesshō) Konoe Motohiro, in Kyoto telling him of this event. But this missive was followed by an alarming story of fire and tempest and a quite untrue account of political conditions in Yedo, which she ascribed to the blunders of Yoshimune. Konoe, it will be recalled, had been in close touch with Hakuseki when he visited Yedo while Ienobu was Shōgun, and was therefore no doubt inclined to take Hakuseki's side. But the entries in his diary, based on his daughter's letters and other reports, though entertaining as gossip, show that the Imperial Court was not well informed on affairs in the East and on the character of the new Shōgun.

2. *Financial Problems*

Yoshimune's attention was soon directed to the finances of the Bakufu. Their condition was deteriorating, although it did not reach a critical point until about 1721; but he saw that economies were needed. His plans for retrenchment included a reduction in the number of hatamoto. With the lapse of time and the growth of families their numbers were increasing, and he refused to recognize inheritance of the rank, especially in cases of adoption. Similar restrictions were applied to the creation of new Fudai vassals. Here, for instance, he would allow newcomers to hold their rank for one generation only. The number of gokenin was also swollen and needed reduction.

Tokugawa Yoshimune

In all these cases of restriction the motive was not entirely financial. It was political in that Yoshimune wished to have the support of a strong, select body of retainers of proved loyalty. He had brought with him from Kii some of his trusted retainers, but gave them no privileges. Unlike his predecessors he had no favourites to protect. One of his ablest men who had made and announced a decision without informing the Bakufu Council was summoned to appear before the Council, rebuked, and obliged to apologize for his error. Yoshimune did not interfere. He was welcomed by the Fudai officers who had been overruled by the Chamberlains and other favourites appointed by his predecessors, and he showed every sign of intending to govern directly. He made no move to fill vacancies in the list of Rōjū, and for appointment to other offices he examined candidates himself. He surprised his officials by encouraging direct appeals, and he installed complaint boxes (meyasubako) for that purpose.

In these and other ways he strengthened his personal authority. He meant to be the sole ruler. His reading of the political situation convinced him that it had deteriorated largely because the traditional social order was breaking down and the military class was losing its control to the rising class of rich merchants and landowners. It was also, he soon discovered, necessary without delay to examine and repair the finances of the Bakufu. His own inclination and the need to make some drastic changes combined to fill his mind with a determination to return to the early days of Ieyasu's rule, a determination that was in part carried out. This return to an earlier and successful system of government came to be known as the Kyōhō Reform, named after the Kyōhō era (1716–36). Yoshimune disliked the Confucianist elements in the policies of his predecessors, and wished to revert to the principles upon which the Tokugawa Bakufu had been based. He is often quoted as saying that he wished "in all matters to obey the laws of Gongen Sama," but there is no written record to confirm this, or any other public announcement of policy. "Gongen," or the Avatar, it will be remembered, is the posthumous name of Ieyasu.

As to concrete measures, he decided, like many oriental rulers before him, that the general standard of living should be lowered; and accordingly he reduced his own expenditure and restricted that of the government.

In 1722 he summoned the leading Bakufu officials and put before them the exhausted condition of Bakufu finances. Poor harvests in 1720 and 1721 had caused a fall in tax revenue, and great expenditure had been needed for repairs to the Ōigawa embankment. For such reasons it had been necessary to call upon hatamoto and go-kenin to accept a cut in their stipends. All officials must now make the greatest possible efforts in their respective posts, and a special Finance Commissioner was to be appointed.

Shortly after this conference the Bakufu issued an order to all daimyos stating that "regardless of shame" ("go chijoku wo kaerimizu") it had been decided to call upon them to contribute 100 koku for each 10,000 koku of their revenue. In return their period of residence in Yedo would be reduced by half, thus reducing their expenditure. This contribution—it was called "agemai," or offered rice—amounted to the respectable sum of 1,750,000 koku. It was about half the total amount of stipends payable to hatamoto and go-kenin, so that the urgent need was met. Other measures were devised to reach a balance between income and expenditure, and Yoshimune paid special attention to the salaries of his officials, with a view to encouraging good service.

His plans for increasing revenue were far-sighted. Since the chief source of revenue was the tax upon agricultural produce, the area under cultivation must be increased. Consequently a great scheme of development must be put in hand. An order was published throughout the country to the effect that, whether in Tokugawa or private domains, positive measures should be concerted by the competent authorities and the farmers to bring new land under cultivation. Since most of these schemes involved considerable capital expenditure on drainage or embankment, by implication the support of the wealthy merchants of the cities was invited; and the Deputies in Bakufu territory were told that they would be granted one-tenth of the tax accruing from newly developed farmland.[1]

The chief development schemes undertaken or approved by the Bakufu under Yoshimune were as follows:

1722—An area in Shimōsa, producing 50,000 koku.

1723—A large area in the Tamagawa basin, including the districts of Mitaka, Koganei, and Kokubunji, which are now part of Tokyo city.

1727—Land in the Tamagawa and Arakawa basins, which by a joint irrigation scheme was converted into rice fields producing 150,000 koku.

[1] Students should note that the estimates of rice production on page 353 of Murdoch's Volume III are much exaggerated. The figure of 60 million koku is fantastic. The average annual consumption of an adult was one koku, and the population at this time was of the order of 30 million. Allowing for storage, it is unlikely that the annual production much exceeded 30 million koku. More land was brought under cultivation after Yoshimune's death, though not for rice alone.

An improvement in the revenue of the Bakufu from land tax after about 1735 was due almost entirely to the opening up of new farmland in Tokugawa domains.

Yoshimune was not alone in promoting the development of new farmland. Most of the daimyos encouraged any plan that promised to increase the product of their domains. There are no exact records of the area brought under cultivation at this time, for (after Hideyoshi's Kenchi) there was only one land survey purporting to cover the whole country. That was in the Genroku era (around 1700), and it was imperfect and unreliable. But while giving no details of separate fiefs, it shows that there was an all-round increase in the area under cultivation. The constant enlargement and improvement of irrigation works testifies to such an increase, and in some domains specialists in irrigation practice were engaged.

Separate villages also carried out irrigation works on their own account, especially in digging channels and in constructing ponds and tanks or other reservoirs, thus furnishing a water supply for new fields. They were able sometimes to avoid surveys or to deceive the surveyors to their own advantage, and there is no doubt that many farmers of the standing of nanushi (headmen) lived a very comfortable life, as can be seen from account books recording the purchase of goods in great variety.

It is pertinent here to make some observations on the accuracy of land surveys in general. Anybody who has travelled through rural areas in Japan must have been struck by the great variety in shape as well as size of both wet and dry fields. Surveyors were instructed to measure the length and width of each field, but rectangular fields were scarce. Dry fields were often on a slope, following a contour, and many could not be measured by a rod but only by guesswork. The shape of wet fields was also frequently irregular, since they had to fit the pattern of irrigation, to say nothing of boundaries between plots of different ownership. It may be generally assumed that there was a very high factor of error in estimating the area of irregularly shaped fields, and no doubt the villages took advantage of these conditions in giving information to the surveyors. In the Genroku survey alluded to above there was no serious attempt to measure areas, and the yield was estimated by the visual examination of a specimen plot at harvest time. Consequently official statements of the value of land in terms of koku must be regarded as indications of magnitude and not as accurate descriptions.

Among the remarkable features of Yoshimune's method of government was his readiness to listen to complaints. One of the gravest offences under the mediaeval law and until the first quarter of the eighteenth century had been the "direct appeal" (jikisō) for justice to the Shōgun, which was punishable by death. In 1716 the Yedo government proclaimed that a great number of appeals and suggestions had been addressed to high officials, and that upon examination not one of them had been found of use. Indeed had they been adopted they would have had undesirable results. Therefore, in the future, except when opinions were asked for by the government, persons responsible for such statements would be punished.

The true cause of this seemingly reactionary policy of the Bakufu was the discovery of an organized business of bribery by which merchants and others persuaded officials to put their proposals before the Rōjū.[2] The reaction against this practice was extreme, since now, irrespective of their nature, all kinds of prayers and claims were forbidden. This was due to the generally old-fashioned attitude of the Rōjū, who clung to their belief that policy should not be based on public opinion. Nevertheless under Yoshimune's influence the proclamation of 1716 was reversed in 1719. Appeals and suggestions would now be examined, and their originators would not be punished even if their views turned out to be unsound.

The three junior Rōjū were ordered to adopt suggestions which promised to be of use to the people in general, such as methods for increasing the crops, or making good use of their earnings, or otherwise behaving as model citizens. Yoshimune was not afraid of direct appeals. In the New Year celebrations of 1718, returning from worship at a family shrine in Ueno, he was approached by a townsman carrying a petition. This offender was seized and bound by police officers, and was about to be handed over to the magistrates for punishment when Yoshimune stopped them, and ordered them in the future not to arrest such persons but to see that their petitions were examined by the municipal authorities. These incidents are trivial, but they show a great change under Yoshimune's guidance in the attitude of the Bakufu towards social problems.

In his effort to cope with the financial stringency by which the government was harassed Yoshimune resorted to measures that deserve some detailed study, since they reveal weaknesses in the political system which he was striving to reform. The fault was doubtless not with

[2] Even the austere Hakuseki was offered a bribe on one occasion at least.

him, but with the permanent officials whose business it was to carry out his policy.

As we have seen, one of his first cares was the problem of the livelihood of the warrior class, who were suffering from a rise in the cost of living. To give effect to his wishes the civil servants resorted at once to the traditional method of issuing edicts. These were designed to reduce expenditure by enforcing thrift. Known as Economy Orders they were of a kind that had been issued repeatedly and without effect since the foundation of the Minamoto Bakufu in the Middle Ages, and indeed since antiquity. Sometimes such injunctions had been attempts to make samurai live according to their station; but these were intended to check expenditure, which began to rise as life in the now flourishing towns became more and more difficult for families on a fixed income.

In 1721 Yoshimune ordered all officials to reduce the normal expenditure of their departments, and even instructed them to state their objections when they were instructed to carry out measures which seemed to them too expensive. In 1722, while working on a full revision of financial policy, he explained the government position to daimyo and hatamoto alike, calling upon them to reduce their standard of living. In 1724 the Bakufu issued orders limiting private expenditure on ceremonies, clothing, household furnishings, and similar objects. Such orders were repeated almost annually for the next twenty years.

They are given in detail in the official collection of Bakufu Orders ("O Furegaki"), which contains under the heading Economy Rules a number of documents bearing dates from 1640 to 1743. They are worth examination for the light which they throw on social changes that accompanied the growth of a thriving bourgeoisie in the great cities and, though on a lower scale, the more prosperous castle towns.

The collection styled "O Furegaki Shūsei," which has been well described as the records of a police state, contains under the heading of Economy Orders a number of documents dated from 1640 onwards. Those issued under Yoshimune's rule are very detailed, as the following extracts from the orders of 1724 will show:

—It has been repeatedly ordered by the Shōgun that economy must be observed in all such matters as the exchange of gifts and expensive entertainments to celebrate weddings. Henceforward these rules are to be obeyed as follows:

—Women's dress has of recent years become more and more showy. Hereafter even the wives of daimyos shall not use more than a small amount of gold-thread embroidery in their garments and shall not wear dresses made of costly fabrics. Female servants are to wear simple clothing appropriate to their position, and in every town the fixed price of these articles must be publicly announced.

—Expensive lacquer ware is not to be bought, even by daimyos. The chairs, chests, and workboxes of their wives are to be of plain black lacquer, with no more than a crest as ornament.

—Nightdresses, coverlets, mattresses, and so forth are not to be of fine embroidered fabrics.

—The number of palanquins at a wedding procession shall not exceed ten.

These particulars will give a general idea of the trend of fashions and of the failure of the Bakufu to enforce its sumptuary rules.

Apart from these public notices the Bakufu approached by word of mouth daimyos of over 10,000 koku, requesting them to reduce their outgoings. In 1729 a further public announcement was issued, pressing for obedience of these edicts and conceding that, owing to a fall in the price of rice, persons on a rice stipend were in difficulties. They would therefore not be expected to pay more than 5 per cent interest on debts contracted since 1702. At the same time the need for economy in food, dress, and social intercourse was stressed as before.

It need scarcely be said that these rules were not obeyed. The indigent samurai could not afford luxuries, and the well-to-do townspeople and farmers could not be induced to lead a simple life when they were enjoying some prosperity after penurious years. The Economy Orders were repeated again and again until as late as 1743, but of course to no effect. They were the work of clerks afflicted with an itch to scribble, and even if they had been issued by higher authority, they would have failed, since the Bakufu could not direct industry and control prices by mere fiat.

The currency problem has already been discussed, and we many now turn to Yoshimune's further efforts to restore the national economy.[3] His policy so far had been one of contraction and retrenchment, but its results were not satisfactory. Indeed by about 1722, when his currency reform was showing signs of success, the general economic condition was growing worse, thanks not so much to mistaken treatment as to

[3] It may be useful here to recall the several coinage changes. 1615—"Keichō": gold "koban"; 1695—"Genroku": gold and silver content of coins reduced; 1714—New issue: the return to Keichō standard, known as Shōtoku issue (Hakuseki's plan); 1718—New currency order of Yoshimune, establishing currency on Shōtoku basis for gold and silver.

storm damage to the crops over a very wide area in the summer of 1721. It was in the late autumn of this year that the Bakufu was obliged to delay payment of stipends to hatamoto and go-kenin. The Treasury could have scraped together enough to satisfy the poorest of these hereditary Tokugawa retainers if it had not at the same time been pressed to pay debts incurred by the Shōgun Tsunayoshi and his successors for articles supplied to the Castle by purveyors of all kinds. The merchants were so anxious for payment that they agreed to a reduction of their claims by one-third, and the amount thus paid out was as much as would have sufficed for the stipends of all the retainers in question for a whole year. In addition to these outgoings the cost of the Ōigawa embankment and other development works proved almost overwhelming.

At this point Yoshimune himself took a hand. He abolished the customary monthly rotation of duties among the Rōjū and appointed a special Finance Commissioner to take charge of financial policy, Mizuno Tadayuki by name. He thus created an effective Treasury department (the Kanjō-Kata), with special bureaux for estimates, accounting, auditing, and other branches of control. Its staff was gradually increased, and by 1735 it was the largest government office.

Such was the system of financial administration. It remains to examine its practical working. We have seen that the contribution (age-mai) of the daimyos of 100 koku in every 10,000 provided temporary relief for half the year (1722). The next step was to find permanent sources of additional revenue.

The revenue from new farmland in Bakufu domains was not of course immediately available, and therefore the new source had to be found either by increasing the tax upon the existing product of wet and dry fields, or by more effective methods of collection.[4] The latter course was adopted, and the basis of assessment was raised by a piecemeal revision of the surveys. This naturally disclosed considerable increases of cultivated area and product in certain areas, and therefore a greater taxable capacity. Here Yoshimune's government showed good sense by authorizing the collectors to make liberal allowance for poor crops due to bad weather and other misfortunes suffered by the farmers. But in 1727 the Bakufu felt obliged to raise the tax from 40 per cent to 50 per cent of the crop. This was an onerous impost, but again the Deputies

---

[4] The various methods of calculating the rent or tax due, whether in kind ("kemi") or by a fixed sum for a given period ("jōmen") are described in Thomas C. Smith, *The Agrarian Origins of Modern Japan* (Stanford, Calif., 1959), pp. 152ff.

13

14

15

16

17

18

(Daikan) in Bakufu domains were ordered to adjust their demands to local conditions.

Apart from increasing the production of rice, Yoshimune's government took steps to encourage industrial production of cotton goods, vegetable oils, and similar articles for consumption mainly in the towns. These directly produced little more revenue, but they added to the general prosperity and, at the same time, permitted a small increase in foreign trade. Thus, by exporting to China in addition to copper such articles as seaslugs, shark fins, and other delicacies, together with lacquer ware and similar products of Japanese craftsmen, the way was prepared for increased imports from China. It should be noted, however, that the most valuable export at this time was copper. The Dutch merchants in Nagasaki were anxious to take great quantities for shipment in their own vessels, but the Japanese authorities restricted their annual supply after Arai Hakuseki's report on foreign trade in 1714. The orthodox doctrine in Japan was opposed to imports, which were confined to such necessities as medicines and books—and sugar, then a rare luxury. It should be added here that little reliance can be placed upon statistics of the import trade of Nagasaki, since smuggling on a large scale was regular and continuous.

Efforts to reduce the deficit in Bakufu finances began to show results before 1730, when a small favourable balance of about 120,000 ryō in gold was deposited in the treasure vault of Yedo Castle. As a sign that there was now some money to spare, in 1728 Yoshimune made a ceremonial progress to the mausoleum of Ieyasu at Nikkō, a costly act of piety which had lapsed for want of funds sixty-five years before, in Tsunayoshi's day. Shortly afterwards Yoshimune cancelled the obligation of the daimyos to make their annual contribution of 100 koku for each 10,000 koku of their revenue.

This period of financial plain sailing did not last long. New difficulties arose, obstacles which could not be surmounted by the issue of regulations. In 1730–31 the price of rice on the Dojima Exchange fell to a very low level. Erratic price movements were in general to be expected in a closed country depending upon good weather for its staple food crop. In the early years of the eighteenth century, a fluctuating metallic currency and a loose control of national finance, together with frequent poor harvests, had driven the price upwards, and this condition persisted until 1720–22, when it reached a peak of from 70 to 80 momme of silver per koku. But from 1723 a series of good harvests brought the price down to 40 momme, and by 1730–31 it reached the minimum at 22—this of course at a time when the coinage was quite free from debasement.

Such a steep fall, while gratifying to the individual consumer, caused a grave disturbance of the national economy, in which rice figured as a medium, or at least a standard, of exchange. The first to suffer from the low price were the members of the military class who received their stipends in rice, which they were accustomed to sell for cash, usually through the medium of a fudasashi, or broker. The rural population were also affected, since they depended (apart from their own consumption) upon the sale of all their surplus produce for cash to meet current expenditure.

Then a year later—in the summer of 1732—great areas of standing crops in western Japan were attacked by insect pests. Their ravages caused a famine in which over two million suffered, and more than ten thousand died of starvation in spite of the prompt supply of rice from government storehouses to the suffering districts. The market price now rose to such a height that the authorities were at a loss for remedies. In some towns, including Yedo, there were serious riots in the early days of 1733, stimulated by the anger of the citizens when they found that speculators were trying to "corner" food. These were the first of a kind of riot known as "uchikowashi," or smashes, which were in later years to become frequent and widespread. Similar violent disturbances took place in other parts of the country, until a tolerably good harvest in the autumn of 1733 brought new rice to the market in quantity and at a fair price.

This change, however, did not relieve the anxiety of the government, for now the price went down to about 40 momme and, as before, struck a blow at the daimyos and other members of the military class who depended upon the sale of their rice for funds to support the administration of their domains and (a heavy load) the cost of annual attendance in Yedo.

The storehouses in Ōsaka were now crammed with rice,[5] but the brokers and their clients the speculators held off buying, so that the price remained low. At length, in November 1735, the government had to intervene, by fixing an official price, ordering Yedo merchants to buy at not less than one ryō for 1.4 koku, and Ōsaka merchants at not less

[5] The Rice Exchange complained to the Bakufu at the end of 1731 that whereas normally when the "new" rice came in, the stock of "old" rice in the warehouses was rarely more than 150,000 sacks (hyō), it had now increased to 600,000 in 1730 and in the current year to 1,300,000. The daimyos rushed their supplies to the market, eager to obtain cash for their current needs, even at a sacrifice.

than 42 momme a koku. If lower prices were paid, the buyer would be fined 10 momme for each koku. These regulations, which were complicated by the normal variations of kind and quality of rice, proved unworkable.

Consequently in the decade ending about 1745 the price of rice fluctuated wildly, and the Bakufu was obliged to make great efforts to regulate its movements. Indeed the chief preoccupation of Yoshimune in these years (he retired in 1745 and died in 1751) was to find an effective remedy for the evils brought about by the ups and downs of quotations on the Rice Exchange. So much did these matters demand the attention of the government that Yoshimune was called by the irreverent citizens Kome Shōgun or Kome Kubō—the Rice Shōgun.

It has been necessary to describe these monetary acrobatics in what may seem excessive detail because they combine to demonstrate that the national economy was governed by rice, which was at the same time the staple food and the basic medium of exchange. Consequently the hazards of climate and disease dictated the action of the rulers in vital political and social matters. So dominant was rice that a shortage had the effect of a currency deflation. A state in which financial stability is so lacking must obviously be difficult to govern, and indeed most of the troubles which Yoshimune had to face were of financial origin and of their nature insoluble in the contemporary framework of Japanese society.

The foregoing statistics show clearly that during the decade following the year 1730 (in which revenue and expenditure balanced) the efforts of the Shōgun to keep the finances of the Bakufu upon a sound and stable foundation ended in collapse. The cause of this collapse was a resort to manipulation of the coinage. In 1714, as we have seen, the gold currency was sound, but in 1736 the government reverted to a debasement which eased the situation by stopping the fall in the price of rice. Yet the problem was not solved. Still the samurai was caught in a trap between receiving payment in rice which was cheap and buying goods that were dear.

For an understanding of the subsequent course of Japanese history, both political and economic, it is important to understand that the conditions of stability were a sound currency, a balance between revenue and expenditure, and an adequate food supply. But these were rarely present together in a country liable to damage by typhoons, cut off from imported supplies, and divided into a number of separate jurisdictions over which the central government could exercise only a limited control.

In his efforts to increase the revenue of the Bakufu, Yoshimune turned his attention to the yield of tax upon cultivated land, and appointed two officials to increase the amount by rigorous methods of collection. One of these was Kamio Haruhide, a Rōjū celebrated for his harsh methods, who is reported to have said: "Peasants are like sesame seed. The more you squeeze them the more oil you get."

The amount of tax collected from this source had fallen during the ten years ended in 1736, doubtless owing to the resistance of the farmers. Now, thanks to the oppressive methods of Kamio and his colleagues, by 1744 it had reached 1,800,000 koku from a low level of 1,320,000, and the assessed product (kokudaka) of all Bakufu domains stood at 4,600,000 koku, the highest point reached under Tokugawa rule.[6] But this addition to Bakufu revenue was not permanent. The collection of tax could not be maintained at so high a level. The collapse of the rice markets, the fall in prices, the storms and the famines, combined to diminish the financial strength of the Bakufu until by 1745 it had entered upon a slow decline. By about 1770 the annual tax collection stood at from 1,100,000 and 1,200,000 koku.

3. Rural Society

The reasons for this decline are manifold, but there is no doubt that it was due in part to a great change in the nature of rural society, which had already in the early years of the eighteenth century begun to lose its close organization on family lines and to break up into a number of loosely connected elements. It is sometimes suggested that these rural communities, or many of them, fell into a state of hopeless poverty owing to misgovernment by the feudal authorities. But there is little foundation for such views. It is true that there were seasons of famine due to natural calamities, but there is nothing to show that (apart from such abnormal losses) the total agricultural product diminished. It is hard to believe that the prosperity of town life and the development of a remarkable urban culture was accompanied by a fall in the output of the farms.

The truth is that the character of the rural economy had begun to develop on new lines, thanks largely to the spread of a money economy

---

[6] During the first twenty years of Yoshimune's rule, rice production of all Bakufu domains remained fairly stable at about 7,000,000 koku. From this about 2,500,000 koku should be deducted for the income of hatamoto, leaving an annual balance of about 4,500,000 koku for storage in Bakufu granaries from 1716 to 1736. This came from the land known as "kurairi-chi."

or, to put it in simpler terms, to an increase in the amount and the variety of cash transactions. The evidence is clear in numerous records written by the farmers themselves, including well-kept account books, which clearly indicate a rise, not a fall, in production, and (it may be added) a spread of education.

The well-to-do farmers, men of the nanushi class, had some knowledge of the Chinese classics. Many were familiar with the great anthologies of Japanese poetry, and often haiku parties were given in their houses. Most villagers knew verses of the great poet Bashō, and some had memories of him as he passed through on his pilgrimages towards the end of the seventeenth century.

The change in the character of the economy was inevitably reflected in the changing structure of the village. The family relationship between the hon-byakushō (independent farmer) and his workers began to break down. The group which had cultivated the land in a corporate effort split into a number of small units no longer maintained by the hon-byakushō but earning a living partly by farm work and partly by day labour for merchants or artisans in the towns, or by the sale of articles of handicraft made in the village from materials available on the farms. The relationship of the workers with the hon-byakushō is no longer that of a kinsman to the head of a family but that of a tenant owing rent to a landlord. Such tenants were of necessity poor and were bound to eke out a livelihood as hired labourers or by home industry. Thus the villages now consisted of a few rich households and a large number of poor peasants. It was these latter who suffered most from natural calamities and who most frequently turned into vagrants and nuisances.

It is difficult to see how this condition could have been remedied by any simple political decree. It was a situation in which agricultural production rose and yet brought poverty with it. There was a weakness in the control of the villages by the Bakufu and the daimyos, for the members of the military class were no longer living upon the land which provided their incomes and were therefore out of touch with the peasants. They were influenced by the normal conservatism of feudal thinking and had fixed ideas about such matters as assessment (kokudaka) and tax. As the production of rice and other crops increased, the revenue of the landlords also improved, but the well-to-do farmers devised ingenious methods of thwarting the efforts of the military to impose further levies upon them. It was only the poorest peasant who found it hard to resist and was goaded to reprisals.

Thus the once peaceful village was at times disturbed by internal strife. Rich peasant was against poor peasant, especially in the matter of public imposts, of which an uneven distribution bore heavily on the weakest. Families which had large holdings claimed powers of decision in matters of importance to the village as a whole, thus giving rise to quarrels ending in violence. These were known as "komae sōdō," or "lesser-family risings," which were clashes within a village. More serious were risings of "ōmae," or "greater families"—that is to say, risings led by the principal farmers in a number of villages and known by the generic name of Hyakushō Ikki. These would include both rich and poor peasants and were directed against extortionate fiscal methods of daimyos or Bakufu officers. In some of these risings the poor peasants displayed a desperate courage. They were serious matters and testified to a basic fault in the agrarian system, but not to its inefficiency in production, for there can be no doubt that even during these troubled phases the total product was rising and so was the general standard of living. What was at fault was the conservative outlook of the Bakufu and the daimyos, who still imposed excessive taxation upon the farms in an endeavour to meet their own increasing debts.

With regard to urban development, Yoshimune was generally interested, but his particular care was devoted to improving the municipal administration of Yedo. He introduced measures to prevent the spread of fires, which were the curse of the city, called by the citizens with wry humour the Flowers of Yedo (Yedo no Hana). He appointed municipal officers of proved capacity and named as magistrates men of high character. The wisdom of his choice is celebrated in a popular work of fiction known as Ōoka Seidan ("The Judgments of Ōoka"), based upon the brilliant detection of crime by his Chief City Magistrate.

4. Yoshimune's Scientific Interests

We may now leave aside Yoshimune's handling of economic issues and turn back in time to examine other aspects of his rule. Though not a scholar himself, he was a man of wide interests. He was fond of field sports, and he enjoyed taking his military subjects on exhausting manoeuvres or great battues on the Kantō plains or the slopes of Mount Fuji; but he also speculated a great deal about the world outside Japan, and as early as 1720 he relaxed a ban on certain books from China which had been first imposed by his predecessors out of fear of Christianity almost a century before. The censorship upon imported books had been so severe that in 1695 the officials at Nagasaki had been instructed by Yedo to destroy a Chinese book, a guide to Peking in several volumes, because it mentioned the tomb of a celebrated missionary, Father Ricci, who had served the Chinese court as an adviser on astronomy until his death in 1610. This ban did not extend to books in European languages, since only a few specialists known to the authorities could read them; but danger was seen in Chinese works because they might contain Christian propaganda. In his announcements of 1720, Yoshimune, who was interested in scientific ideas, decreed that books which did not contain accounts of Christian teaching might be imported and circulated.

He was especially concerned to furnish Japan with a new and reliable calendar, for apart from his own curiosity, it was according to Chinese practice the duty of a ruler to ensure the performance of his functions and those of his officers at correct times. Like the Romans the Chinese believed in the influence of the heavenly bodies, and astrology played an important part in shaping the conduct of both the sovereign and his subjects. Yoshimune made enquiries of an assistant to the official astronomer and was told of one Nakane Jouemon Genkei, a Kyoto silversmith, who could give good advice on making a correct calendar. Genkei was summoned to Yedo and received by Yoshimune, who was pleased with his speech and demeanour. Genkei was instructed to read a recent Chinese book, but found that it was only an extract from a Chinese version of a complete Western work. He told Yoshimune that no progress could be made so long as Chinese translations of Western books were kept out of Japan for such absurd reasons as a mere mention in the text of something related to Christianity or Christians.

This was the principal reason why Yoshimune removed the prohibition of imported books. His interest in natural science was exceptional for his day, and it turned his attention to foreign countries, so that he followed Arai Hakuseki in feeling that Japan must enter into relations with the world outside. It is clear from contemporary writings that by the beginning of the eighteenth century many scholars in Japan were already thirsting to learn more of the arts and sciences of European countries than could be acquired by occasional contacts with visiting foreigners, such as the Dutch merchants from Deshima and learned men who sometimes came with the Dutch missions to Yedo.

Yoshimune himself had in 1719 invited to Yedo an interpreter from Nagasaki named Nishikawa Joken, who was known as a student of astronomy. He had made a large terrestrial globe with the help of a skilled mechanic from Kii, and had himself used a telescope imported from Holland for observing the heavens. At his orders officials were sent to ask the Dutch residents in Nagasaki questions about eclipses, tides, the movements of celestial bodies, and so forth, but the Hollanders could not give him satisfactory answers. It was not until more than twenty years later (1744) that Yoshimune had an observatory built in Yedo.

By using apparatus of this kind his specialists discovered errors in the existing calendar, and set about its reform, which was not completed until after Yoshimune's death. It was put into use in 1754, which was the beginning of the era named Hōreki, or Precious Calendar.

Yoshimune's enquiring spirit led him to search for some means of avoiding the misfortunes which arose from poor harvests due to natural calamities. He saw that some alternative or supplementary foodstuff must be provided. The consumption of meat was very small, since it was forbidden by Buddhist teaching; and fresh fish was a luxury which few could afford. Therefore some nutritious vegetable product must be cultivated. This was found in the sweet potato, which was proposed by a Confucian teacher named Aoki Konyō in 1734, that is shortly after the famine of 1732–33. The sweet potato ("kanshō") was of southern origin and was brought to Japan by way of the Luchu Islands. Aoki became known as Kanshō Sensei, or Doctor Potato. It is a curious coincidence that at about the same time in England an effort was made to diversify agriculture, and farmers were pressed to grow root crops by a nobleman who became known as Turnip Townshend. But the resemblance between the two situations is only superficial, since England had a small population (about seven and a half million) sustained in part by oceanic trade, whereas Japan had a population of the order of 30 million and was virtually closed to imports. When harvests were bad in England, it was possible to relieve distress by importing grain from the Baltic; but no such remedy was available to Japan. A closer parallel would be Scotland in the early eighteenth century, where it was said with some poetic license that "half-starved spiders preyed on half-starved flies."

Aoki Konyō (1698–1769) was one of a number of scholars whom Yoshimune ordered to study the Dutch language. This was a significant act, for it showed that the government was in favour of a breach in the exclusion policy, at least in its intellectual aspects. But it was a long time before Dutch studies were seriously pursued. Yoshimune's order was issued in 1741, and Aoki worked on a dictionary which he did not complete until 1758, after Yoshimune's death. It was naturally imperfect, but it was the herald of a growing interest in Western ideas, an interest which soon spread over the whole country.

5. *Yoshimune and the Vassals*

Yoshimune was not satisfied with reforming the Bakufu itself. He wished to extend his reforming influence to the domains of the great barons. Here he met with some resistance from an unexpected quarter. One of the three great collateral houses (the Go-Sanke), under the leadership of Tokugawa Muneharu, the lord of Owari, opposed his negative, conservative, and thrifty kind of government and called for a more open and unrestricted policy. Life in the castle town of Nagoya was gay and free, no doubt inspired by a feeling that Owari was senior to Kii and that Yoshimune was behaving in a despotic fashion. In 1732 Yoshimune rebuked Muneharu for insubordination, but to no effect. He therefore took strong measures, ordering Muneharu to stay under house arrest. In 1733 he similarly rebuked Munenao, his successor as lord of Kii, for misgovernment in his fief leading to financial troubles and uprisings.

This action seems to have been dictated by anxiety concerning the capacity of his own eldest son and putative successor, Ieshige. Desiring to keep the succession in his own family, Yoshimune created two new Tokugawa houses, his second son, Munetaka, being made the head of a branch named Tayasu (after one of the Castle gates of Yedo) and his fourth son, Munetada, being made the head of a branch named Hitotsu-bashi, after another gate. Both resided within the Castle grounds.

These two new houses and a house of later foundation called Shimizu were to ensure the Tokugawa succession and thus to strengthen the foundations of the Tokugawa dynasty. The three new houses (known as Go-Sankyō, or Three Noble Houses) also served as a check on the influence of the Go-Sanke, who had shown a tendency to stand apart from, if not actively to oppose, the Shōgun in power. The three new houses were granted less valuable estates than the Go-Sanke, but, owing to their near relationship to the ruling house, it was they rather than the Go-Sanke who furnished a successor when the Shōgun had no direct heir. Thus the eleventh Shōgun Ienari was a member of the Tayasu house.

Yoshimune retired in 1745, having held the office of Shōgun for thirty years. He remained in his apartments in the Castle as a guardian of his son Ieshige until 1751, when he died at the age of sixty-eight.

There can be no doubt that Yoshimune was after Ieyasu the greatest of the Tokugawa Shōguns. He has been described as conservative, even reactionary, and it is true that his ideal was to restore the discipline of the first decades of the Tokugawa Bakufu; but he dealt with difficult problems in a rational and unprejudiced manner, without being influenced by the conventions of strict feudal rule. His handling of financial difficulties was sensible and positive, and if he failed here, it was because of a fundamental weakness in the national economy. He was quick to perceive the importance of developing new farmland and in general in increasing production. As we have seen, he encouraged learning and perceived the importance of knowledge of a kind which could be obtained only by studying the achievements of Western peoples. He made the first breach in the policy of seclusion.

It cannot be said that he was popular, for his reforms were bound to displease one class or another. He was blamed for misfortunes which should have been attributed to natural forces beyond the control of a Shōgun. His last years were darkened by the current economic crises, and he who had been hailed by the citizens on his accession was made the subject of vulgar lampoons.

6. *Legal Reform*

No authoritative code of law existed in the early days of Yoshimune, when suits were judged in accordance with precedents furnished by decisions of the City Commissioners (Machi-Bugyō) of Yedo. In 1717, however, an official named Ōoka Tadasuke recommended the codification of the law as it was then interpreted. Thanks to pressure from him and to advice given by such prominent persons as Muro Kyūsō, Yoshimune agreed that a text of the laws should be drawn up, and an order to establish a code of law was issued by him in 1720.

The document drawn up in compliance with this order was completed in 1742. It was known as the Code of One Hundred Articles, or *O Sadame Gaki Hyakka-jō*. It was slightly amended by Ienari and became what was then known as the Kansei Code. Its punishments were less severe than those laid down in previous orders, and it placed limitations on the use of torture. There are several extant versions of this document, some of which are spurious; but the best text is to be found in the collection known as *Tokugawa Kinrei-Kō*. The basis of the code was a document drawn up in Ieyasu's time, which in its later forms contained additions or amendments made by the second and third Shōguns. It may be regarded as a statement of the principles, social and political, of the Shōgun's government rather than a penal code.

CHAPTER XIV

THE BAKUFU IN DECLINE

1. *Yoshimune's Successors*

Y O S H I M U N E was succeeded by two feeble and incompetent Shōguns in turn. The ninth Shōgun, Ieshige, succeeded his father in 1745 at the age of thirty-five; and Ieharu, the tenth Shōgun, Yoshimune's grandson and his favourite, held the office from Ieshige's demise in 1760 to 1786, when he died at the age of sixty.

Ieshige was a sickly child, whose weakness as an adult brought him the nickname of Shōben Kubō, or the Bed-Wetting Shōgun. His health was impaired by juvenile excesses. He stammered so badly that his speech was incomprehensible. It had to be interpreted by his companion, a young samurai named Ōoka Tadamitsu, who had grown up with him and whose indispensable services were rewarded by frequent promotion until, after Yoshimune's death in 1751, he reached the rank of Chamberlain (Soba-yōnin) with a stipend of 20,000 koku. This was an important post, since owing to Ieshige's handicaps the Chamberlain in close attendance upon him exercised as his mouthpiece and deputy a high degree of political power.

Ieshige despite his physical defects was not mentally deficient. He wrote an essay on the game of chess; but he was quite unfitted for the task of government, being dissipated and erratic. The Council of Elders (Rōjū) had to depend upon Tadamitsu for an expression of the Shōgun's wishes. This awkward situation did not, however, prevent the Elders from exercising their proper functions. After Yoshimune's retirement (1745) the leading Fudai daimyos (such as Hotta Masasuke and Matsudaira Takemoto) ostensibly governed on behalf of the Shōgun in the customary manner, although in fact Tadamitsu, by a tactful use of his influence upon Ieshige, was able to exercise a ruler's authority. Thus the incapacity of Ieshige tended to put power into the hands of the senior Chamberlain, where it continued to reside for many years.

In 1760 both Ieshige and his Chamberlain died, and Ieshige's son Ieharu took his place, being at that time forty years of age.

Ieharu as a boy had been Yoshimune's favourite and would have become Shōgun upon Yoshimune's retirement but for the Tokugawa family rule of succession, which Yoshimune preferred not to disregard. Ieharu was physically robust, but without strength of character. He was intelligent, but so lacking in application that he could not bear to listen to his advisers for more than a few moments. He was moreover slovenly in his person, lazy, and untidy. In such circumstances the incompetence of a ruler has results graver than occasional administrative blunders. It opens a way for the rise of ambitious and unscrupulous characters, whose conduct of affairs is based on selfish motives. Events under the rule of Ieshige and Ieharu amply illustrate this danger.

As we have seen, after the death of Yoshimune, government was in the hands of the Chamberlains, who transmitted orders to the executive body. These were Ōoka Tadamitsu and a remarkable man named Tanuma Okitsugu. The office of Chamberlain had grown in political importance during the rule of Tsunayoshi, when Yanagisawa exercised great power, and under Ienobu and Ietsugu such men as Manabe were influential as advisers. Thus the authority held by Tadamitsu was customary and indeed essential in view of the incapacity of the sickly Shōgun; nor did he abuse the powers which he came to exercise as Junior Elder (Wakadoshiyori), a post he held until his death in 1760.

Tanuma Okitsugu was a man of similar origin, but of much greater ability and strength of mind. During the lifetime of Tadamitsu he played no prominent part, but later he was able to dominate the political scene by sheer force of character and by extremely dishonest or, let us say, unconventional methods. His success calls for some scrutiny of his career, which reveals a decline in the integrity as well as the competence of the Bakufu after Yoshimune's death.

2. The Tanuma Regime (1767–86)

Tanuma Okitsugu's father was an ashigaru (foot soldier) in the service of the Kishū branch of the Tokugawa family, who, when Yoshimune moved to Yedo as Shōgun, was included in the company of hatamoto and promoted to a modest office with a salary of 600 koku. Okitsugu followed his father on the road to promotion. He first became a page in the apartments of Ieshige at the age of sixteen. In the following year his father died, and he became head of the Tanuma family. On Yoshimune's death in 1751 he rose to the rank of Chamberlain in the service of Ieshige, then Shōgun—a remarkable success for a man of of such humble origin. By 1760 he had become a favourite of the new Shōgun, Ieharu. Thereafter he made rapid progress. His talents were recognized, and within a few years of his appointment he was granted a stipend of 10,000 koku and thus ranked as a daimyo. By 1767 he had risen to the rank of Senior Chamberlain and was promoted to the lordship of Sagara, holding a castle and a revenue of 20,000 koku, which was soon raised to over 50,000 koku.

He now aimed even higher, for he coveted the most powerful office under the Shōgun, namely the presidency of the Council of Elders. This post was then held by an important Tokugawa kinsman, Matsudaira Takemoto, whose rank and integrity together were for a time an obstacle to rivals; but his death in 1779 gave Okitsugu an opportunity to seize a monopoly of power.

The Rōjū in general were unable or unwilling to resist Okitsugu, who dominated them, and he soon took Takemoto's place. Thenceforward he exercised untrammelled authority for the best part of a decade. He was a man of insatiable appetites. In his rise from humble origins he had studied the weaknesses of his superiors and his colleagues, and learned by experience how to play upon them. With this knowledge he was able to satisfy his lust for power and his greed for possessions. He married a woman related to a mistress of Ieharu, and through her he was able to influence Court ladies. He knew that behind the curtain they had power to shape policy in so far as it was determined in the Shōgun's apartments. He took care to become well acquainted if not intimate with some of them. Indeed he made a special effort to secure as his own mistress a friend of Ieharu's favourite, and through her he bribed most of the ladies-in-waiting and the less exalted concubines.

Women's hair styles, ca. 1760

As to Tanuma's relationship with Ieharu there is an interesting passage in a nobleman's diary (*Shimmei-In Den Go Jikki*) suggesting that Ieharu was not entirely deceived by Tanuma and that Tanuma had some respect for Ieharu's judgment. But Tanuma's purpose was not to bring direct influence to bear upon the Shōgun. He had a lively appreciation of the power of money, and his purpose was to obtain that power for himself through the accumulation of great wealth, partly by accepting bribes but principally by investment in profitable enterprises. He made no attempt to conceal his approval of bribery. Indeed its habit was far from uncommon in official circles before his day, and he differed from most of his predecessors only in the scale of his exactions and in the open way in which he resorted to such malpractices. He is alleged to have said: "Gold and silver are treasures more precious than life. A man whose wish to serve is so strong that he offers bribes for an appointment shows thereby that his intentions are loyal. . . . I myself go every day to the Palace, where I labour painfully for the country, my mind never at rest. It is only when I return home and find presents from many families piled up in the long gallery of my house that I feel at ease." His clients thronged at his gateway and grovelled before him as they offered gifts. But in his household one thing of importance was missing. In reply to a visitor who had said that Tanuma must possess every kind of treasure, a bystander observed that what was undoubtedly lacking was a weapon or a suit of armour stained with blood from the battlefield.

Among the clients who brought bribes to Tanuma were important people like Ii, the Lord of Hikone, who wanted an appointment as Tairō (which he obtained), and Daté, the Lord of Sendai, who desired a Court title. Even the strict Matsudaira Sadanobu sought appointment to the fourth Court rank and to that end made suitable offerings to Tanuma. Less important posts could be obtained at fixed prices, such as 2,000 ryō for the office of Nagasaki Bugyō, or 1,000 ryō for an appointment as Censor (Metsuke). Among the presents designed to attract Tanuma's special attention was a large box said to contain a life-size doll, which turned out to be a beautiful young girl richly attired.

Tanuma was not the only high officer who took bribes, for such important functionaries as the Finance Commissioners were also open to persuasion. In the light of such practices it will be asked what government was like while Tanuma was chief minister. History and tradition tend to dwell upon his misdemeanours and attribute to them the faults of the Bakufu during his lifetime. But he was a symptom rather than a cause of those faults, for corruption was already rife after Yoshimune's rule, though he had tried to arrest it; and in fact Tanuma did not peculate, but took positive steps to protect official funds and to reduce the expenditure of the government while increasing its revenue by constructive methods. During his term of office he found time and occasion to encourage important riparian works and (in 1785) he sent a party of officials to study conditions in Yezo (Hokkaidō) and Karafuto (Sakhalin) with a view to their development. He also encouraged an increase of the Nagasaki trade, which had been reduced on the advice of

Arai Hakuseki; and for that purpose he stimulated the production of copper for export.

In these and other ways Tanuma and his family were extremely active, and the old, conventional view of Okitsugu as nothing more than a greedy rascal is not held by modern Japanese historians. His term of office was brief, for he became a Soba-yōnin in 1767, a Rōjū in 1772, and was deprived of his title and office in 1786, following the death of Ieharu. Indeed his downfall was as sudden as his rise. The murder of his son (Okitomo) by a man named Sano Zenzaemon was a sign of the growing antagonism which he had invited. This was in 1784. Shortly after being deprived of his office in 1786—in the same month—grants of land worth 20,000 koku were cancelled, and he was ordered to relinquish his residence and his warehouses in Ōsaka within three days. He was to stay in retirement and to convey such property as was left to him to his grandson.

Having examined the political background as it appeared during the rule of Ieshige and Ieharu—that is from 1745 to 1786—we may now turn to the attitude of the country towards the Bakufu for evidence of its decline in public esteem. For this purpose it is pertinent to cite the main events, both social and political, of the period under review.

3. Anti-Bakufu Sentiment

There can be no doubt that in Tanuma's day the Bakufu as an administrative organ had reached a hazardous state of inefficiency and confusion. There were many who deplored its weaknesses and doubted its stability. Some indeed, while not going so far as to plan its overthrow, thought that the time was ripe for a restoration of Imperial rule, and several worked for that end. Clearly the warrior spirit and the warrior ethos, as represented by the Bakufu, were in decline.

It must be recognized, however, that the authority of the house of Tokugawa as a central government, its power to coerce even the most independent and mutinous daimyos, was not impaired by its administrative incompetence. Despite its weaknesses in matters of secondary importance it was a powerful, self-regulating organ of national scope. The system of checks and balances formed by the strategic location of the vassals, which had been worked out by the first three Tokugawa Shōguns, was a permanent source of strength. No feudatory dared disobey an order from Yedo, or he did so at the risk of losing his fief and even his liberty. In fact it was easier for the Bakufu to handle obstreperous barons than to suppress the risings of angry peasants. Despite its faults the Bakufu was Leviathan. Moreover, it must be remembered, irrespective of the guidance of the Bakufu, many of the great fiefs were extremely well governed, and thus contributed, however unintentionally, to the general stability of the Tokugawa regime.

Subject to these considerations, it is worth while to examine some of the active forms of expression of sentiment hostile to the Bakufu during the eighteenth century.

Seemingly as a reaction against the strict rule of Yoshimune, several movements hostile to the Bakufu developed soon after his death. Most remarkable among them was a school of thought encouraged by one Takenouchi Shikibu, son of a country doctor and therefore not strictly speaking a man of samurai rank. Leaving his home in Echigo he took service in Kyoto in the house of an important Court noble, Tokudaiji Kinshirō. There he studied the teaching of the Shintō sect called Suika Shintō, and at the same time attended lectures on military science. He soon came to hold views antagonistic to government and proclaimed the Shinnō-Ron, the doctrine of loyalty to the Throne, which was to divide the country in the nineteenth century. He contended that if the Court were to make a serious effort the whole country would support it, and his lectures attracted a number of Court nobles. News of this movement came to the ears of the Emperor Momozono, and was seriously discussed at his Court, but the heads of the senior noble families were against a clash with the Bakufu. They informed the Kyoto Shoshi-dai of Shikibu's views, and he was speedily arrested and expelled from the city in 1759.

Shortly after this event a teacher of military science, one Yamagata Daini, was reported to be plotting against the Bakufu. This man was the son of a labourer in Kōfu, and there had become a retainer of Ōoka Tadamitsu, whom he served well. But on the death of Tadamitsu he made his way to Yedo, where he set up as a teacher of military science in 1760. His teaching was hostile to the absolute rule of the Bakufu, which depended upon force. He approved of the military virtues, but he was in favour of the "Kingly Way" (Ōdō), that is to say of Imperial rule. He attracted the attention of a senior retainer of the daimyo of Kobata, one Yoshida Gemba, who discussed with him the need of reforms in the administration of the fief. This aroused the opposition of some of Gemba's colleagues, who accused him and Daini of plotting a revolt. These matters came to the notice of the City Commissioners, who also learned that a disciple of Daini, one Fujii Umon, had openly used violent language in condemning the arbitrary methods of the Bakufu. On investigation they found no evidence of a plot, but

Daini was condemned to death, and Umon sent to prison. The revenue of the Oda family was reduced and Gemba with his associates was punished. Takenouchi Shikibu was also interrogated, but there was no evidence against him. He was banished to Hachijō because he had disobeyed an order to leave Kyoto.

These events have been related here in some detail bcause they show that the leaders of the Bakufu were determined to suppress the loyalist movement. Their nervousness was displayed by the erratic handling of the problems with which they were confronted. It varied from extreme severity to alarming weakness at a time when steadiness was essential. Their lack of understanding is clearly shown by the growth of serious rioting after an extremely harsh corvée had been imposed upon the peasants in the country along the highway from Yedo to Nikkō, where the mausoleum of Ieyasu had been built.

4. Agrarian Riots

In ordinary times there was a regular flow of officials and pilgrims between Yedo and Nikkō, a distance of about one hundred miles. The necessary porters and horses were furnished to officials by villages along the road, in accordance with the customary levy known as "sukegō" (corvée). But for this very special occasion of the pilgrimage to Ieyasu's tomb, the Bakufu planned the procession on a grand scale. It was to include all members of the Tokugawa family, Court nobles, the great vassals, and their retinues. For their transport and lodging the peasants in the area through which they passed were ordered to provide porters, horses, and housing on a lavish scale or, if horses were not to be had, cash payments at extortionate rates.

This levy was extended to peasants at a long distance from the direct road to Nikkō and became so onerous that towards the end of the year 1764 there were agrarian risings on a large scale in the provinces of Kōtsuke and Musashi. The number of peasants taking part in this revolt is said to have reached 200,000, which was of the same order as the Shimabara uprising of 1637–38. Its origin and its size show that the leaders of the Bakufu were ignorant of the state of feeling in the country and incompetent to deal with the situation which their ignorance had created. An effort to appease the rioters had some temporary success, but by the end of the year tens of thousands swept through the countryside and attacked storehouses in Kumagai, smashing their contents. It was nearly a month before the Bakufu could suppress this disorder in the Kantō, the base and stronghold of the House of Tokugawa.

Subsequently agrarian rising occurred in other parts of Japan, causing great anxiety to the government, whose endeavours to suppress or prevent them met with little success. Rewards were offered to those who would give warning of risings or mass absconsions planned by farmers. At the same time, daimyos in whose territory such riots took place were told that they might call for help from neighbouring domains, but must not use firearms. Sometimes risings within a fief were concealed from the Bakufu, while attempts to conciliate the peasants were made by the daimyo or his deputies; but this moderate action only encouraged further insubordination and thus led to the use of force against the rioters. There were, however, some domains in which there was only a small military establishment, and they were obliged to appeal for help to the nearest Tokugawa deputy (daikan).

In 1770 the Bakufu issued an order denouncing the conduct of the peasantry and promising rewards (including promotion to the rank of samurai) to informants who would disclose the plans of the rioters. Such facts reveal the incompetence of the Bakufu, its lack of decision, and its shifts of policy. It was clear that some change of government was needed, some strong central authority in determined hands.

CHAPTER XV

ECONOMIC DEVELOPMENT
AND SCIENTIFIC KNOWLEDGE

1. *Tanuma's Policy*

T A N U M A   O K I T S U G U' s   hunger for bribes is so sensational that some
historians have been inclined to dwell upon it and to neglect his positive
contributions to the national economy, which were of the same nature
as those of Yoshimune. In fact Tanuma's policy was not original but
led to a further development of measures planned by Yoshimune. Tanuma's action cannot be treated separately from the political situation
reached under Yoshimune, especially in its financial aspects. One of
the features of the Kyōhō Reform (1716–36) was the trend of Bakufu
policy towards an increasing use of commercial capital. Furthermore,
it should be recalled, Yoshimune had already developed a kind of civil
service control of financial policy by his appointment of special officials
to deal with financial problems—the Kanjō-Kata.

Whereas in the capital there was a deplorable atmosphere of corruption and debauchery in the Shōgun's entourage, in less elevated
circles there was much activity in trade and industry fostered by Tanuma, and a new intellectual activity which, it may be argued, arose
from the discontent of thoughtful men who felt that the feudal society
was stagnant. Expressions of this feeling were various. Tanuma, besides encouraging productive industry, provided funds for bringing
new land under cultivation, thus continuing the policy favoured by
Yoshimune in (for example) promoting riparian works in order to
increase the area of irrigated land. After a great eruption of the volcanic
Mount Asama in 1783 had raised the bed of the Tonegawa, preventive
work on a great scale had to be undertaken. The cost of carrying it out
was borne by two millionaires, one from Yedo, one from Ōsaka; and
when it was completed a large share of the new cultivable area was to be
allotted to them. A series of misfortunes caused this enterprise to be
abandoned upon Tanuma's resignation; but perhaps his boldest departure was to promote trade with Russia by developing the northern
territory of Japan—the Hokkaidō and Sakhalin.

A plan for such an undertaking had been suggested by one Kudō
Heisuke, a physician in the Sendai fief who had studied the Dutch language and took a special interest in foreign countries. At this time Rus-

sia was advancing across Siberia and Kamchatka to the coasts of
Chishima (the Kurile Islands), and certain Japanese traders from the
Matsumae fief (Hokkaidō) were with the daimyo's approval secretly
trading with Russians in the neighborhood of Kunashiri Island. This
fact came to the knowledge of Kudō through a rōnin from Matsumae,
and in 1783 he submitted to the Rōjū a description of the Aka-ezo, the
Red Northern Islanders, that is to say the Russians. In this document
he pointed out that Russia was growing in strength in the northern
region. Her illicit trading must be stopped, but for that purpose it
would be prudent to trade openly with the Russians and to apply the
profits thus earned to the development of the whole region.

Kudō's idea was taken up by Tanuma, who in 1785 sent a mission
under a Finance Commissioner to make investigations on the spot. One
party studied Chishima, another studied Sakhalin. Early in 1786 the
leader of the mission submitted to the Bakufu a plan for the development of the whole region. In his report he recommended developing as
farmland about one-tenth of the area of the principal island, which is
now known as the Hokkaidō.

In general Tanuma's contribution to economic growth was important. He added to the existing association of recognized brokers (kabunakama) a guild consisting of new merchants in Yedo, Ōsaka, and other
centres. To these he granted special privileges, but in return he taxed
them heavily. This levy, at a time when production was rising, brought
in large sums to the Bakufu treasury. In 1766 a monopoly of copper
had been formed in Ōsaka, and following this similar exclusive privileges were granted to recognized dealers (kabunakama) in iron, brass,
lime, and other staple commodities. Special wholesale dealers (tonya)
in important supplies such as oil, cotton seed, and sulphur were licensed,
and their profits were assured in return for a payment of tax. In fact the
levy on all these monopolies made a valuable contribution to the revenue
of the Bakufu. The tendency to form such special bodies was very
strong, and it is said that in the years about 1785 there were more than
one hundred kabunakama in Ōsaka alone.

The taxes paid were known as "myōga" and "unjō." They were
nominally voluntary payments. If an individual townsman was granted
some privilege he paid "myōga-kin," a thank-offering for an act of
grace by the government; while "unjō-kin" was a direct payment at
rates specified by the government. The direct tax (unjō-kin) was levied
not only upon articles of commerce but also upon apparatus and undertakings, such as water wheels, ferries, wharves, the business of brothels,
and even upon the earnings of individual unlicensed prostitutes, the
furtive practitioners known as kakushi-baita.

For these purposes a special tax office was set up, and it may well be imagined that the grant of licenses was usually dependent upon bribery in this society of dishonest brokers and speculators.

2. Agrarian Distress

The close relationship between the Bakufu as represented by Tanuma and the rich merchants of Yedo and Ōsaka brought advantage to the government, since a good share of the profits from the investment of private capital in productive industry was absorbed by the Treasury. The Bakufu did not interfere when merchant capital was invested in agriculture, but here they were on unsafe ground, for the commercial methods applied to purchasing the produce of the farms were obnoxious to the villages. The merchants fixed the price they were willing to pay at such a low level that the peasants for the most part found that the more they produced, the less they earned in terms of cash. This was an attack upon the class which was the main support of the feudal society; and in the eighteenth century the peasants were not slow to react against what they deemed to be unjust treatment by the ruling class. There are records of uprisings early in the Tokugawa era, but they grew frequent after 1704, and by then they had become endemic. Some of the earliest were on a great scale, as for instance the rising of 84,000 farmers in 1739, against heavy taxation in the province of Iwaki. They wrecked buildings and threatened the daimyo's castle until their demands were met. In other cases, however, the rising failed, and the peasants were cruelly punished.

An interesting example is that of the fief of Kaminoyama in Dewa, where dreadful conditions had resulted from failures of the harvests in the two years preceding 1747. The requests of the peasants were granted, and they were given a supply of rice. But this was not the end of the matter, for shortly after the dispersal of the farmers, the leaders were questioned under torture. The circumstances of the rising had been reported to Yedo, and the Bakufu ordered the executions of the leaders.

In the following decades similar uprisings recurred, nearly all due to misery resulting from famine and plague. The Kurume uprising of about 50,000 men was a protest against an unfair tax. The leaders were punished, some put to death; but the tax was withdrawn. In 1764–65 came the disturbances in Musashi and Kōtsuke already described (Chapter XIV, Section 4). There had been serious riots in Hida in 1773, which, on orders from the Bakufu, were suppressed by troops using firearms. Most cruel punishments were inflicted on the alleged ringleaders, and spies were rewarded for their delations by permission to take a surname and wear swords.

In 1781, certain merchants fixed standards of quality for silk and cotton, and in the market towns of Musashi and Kōtsuke they established trading stations where the product was examined and a certificate of quality granted for a fee fixed in silver at so much for a unit of weight. But when the market for these articles opened at the end of the summer, the usual buyers—the leading department stores like Echigoya and Shirokiya—held back, saying that they were not prepared to buy at prices which included the examination fees. They agreed to buy no silk this year, but to sell only from stock.

This decision angered the villages in areas which depended upon the sale of raw silk, and a number of their leaders led a crowd of over three thousand peasants in an attack upon those who had set up the examination stations. Their houses were smashed and set on fire, and the rioters then marched to the castle town of Takasaki, where they appealed to the daimyo, Matsudaira Terutaka, to abolish the examination fees. A few of them were wounded by the castle soldiers, who attacked them with bows and firearms, but the peasants were not checked. They sent a deputation of six elders into the castle and pressed for a judgment of their case by the Bakufu deputy (gundai), an officer of good repute named Ina Tadataka.

Their claim was considered, and the examination stations were done away with. This was a great triumph for the farmers and a demonstration that action by the Bakufu to assist merchants at the expense of the peasants would in future be resisted by force. But unfortunately for the peasants they were presently exposed to greater dangers than the cupidity of traders, for especially in the decade 1770–79 the country was overwhelmed by natural disasters. In 1770–71 almost every province suffered from continued drought. In 1772 there was a great fire in Yedo only less destructive than that of Meireki (1657), and in this year also the farms suffered from disastrous floods.[1]

In 1773 there was a plague of sickness from which nearly 200,000 persons are said to have died. It spread to the northern provinces where in the Sendai domain alone 300,000 are said to have died of disease or starvation. Nor was this the end of disasters. In 1778 there were floods in Kyoto and in parts of Kyūshū, and an eruption of the volcano on Ōshima Island, followed by an eruption of Sakurajima, the volcano near Kagoshima, in 1779. The great famine of Temmei began in 1783.

---

[1] In the calendar this year was the ninth of Meiwa, i.e., Meiwa Kunen, which the citizens with their sarcastic humour read "Meiwaku," meaning "Consternation."

In the following year from spring to harvest rain was incessant, and during that period an eruption of the volcano Asama caused great devastation. The famine spread to almost every province and continued until 1786–87.

These calamities were attributed by many citizens to the bad government of Tanuma and his son. Of course they were due to natural phenomena rather than to mistaken policies. It is true, however, that the Bakufu made no serious effort to control the price of food; but a more serious aspect of the shortage was the failure of the authorities to give help to the distressed regions. The seclusionist habit of the daimyos was so strong that they for the most part refused to allow food to be sent from their fiefs to their neighbours, even when they knew that not far away peasants were dying of hunger.

A samurai residing in Shimotsuke province described conditions in the following terms: "Although the shortages in the Kantō did not amount to a great famine, the loss of life through starvation in the northern provinces was dreadful. There was nothing to eat but horse-flesh or, when this ran short, dogs and cats. Once these were consumed, people died of sheer starvation in great numbers. In some villages of thirty, forty, or fifty households not one person survived, and nobody could say who had died or when, for the corpses were unburied and had been eaten by beasts and birds."

There are also records, by no means incredible, of cannibalism. The northern provinces were always in danger of famine, since their land was of marginal utility and their climate severe. The famine of 1783, as we have noted, lasted for about five years. It was one of the three great famines in the history of Tokugawa Japan, the others being the Kyōhō famine of 1732–33 and the Tempō famine of 1832–36.

Such selfish policies as those just described contributed to the frequency of famines, especially in regions where normal climatic conditions were severe and harvests were precarious. When famine spread and affected a great area its results were tragic; but food shortage in even small areas tended to spread because the food problem was not treated on a national scale. A striking example is furnished by the famine of Temmei (1783). Though it had been serious even in the previous year, the Tsugaru fief had sent 400,000 bags of rice for sale in the Yedo and Ōsaka markets, and had forced the peasants to pay all land tax in kind. This ruthless action resulted in a shortage of staple foods within the clan. The daimyo's chief officers were alarmed and borrowed 10,000 ryō from the Bakufu, intending to buy rice from neighbouring fiefs; but this plan failed and villagers starved with money in their pockets.

Thus the agrarian system under the feudal regime as it was then administered failed of its purpose and caused widespread discontent. There had already been food riots ("smashes") in Yedo in 1733, but during the Temmei famine the price of rice rose to such high levels that the townsmen took to violent action in all the important urban centres—Yedo, Kōfu, Suruga, Kyoto, Nara, Fushimi, Sakai, and as far west as Kyūshū. In Yedo, where rioting lasted for three days, there was a state of anarchy. The warehouses and residences of the rice dealers were burned down, and special animosity was displayed against the rich merchants who, under Tanuma's protection, had bought up supplies of rice during the famines. There is no doubt that (quite apart from storms and plagues) the rapid growth in an agrarian society of a commercial economy which had been fostered by Tanuma weighed heavily upon the peasants.[2]

This is a fact which is borne out by population statistics of the era. They are meagre, it is true, but there is evidence enough to show that in the century or so before 1720 the population was gradually rising, whereas after that date for a century or more there was scarcely any increase. This phenomenon is not easy to understand. It is only partly explained as a result of deliberate abortion or infanticide during a long period of rural distress. It is better regarded as a sequel of the famines and epidemic diseases which visited the country so frequently during the eighteenth century.

Some historians discern a social origin of these misfortunes, ascribing them to the cruelty of feudal rule and the great gap between rich and poor which was widened by the penetration of a commercial economy into rural life. There is some truth in this, but no benevolent government could have averted the natural calamities which were the immediate causes of distress.

In considering population growth or decline in eighteenth-century Japan it is important to recall that the available statistics were based upon imperfect data. They do not include members of the warrior class, and they could not record the numerous unregistered persons, whether migrants or recent arrivals in a district. The separate fiefs reported their population, but the method of reckoning varied from place to place, sometimes excluding children. Subject to these variables, the movement of population may be regarded as shown with reasonable

---

[2] A very full account of peasant uprisings in the Tokugawa era is given by Dr. Hugh Borton in *Transactions of the Asiatic Society of Japan* (May 1938), in which he estimates the number of uprisings at over 1,000. Since that date new evidence has become available, showing the total to be over 1,600, mostly occurring after 1730.

accuracy in the figures of the national census conducted by the Bakufu every six years from 1721. These show crude totals as follows:

Date	Population in millions	Date	Population in millions
1721	26.06	1768	26.25
1726	26.54	1774	25.99
1732	26.92	1780	26.01
1744	26.15	1786	25.08
1750	25.91	1792	24.89
1756	26.07	1798	25.47
1762	25.92		

The fluctuations in these figures correspond fairly closely to climatic change until 1798, from which year there was a steady rise for three decades. The fall from 26 million in 1780 to 25 million in 1786 and to less than 25 million in 1792 indicates that at least a million people must have died of famine or pestilence within less than a decade.

3. The Condition of the Samurai

Any general observation on the samurai as a class is apt to be misleading, since they vary from the simple soldier on a small allowance to the direct vassal of the Shōgun, the Bannerman (Hatamoto) in receipt of handsome emoluments. Since in times of peace most of these men had no occupation, they created a social problem for the Bakufu. Some description of the difficulties which arose from their unemployed condition has been given in the chapters (III and VI) bearing upon the rōnin revolt of 1651. In the eighteenth century a great number of the most capable members of this class had been absorbed into official life in the capital or in the castle towns, and others had settled in cities where they lived on their small stipends, or adjusted themselves to urban life by working at trades such as making umbrellas or wooden clogs or in clerical occupations. Some, for want of funds, went so far as to adopt the son of a townsman in return for a cash payment, thus conferring upon him the status of samurai. There was a recognized scale of payment for these transactions—some twenty ryō to become an ashigaru, and a thousand ryō or more for higher ranks.

The chronicles of those times, and especially the plays and novels, naturally pay little attention to samurai living a quiet life and struggling against penury. They prefer to depict the brawls and the debauches of such picturesque if disorderly characters as Tamura Daikichi, a man of hatamoto rank who kept a gambling house where bloodshed was frequent, and who when placed under arrest by the City Magistrates, escaped, was captured in a remote village disguised as a monk, and put to death in Yedo. Another such character was a samurai who drew his sword on the attendant in a drinking shop, but was disarmed by blows with an iron rod and forced to run away. It was not for his violence but for his cowardice that he was tried and punished by exile.

These and similar episodes may give the impression that the samurai had lost their prestige and that the authority of the warrior class was waning; but this impression would not be true, for there were a number of serious men who were scholars by temperament and, being members of the governing class, were interested in political issues. They inherited the tradition of the Neo-Confucianist philosophers, but they were living in an age when among educated men a feeling of dissatisfaction was growing throughout the country, and to some thinkers the seclusion policy seemed to be preventing necessary change. It will be recalled that even so conservative a scholar as Arai Hakuseki had sensed that Japan must not lose touch with the outside world.

Another man of learning, Aoki Konyō, celebrated as the expert who brought the sweet potato to Japan, by his encouragement of Dutch language studies had led the way to further enquiries into the nature of Western learning. With official approval he wrote several papers on the Dutch language, and as well as these he had presented memorials on current fiscal and other problems to the Shōgun Yoshimune, who favoured his activities. He also made efforts to improve the condition of the hatamoto, although he himself was not a samurai by birth, but the son of a wholesale fishmonger in Yedo. Unfortunately the Shōgun died before any action could be taken on these proposals, but Konyō continued to press them and made a point of questioning the Dutch "Kapitan" on the annual visit from the trading station at Deshima to Yedo. He died in 1769 at the age of seventy-two.

4. Rangaku

Konyō's encouragement of Dutch studies was approved by the Bakufu, and he was promoted to the office of Chief Librarian (Shomotsu-Bugyō). His success in promoting "Rangaku," or Dutch Studies, was due less to his books than to his influence upon his pupils, chief among whom was one Maeno Ryōtaku, a physician in the Okudaira fief whose contribution is much praised in a work called Rangaku Kaitei (Steps in Dutch Studies) by a scholar named Ōtsuki Gentaku.

Maeno Ryōtaku was sent by his daimyo to Nagasaki, where he consulted Japanese interpreters at Deshima. He made but little progress, probably because the interpreters were not helpful. But his contribution to Dutch studies was important, for he was a pioneer. He visited Nagasaki twice, at his daimyo's behest, and though he learned a vocabulary of a few hundred words he could not use it effectively. He did, however, procure from the interpreters certain books which he struggled to read with such aids as he could procure. He wrote several essays on the Dutch language and on such studies as surveying, geography, and astronomy. His labours were described in a work entitled *Rangaku Kotohajime* (The Origin of Dutch Studies) by his friend Sugita Gempaku. He died in 1803 at the age of eighty.

Following Maeno and Sugita came a number of scholars who profited by the experience of their predecessors, and became more successful exponents of Dutch learning. Among them were the aforementioned Ōtsuki Gentaku, born in 1757, the son of a physician, and Hiraga Gennai, perhaps the most remarkable of them all. These men lived in a time of which it was said: "The wind of Holland blows throughout the land [Oranda kaze seken wo fukiwataru]." The word "Rampeki" was in common use. It meant "the Dutch Craze." It was a craze which affected such practical persons as Tanuma Okitsugu, who encouraged Dutch studies, perhaps not so much as a policy as out of curiosity and a desire for rare objects. But at the same time he was an acquisitive and far-sighted man, always on the look-out to expand and diversify the national economy.

Most of the scholars attracted by Dutch learning were specialists, interested in medicine or astronomy or some other single branch of study; but one of them was a polymath, who sought knowledge over a wide range of subjects. This was Hiraga Gennai, a man whose influence was felt in so many directions that his career deserves some separate notice.

5. *Hiraga Gennai (1728–79)*

He was the son of an ashigaru, whom he followed as herbalist for Matsudaira Yoriyasu, daimyo of the Takamatsu fief in Sanuki province. He was undoubtedly the most versatile and in some ways perhaps the most gifted man of his day. In 1752, in his twenty-fourth year, he was ordered by Yoriyasu to proceed to Nagasaki for study of the Dutch language and of natural science. Yoriyasu was a collector of specimens of all kinds—birds, fish, plants, shells, precious stones—and kept a catalogue which contained descriptions and drawings of these objects under their names in Japanese, Chinese, and Dutch. Gennai, during his stay in Nagasaki, was to gather knowledge which would be of use to Yoriyasu.

He spent a year there, seemingly in desultory studies, and on his return in 1753 he went to Yedo, where he worked under one Tamura Enyu. He specialized in botany, but both he and Tamura were interested in a more comprehensive study of production of commodities in general, whether by agriculture or industry. This branch of learning (named by them "Bussangaku," or the science of production) deserves some enquiry for the light it throws upon social and economic ideas current during the eighteenth century in Japan. But first we should continue an account of Gennai's life, since he may be said to have dominated the "modern" intellectual scene in Japan, however briefly, at the height of the fervent interest in ideas imported from Europe.

While engaged in his studies and other enterprises in Yedo, he continued to receive his stipend from Takamatsu, but he wished to be relieved of his obligations as a retainer. He applied for indefinite leave of absence, and this was granted, but he took offence at a not very onerous condition laid down by Yoriyasu, resigned his official post, and thus became a rōnin. Thereafter he was a disappointed man, devoting much of his talent to fugitive literature of a satirical or scurrilous nature and (under a pseudonym) a number of stage plays; but he continued to engage in serious studies, such as a work on the Classification of Natural Objects (*Butsurui Hinshitsu*), issued in 1763, and an essay upon making an asbestos cloth, issued in 1764.

His interests were almost universal. Apart from adding to his knowledge of scientific matters, he devoted some effort to painting in Western style, showing contrasts of light and shade which could not be portrayed by conventional line drawing. He gave lessons in oil painting to one Shiba Kōkan, who had hitherto practised drawing in the Chinese manner but was later to gain high reputation as an exponent of Western principles of art.

In 1770 Gennai again visited Nagasaki, where he learned to construct an electrical apparatus. He also saw specimens of Kyūshū pottery and suggested to the Bakufu that it should be specially made for export. In 1773 he wrote at the daimyo's request a report on the iron ore deposits in the Sendai fief. In 1774 he wrote his *Hōhiron*, a tract expressing his contempt for modern society, and commenting upon the part played by the haphazard and the irrational in human affairs. He was now a querulous and pessimistic figure. Late in the year 1779, through some misunderstanding or in a moment of frenzy, he attacked and killed one of his followers. He was arrested and died in prison a few weeks later, at the age of fifty-one.

His friend Sugita Gempaku was not allowed to take his body for burial, since it was that of a criminal; but Gempaku was permitted to take the clothes that Gennai had worn. These he buried in a cemetery in Asakusa, erecting a stone on which he had carved an epitaph, saying that Gennai was an exceptional man who liked remarkable things and lived a remarkable life ended by a remarkable death. But this memorial was destroyed by official order.

Bussangaku. This may be translated as the science of production. Of course there were already in the eighteenth century important increases of production in both agriculture and industry, some natural and some definitely planned; but what Gennai and his associates had in mind was an all-round planned increase in the number and quantity of articles produced.

Most of the scientific knowledge so far obtained from the Dutch had been applied to medicine, and had stimulated studies of botany in particular. It was the purpose of Gennai and his school to encourage the production of a great variety of objects for similar purposes. They took the line that the sciences depended upon products, as medicine depended upon herbs. This was a natural view, since they were not acquainted with scientific theories, and the provision of a quantity of useful objects was in their minds the best way of improving the national economy.

In 1757 Gennai's colleague Tamura Enyu, who had travelled widely in Japan to investigate the cultivation of subsidiary foodstuffs and medicinal herbs, opened in Yedo a display of important products. This was in fact the earliest example of an exhibition in Japan, and its success was due in part to the energetic support of Gennai. In 1762 Gennai opened an exhibition of his own, consisting chiefly of medicinal items. In this and other exhibitions during the decade the number of exhibits reached 2,000, and they came from thirty provinces. In his work *Butsurui Hinshitsu* of 1763 (cited above) some of the most important exhibits were described, with drawings and explanations.

It is clear from the nature of the exhibits and the statements of Gennai that the significance of his Bussangaku is that it predicated a planned increase of production and not a mere undirected effort. Gennai, it should be noted, was patronized for his European studies by Tanuma, who was in favour of a rapid increase in the output of both agriculture and industry.

It is also possible that Gennai's idea of making a complete catalogue of objects was inspired by the philosophy of the Chu Hsi school, which held that an understanding of universal reason was to be gained only by investigating everything and ultimately collating the investigations. This is the frame of mind that in the West led to science, but in the East had to fight against sudden enlightenment or revealed religion.[3]

[3] See L. Carrington Goodrich, *A Short History of the Chinese People* (New York, 1959), p. 155.

CHAPTER XVI

THE KANSEI REFORM

1. Matsudaira Sadanobu (1758–1829)

THE NAME of "reform" has been given by some historical writers to
certain phases of government which recurred at intervals during the
rule of the Tokugawa Shōguns from the last years of the eighteenth
century; but it is a misleading label, since it gives the impression that a
new and better form of government was introduced. What really took
place was the revival of an earlier and successful system which had
declined largely from economic rather than political causes. The model
was the so-called Kyōhō government developed by Yoshimune in the
Kyōhō era (1716–36).

Following its decline came what is known as the Kansei Reform in
1787. In that year the need for constructive measures was driven home
to the Bakufu by the repeated failures of the government to suppress
uprisings by both peasants and townspeople. The use of armed force
was occasionally successful in a limited area for a limited time, but it
was clear to thoughtful members of the warrior class that the causes of
revolt must be ascertained and dealt with in a peaceful manner, remem-
bering that the risings were due to conditions which the people found
unbearable.

A reform movement which began late in 1787 was stimulated by in-
tolerable hardships following upon season after season of poor harvests.
In the early summer of that year the price of rice increased to five or six
times the average level. The hungry poor rose in anger, and "smashing"
raids took place first in Ōsaka and then in smaller towns, as we have
already seen (in Chapter XV, Section 2). When the riots had subsided,
the question of future policy came before the Council of Elders, which
had appointed as its president in 1787 (the year after Tanuma's fall)
the young daimyo of Shirakawa in Mutsu, Matsudaira Sadanobu.

Sadanobu was a grandson of Yoshimune and a son of the head of
the Tayasu branch of the Tokugawa family. He was adopted by the
House of Matsudaira, thus succeeding to the Shirakawa fief of 110,000
koku. Imbued with Neo-Confucian idealism, he devoted his energy to
the improvement of this domain, paying special attention to the revival
of villages ruined by successive calamities. At the height of the Temmei
famine (1783), which afflicted the northern provinces in particular, he

had promptly brought a great supply of rice to Shirakawa, with the result that there were no deaths from hunger in his fief.

He played an important part in the choice of a successor to the Shōgun Ieharu, who died in 1786. Tanuma Okitsugu and certain Tokugawa claimants intrigued against him, but they quarrelled among themselves, and with Sadanobu's support Ienari, of the Hitotsubashi line, succeeded as eleventh Shōgun in 1787. He was a minor, born in 1773, and was under tutelage until 1793. Tanuma was dismissed and disgraced, and Sadanobu stated his wish to join the Council of Elders (Rōjū). He submitted a memorial explaining his desire to undertake a reform of the Bakufu. His plan was approved by the Three Houses (Go-Sanke), but met with opposition from some of the older ladies-in-waiting, who had fallen under Tanuma's spell, and from some of Tanuma's supporters among the Rōjū. It was not until the urgency of reform was brought home to them by the riots in the summer of 1787 that they gave their consent.

Sadanobu then presided over a select committee of the Rōjū and introduced a number of remedial measures, in the control of finance, in the selection and promotion of officers of state, and in the suppression of bribery and other dishonest practices that had marked the Tanuma regime. He was then in his thirtieth year. Besides presiding over the Council of Elders he was appointed to the office of Hōsa, or Adviser to the Shōgun, in which in practice he exercised the power of a Deputy or Regent.

The offending officials were not dismissed, but put on their good behaviour. Tanuma and his associates soon found the wind of reform too bleak for their comfort and, as we have seen, were suitably punished. The former Finance Commissioners (Kanjō-Bugyō) were heavily fined for malpractices and reduced in rank. Certain subordinate officials found guilty of theft, corruption, and malversation of funds were condemned to death or banishment, while the merchants who had been privy to their misdeeds were similarly dealt with. At the bottom of the scale even small traders and rice brokers were included in the pursuit, and at the top a number of political leaders of the highest rank were deprived of office because of their relations with Tanuma, among them the Tairō Ii and several Elders such as Abe and Mizuno.

Having seen how Sadanobu set about his business, let us now turn to his character, since it accounts for much that happened while he was in power. He was a man of great piety, and was regular in his devotions, calling upon the spirit of Ieyasu to help him to carry the heavy burden of government. He was articulate, even eloquent. His object

19

20

21

22

23

was to restore the foundations of Bakufu government, the pattern being that of the reforms commenced by Yoshimune, his grandfather. In January 1788 he prayed at the Kichijō-In of Reiganjima in Yedo, offering his own life as a sacrifice for one year in which there would be a good supply of cheap rice so that the people need not suffer. He had already displayed unusual capacity in the government of his own fief. He was, moreover, a learned man, and had published a number of treatises on politics, economics, and the arts, among them an essay on the nature of government in which he expressed equalitarian views, such as "The peasant working in the fields under a blazing sun is a man, no less than a daimyo leading an easy, well-fed life." He also declared that the domain ruled by a daimyo was not his property, but belonged to the nation; and he observed that where there is distress, the people dare not complain, but the ruler is responsible for their condition.

Sadanobu had a literary gift, and wrote copiously. A memoir which he wrote under the title of *Uge no Hitogoto* for the instruction of his descendants has fortunately been preserved. It gives a most interesting account of his official career and his personal views. It reveals him as a man of high principles, whose attitude towards the people he governed may perhaps best be described as tutorial. He was, as will be seen from the account of his regime which follows, humourless and without imagination. He was criticized in his day by an opponent to his views who, in a memorial to the Shōgun, described him as talented, but narrow-minded, a man who meant to do good but only did harm.

2. Sadanobu's Policies

Sadanobu was in a strong position. Thanks to his family connexions and his acknowledged gifts, he was acceptable as a personal adviser to the Shōgun Ienari, much as Hoshina Masayuki had served the Shōgun Ietsuna. He was in fact almost a Deputy Shōgun, though he took care not to behave in an arbitrary manner and was at pains to consult the Elders and other influential persons. He was confronted by many serious issues, but his first and most difficult task was to regulate the finances of the Bakufu, not by manipulating currency but by a genuine balance of revenue and expenditure.

The situation in 1787 was that the Treasury was almost empty, and in 1788 a deficit seemed unavoidable. The decennial average of excess of revenue over expenditure had fallen from about 250,000 ryō per annum in 1772–80 to zero, and there was no gold or silver in the Treasury chest, which had held three million ryō in 1770. When this situation was revealed to the Rōjū, they were both surprised and alarmed, for they were ignorant of financial matters. To meet the deficit, short of borrowing from rich merchants, there was only one course to take. The annual expenditure must be reduced. This was done, and by 1793 ordinary revenue was slightly in excess of ordinary expenditure. There were, however, heavy items of extraordinary disbursement, for such purposes as rebuilding palaces destroyed by fires in Kyoto. It seems appropriate to observe here that the annual loss of property in Japan through fire was immense.

To meet such demands an increase of revenue had been achieved by reviving (1789) Yoshimune's system of contribution by daimyos, and making its rules more stringent. In general Sadanobu's policy in economic matters was negative, for he was disposed to control and restrict rather than to expand—a feature which is plainly revealed by a great increase of severe measures against large commercial undertakings and against moneylenders. The number of punishable economic actions grew apace.

Perhaps the best, or at any rate the plainest, example of his actions designed to put an end to extravagance is his treatment of the brokers (fudasashi), whose business it was to advance money to samurai on the security of their rice stipends. The fudasashi as a class made outrageous profits and were notorious for their patronage of the most luxurious establishments in the pleasure quarters of Yedo. They were the most prominent and the most numerous of the great spendthrifts of the day. The wealthiest among them were those who advanced money to the Shōgun's direct retainers, the hatamoto and the go-kenin, on the security of their rice stipends. These brokers drove a hard bargain. They had already been checked by the Bakufu some years before, and now Sadanobu struck a blow at them by reducing the rate of interest on such advances and warning the fudasashi that they would be severely punished if they disobeyed his order. The hatamoto took full advantage of this protection, and in 1795 they rioted in the streets and treated the brokers with such violence that the City Commissioners had to send a daily patrol to the district where the hatamoto were creating disturbances. Thus the Bakufu found itself in the awkward position of having to punish members of the principal military force serving the House of Tokugawa and committed to preserving the peace.

Sadanobu was naturally unable to cure the essential defects of the feudal system over which he presided. He had to attend to immediate problems, and of these there were plenty. He must regulate prices and in other ways succour persons or classes in distress. He must repair the damaged finances of the Bakufu, and in general relieve the anxieties of the people. On the whole his policy was conservative. He tried to make the best use of existing institutions. In financial matters his chief object was to reduce or check expenditure, to moderate the wild profit-making of the past years, and in general to restrain the money economy which was now dominant and to put in its place a land economy. In order to carry out a policy of retrenchment, immediately after taking office he ordered a reduction of current expenditure for three years, and after that, within five years, a balance of revenue and expenditure was to be restored. In the Bakufu Treasury there had been over three million ryō in gold and silver in 1770. By 1787 the chest was nearly empty, by 1790 it was being replenished.

His economic policy thus had some temporary success. He decided upon some simple currency reforms, which appear to have been effective. There was no social disturbance due to a shortage of food during his term of office, that is from 1787 to the close of the century. Indeed there were good harvests for a decade or more; and he dealt with speculation on the rice market by supervising the leading Ōsaka rice merchants and where necessary punishing them severely. This was a temporarily effective measure, and he continued his efforts to keep prices down. He provided against famine by ordering all daimyos to form a reserve of rice by setting aside annually for five years fifty koku for every 10,000 koku of their revenue.

He considered that the fundamental cause of high prices was a lack of balance between production and consumption, which he thought could be remedied by restraining commerce and encouraging agriculture by drainage, irrigation, afforestation, and other methods. He abolished or reduced the corvées hitherto imposed upon peasants. These were reasonable and beneficial measures, but he made a serious mistake in his endeavour to check a fall in the population of villages and a flow of villagers to the towns. He even tried to reduce the subsidiary work of the farmers in growing tobacco, indigo, and other subsidiary crops. It is very doubtful whether Sadanobu's agrarian policy had any real success. While he was announcing benefits, the tax-collectors were imposing their levies without mercy.[1] It is characteristic of Sadanobu's administration that its benevolent theories were rarely put into full practice.

His edict of 1790 ordering peasants to return to the land was meant to reduce the population of Yedo and increase the rural population. It

---

[1] See the memorial of Shibano Kuriyama in *Keizai Taiten*, Vol. XXVI.

is doubtful whether this policy served any useful purpose. It was too conservative. It was putting the clock back. Its chief interest is in the light which it throws upon Sadanobu's qualities as a statesman. Despite his ideals and his hard work he was at the mercy of his theories and lacked practical wisdom. In his attempt to go back to Ieyasu and Yoshimune he was in fact a reactionary in an era of inevitable change. What is usually called the Kansei Reform was, it is true, a phase of good government in intention, but essentially this was a period free from the famines and other disasters which had marred the previous decade. It was circumstances rather than policy which produced good results.

While Sadanobu paid close attention to the purely monetary aspects of the national economy, it is clear that he was blind to the importance of developing its other features. He did little to encourage either productive industry or commercial enterprise. He seems to have supposed that such action would lead to a rise in prices, which he was most anxious to prevent. He wrote an "Essay on Prices" (*Bukkaron*), and the Bakufu endeavoured to keep prices down by manipulating the market for gold and silver to be used in coinage. This complex task had poor success, and better results were obtained by regulating the rice market, the basis of the economy. All attempts to "corner" the supply of rice were forbidden under severe punishment.

In so far as the great efforts of Sadanobu were directed to permanent reform, his policy was not successful. It had some visible effect for a few years between 1787 and 1794, but it was soon confounded in a great river of events and left hardly any trace. Judged by direct results it was a failure, but it cannot be dismissed as such, since it marked an important stage in the history of the Bakufu, a different view of its functions.

3. *The Bakufu and the Court*

It will be recalled that in the seventeenth century the relations between the Imperial Court and the Bakufu had been amicable, but that Yoshimune, though respectful, did not pay much attention to the Throne. In the years about 1760, however, there was a strong loyalist movement which disturbed the Bakufu, and a number of conspirators who had plotted a rising were punished in 1766. An underground movement nevertheless continued, not so much for the purpose of restoring power to the Imperial House as to ensure a reasonable income to the Emperor and his nobles. In 1774 some stewards and Bakufu officials were severely punished for swindling the Court, and again in 1778 similar peculation was laid bare by Sadanobu himself, who had visited Kyoto to discuss the rebuilding of the Palace, which with a great part of the city had been burned to the ground in a disastrous fire early in the year. In his journal he gives a detailed account of his sojourn, of his discussions with Court nobles, and of an audience with the Emperor, by whom he was amiably received.

The relations between the Bakufu and the Court then seemed cordial, but they were soon to deteriorate, for there was a dispute as to the powers of the Emperor after the retirement of Go-Momozono. The new sovereign, Kōkaku, had to apply to the Bakufu for permission to grant ranks and titles to the abdicated emperor (1789). It would seem that the Bakufu could not reasonably object to this act of piety, but in fact Sadanobu let it be known that he could not approve. The Throne and the Bakufu were thus at odds, but somehow or other the dispute was patched up. Yet feelings at the Court remained hostile to the Bakufu, and Sadanobu not without reason suspected that a strong sentiment against Yedo prevailed in Kyoto. It was encouraged by the zeal of a young student from Yedo, one Takayama Masayuki, who publicly venerated the Emperor while kneeling on the Sanjō bridge and facing the Palace.

These episodes were of no great importance at the time, but they make a significant prelude to the loyalist movement which, in due course —in less than a century—was to destroy the Bakufu and revive the power of the Throne.

4. Intellectual Trends

There was no end to Sadanobu's belief in the power of learning to improve morals. He thought that the true remedy for the evils of the day was to be found in the practice of Confucian teaching. He was himself an enthusiastic seeker after truth and a convinced believer, so that it was natural for him to choose a Confucian ethic as the basis of the cultural policy which he intended to follow.

In that policy the most important feature was the renovation of the Confucian college (the Shōhei Gakumonjo) and the banning of any other teaching than that which it prescribed. At that time the college was in a poor condition, torn by dissensions and without strong direction. Sadanobu was perturbed by this situation and set about clearing up its disorder, notably in the first place by removing traces of the influence of Tanuma and appointing new professors, exponents of the

Chu Hsi school who were scholars of high reputation in harmony with the reform spirit which animated those days. A new President of the college was appointed, a Matsudaira who was adopted into the Hayashi family and was named Jussai.

There was little room for academic freedom in Sadanobu's scheme. In 1790 an ordinance was issued prohibiting any other teaching than the form of Chu Hsi doctrine in which he himself believed and which spread widely to the detriment of other beliefs. The official school brought great pressure to bear upon other schools, which they regarded, and indeed persecuted, as unorthodox. One of the victims of this persecution was the distinguished philosopher Ogyū Sorai. In so far as this was Sadanobu's work it is an instance of his nervous dread of the unorthodox.

Yet he was not an obscurantist and was not a prejudiced believer in the Chu Hsi philosophy. Indeed, although he tried to control and unify thought for political purposes and did not listen to the protests of scholars, he never went out of his way to punish dissidents. His government did, however, in 1790 issue orders for the censorship of certain publications, such as lewd pictures and pornographic books, and to this list were added works which ridiculed the government. In the following year Santo Kyōden, a popular writer of comic works, was punished for such an offence. More surprising was the punishment in 1791 of a scholar named Hayashi Shihei for publishing a work on maritime defence called *Kaikoku Heidan,* a theme of great importance at that time, when Japan had neither a navy nor a merchant fleet useful for defence. But Hayashi's work was well timed, for a few months after his arrest a mission from Russia arrived at Nemuro in Yezo (the northern island now known as Hokkaidō).

Sadanobu was aware of the truth of Hayashi's charges, but did not approve of disturbing statements. It was not wise to alarm the people. It is one of the ironies of history that while these minor anxieties occupied the minds of the rulers of Japan, a more pressing danger than uncensored books seemed to threaten them in their foreign relations; for in the north there was already trouble with Russians, and the Ainu living on Kunashiri (the nearest of the Kurile Islands to Yezo) were in constant revolt. News of the appearance of foreign ships off the shores of Japan gave the Bakufu real cause for anxiety. This was no time for philosophical argument. The minds of thinking men had to be applied to grave questions of national policy. How was the government to deal with this undoubted threat to the national policy of seclusion? The problems of reform, as they were seen by Sadanobu, had to give way to solid realities.

In the summer of 1792 a Russian naval officer reached Nemuro in a Russian vessel which was on an official mission to repatriate some Japanese castaways and to propose the opening of diplomatic and commercial relations, proceeding to Yedo for that purpose. Nemuro was in Japanese territory, being a harbour in the island Yezo, and therefore by Japanese law the vessel had no right of entry. Sadanobu ordered preparations for coastal defence, and in 1793 he inspected the coasts of Izu and Sagami. In the following year he resigned his office as Regent, not because he felt that his policies had failed, but because his critics blamed him for all the difficulties with which the government was now confronted. He had incurred the ill will, the jealousy, of the Shōgun Ienari, who was anxious to direct the Bakufu and did in fact continue to rule until 1837, thus holding office for fifty years.

Ienari contributed little to the prosperity of the state, for most of his actions resulted in the failure of undertakings which Sadanobu had planned in the national interest. Not satisfied with Sadanobu's resignation of the office of Regent, he went so far as to remove his name from the list of Rōjū, a mean action which was inspired by the envy of Sadanobu's rivals or his enemies in the inner apartments of the Shōgun's palace.

There was little sympathy for Sadanobu among the citizens. They had tired of his attempts to dictate their behaviour and they disliked his reforming zeal. Popular feeling was expressed in lampoons, in songs and verses which played upon the names Tanuma and Shirakawa. They said that they preferred a muddy pond (numa) to a clear stream (shirakawa). Less vulgar critics attacked him for what they saw as his pretentious and inefficient character, but there can be little doubt that on balance his administration was effective in clearing up the irregular situation left by Tanuma and in preventing, or at least postponing, a serious decline in the authority of the Bakufu. He was a conservative man, and attempted no radical changes; but in the opinion of some Japanese scholars his efforts and those of his trusted colleague Matsudaira Nobuaki (who took his place as Rōjū) combined to prolong the authority of the Bakufu for thirty years after the withdrawal of Tanuma.

5. The Russian Approach

Russian expansion eastward across Asia goes back a long way, but Russian geographers do not appear to have known much about Japan until late in the seventeenth century. They had some information from Dutch sources and from the descriptions of Atlasov, an explorer sent to Kamchatka, who in 1700 reported to Moscow on the Kurile Islands and their proximity to Japan. His knowledge was derived from a Japanese castaway named Dembei. This man and other survivors of a devastating storm at sea managed to reach Kamchatka, and Dembei was fortunate in that he was taken into the care of Atlasov and sent on to Moscow. There he was received in 1702 by Peter the Great, who displayed a great interest in such particulars about Japan as Dembei could convey to him. In that year he isued a decree ordering preparations for intercourse with Japan. Thenceforward there were increasingly frequent Russian voyages from Kamchatka designed to reach Japanese territory, while in Moscow studies of the Japanese language were begun.

Among the early voyages was one in 1721 from Okhotsk, under the command of scientists commissioned to find a route to Japan by way of the Kurile Islands. Such voyages continued at intervals until 1792, when Lieutenant Adam Laxman, son of a professor of natural science at Irkutsk, arrived as a member of an expedition sent by Catherine the Great in a vessel named *Ekaterina*, which from Okhotsk had proceeded down the Kurile Archipelago. It was this visit which caused alarm in Yedo and hurried Sadanobu's resignation.

Laxman was kindly treated by Japanese officials while waiting at Nemuro for a reply from Yedo, for Japanese and Russians had been in contact for several decades in Yezo and the neighbouring islands, and their intercourse was friendly. He sent his letters of instruction to Yedo, to show that he was under orders from his sovereign to proceed there in order to open negotiations for trade and residence. He also was to repatriate several Japanese castaways, including a remarkable man named Kōdayu, who was teaching Japanese in Irkutsk and had been protected by a scholar in that city, Professor Eric Laxman, the father of Adam Laxman.

Adam Laxman's mission put Sadanobu in a quandary, which he resolved in a manner familiar to harassed statesmen—by procrastination. Laxman was given to understand that if he wished to be admitted to Nagasaki, he must go there and like any other visitor ask for permission to enter the harbour. Nagasaki was the only port in Japan where foreign ships might call. Laxman was not satisfied with this response, and sailed away to return to Russia. The Russian government was not interested enough to put direct pressure upon Japan, but did not abandon the idea of closer relations. A few years later another Russian vessel appeared. This was in October 1804, when the warship *Nadezhda*, carrying an ambassador from the Tsar, entered Nagasaki harbour. The ambassador, Vasilii Rezanov, was treated politely enough, but he met nothing but delay and obstruction for several months. In March 1805 he was told that instructions had come from Yedo, and he must leave forthwith. This he did.

At this time the political situation in Yedo was confused. Sadanobu though out of office could still exert some influence as member of a group of high officers of state that included Matsudaira Nobuaki and other councillors. They were able for a time to control the incompetent Shōgun Ienari, but soon after the turn of the century they began to lose their authority, and while this change in the character of government was taking place, the Bakufu received a severe shock from a critical tension in the country's relations with Russia which was produced by the treatment of Rezanov.[2] But the government's reaction was entirely negative. It did nothing but refuse the Russian requests.

The reason for this change of front was (rather than pressure from the Dutch as is sometimes suggested) nothing but a complete loss of the positive and active character which had been displayed by the Bakufu in the exercise of its power a decade before.

After Rezanov's departure no Russian attempt was made to establish a position on the main island of Japan, but there were frequent raids on Yezo and the Kurile Islands inspired by Rezanov in a spirit of vengeance for his humiliation in Nagasaki. He had made his way to Alaska and thence to San Francisco, where he began preparations for an expedition against Sakhalin. He engaged the services of two Russian naval officers (Khostov and Davydov). In 1807 these two attacked settlements in Sakhalin and Yezo and then, loaded with booty, sailed for Okhotsk. They left a letter stating that they would return and attack the Japanese settlements unless Japan and Russia came to terms. They had of course no authority to make such statements, for the government at Petersburg had no knowledge of their actions.

Their attacks were so flagrant that the Bakufu was bound to retaliate. There were many opinions as to a suitable policy, and unaware that the two officers had no authority for their raids, the Japanese decided that they must prepare to resort to arms against Russia. But first their own defences must be strengthened. They sent contingents to strategic points in Yezo, reinforcements went to Etorofu, and the defences of the northern shores of the main island were strengthened. Since the two Russia officers had left word that they would return to Sakhalin

[2] Rezanov lost interest in Japan when he saw fine prospects in California. He hoped to make it a Russian possession and might well have succeeded, since there would have been only feeble opposition from the Spanish colonists. But his health failed and he died in 1807.

and Etorofu for an answer, a reply was drafted which stated that Japan
would not submit to threats and would fight if the Russians persisted
in sending ships to attack her territories.

Apart from these verbal skirmishes the position remained much as
before, until in the summer of 1811 a Russian cruiser, the *Diana,* drew
near the shore of Etorofu in order to fix its position. The captain, Vasilii Golovnin, had no intention of clashing with the Japanese. He sent
an ensign ashore to make enquiries, and followed himself, to find the
ensign in conversation with Japanese soldiers. His innocent visit, however, aroused the suspicions of the Japanese officers who had soon appeared on the beach and had asked questions about Khovstov and Davydov. Soon after this meeting Golovnin moved to an anchorage off
the shore of Kunashiri, near to a strongly garrisoned fortress. He went
ashore with several officers and spoke to some Japanese on the beach;
but after some conversation all pretence was suddenly dropped. Golovnin and his men were captured, bound, and led away to another part
of the island. They were cruelly treated and ultimately imprisoned in
Hakodate. There they had been held in captivity for two years when
the *Diana* was brought to Hakodate and allowed to take them away.
The reason for this change of mind was a declaration by Russian officials that Khostov and Davydov were acting against their orders. The
Russians at this time had proposed an exchange of prisoners.

Golovnin had gained the esteem and affection of his captors, and
when he left there was a festive farewell gathering in which Russians
and Japanese took part in great harmony. The Japanese crowded round
their one-time prisoners with gifts and kind words, and some were on
the verge of tears at parting. As the *Diana* was towed out the Japanese
and Russians exchanged thunderous cheers. Such behaviour was typical of the intercourse between Japanese and Russians, which combined
fear and attraction. Golovnin's was the last important attempt to establish good relations with the Japanese in the Kuriles. This intercourse,
like a love affair with its quarrels and embraces, played an important
part in revealing to the Japanese their own weakness and in opening a
breach in the policy of seclusion.

In 1808, a year after the *Diana* sailed from Kronstadt, an English
frigate sailed into Nagasaki in search of Dutch prize, for at that time
Holland, ruled by a French king, was an enemy of Great Britain. This
was H.M.S. *Phaeton,* a crack vessel, one of the "Saucy Channel Four"
which did good service during the Napoleonic wars. Her captain, seeing that there were no Dutch ships to make prize, decided to leave, but
first demanded a supply of food and threatened to bombard the harbour if it was denied. The Governor of Nagasaki was ready to resist,

but it turned out that the defences were weak and the defenders mostly absent or incompetent. Supplies were furnished. The intruder then sailed out on a fair breeze, and the Governor committed suicide that evening.

This episode shows clearly, as well as the inadequacy of the defences of Nagasaki, the poor spirit of the defenders and the daimyos who were responsible for its protection. It was not until after the *Phaeton* incident that the harbour defences were strengthened and improved.

The visits of the *Diana* and the *Phaeton* were by no means the first arrivals of foreign vessels (other than Chinese and Dutch) at Japanese ports after the seclusion edicts. An American merchant ship, the *Eliza,* had arrived at Nagasaki in 1797 and returned annually until 1803, at first bringing cargoes for the Dutch, since the Netherlands had at that time no ships available.

This was a time when European maritime states were encouraging voyages of exploration in all oceans. The British Admiralty in particular sent suitable warships on peaceful surveying missions in the interests of cartography. Broughton's voyages in the North Pacific were of this nature, and innocent of any hostile purpose; but the Japanese were not aware of this and were so alarmed by reports of his visits to points in Sakhalin from 1795 for a year or more that the Bakufu sent officers to persuade him to leave.

Further breaches in the seclusion policy were made by the arrival of English ships at Japanese ports—in 1817 and again in 1818 at Uraga, in 1824 at Ōtsugahama in Hitachi, and off the Satsuma island of Taka-rajima in the same year, when there was a fracas between the English sailors and the islanders. This incident caused the issue in 1825 of a new edict, known as the "ninen naku," or "no second thought," expulsion order. Hitherto the occasional visits of foreign ships had not been forcibly prevented when they came in search of water and fuel; but now the local authorities were ordered to destroy any vessel that came close in shore, and to arrest or kill any members of its crew that might land. These sudden changes of attitude betrayed a lack of resolution in the Bakufu. In fact they were evidence of the sheer loss of forceful initiative which had overcome the Bakufu in those years. Its policy was one of ease and comfort. It even withdrew from the direct government of Yezo and returned the responsibility to the daimyo of Masumae.

6. Sumptuary Laws

In most periods of Japanese history one finds examples of sumptuary legislation intended to promote economy and invariably failing to produce the results desired. Sadanobu's government issued some of the most ridiculous laws of this kind. Whether Sadanobu himself was directly responsible for these measures is not clear, but he was a solemn and not very imaginative man and may well have approved of them. He certainly was given to interfering in the daily life of the people, and towards the end of his term of office he had lost all the popularity he may have enjoyed.

His endeavour to regulate and reduce the expenditure of the towns-people was continuous. It took the usual form. He forbade the use of barbers and hairdressers. He ordered the arrest of prostitutes in the city, and had them sent to the Yoshiwara (the great Yedo brothel quarter) for a term of years. He ordered separate accommodations for men and women in the city bath-houses, thus depriving the citizens of their favourite resorts for social intercourse, the hairdresser's shop and the public bath-house. He forbade betting and gambling, thus depriving gamblers of their livelihood and (it was said) driving them to robbery as a trade.

Worse than these attacks upon the simple pleasures of the people, the authorities had recourse to a system of spying, intended to secure obedience to the rules. The spies would mix with the customers and denounce them for some careless remark, or they would accept bribes and thus make it necessary for more spies to keep a watch upon their colleagues. In fact there were spies in all quarters of Yedo and also of Ōsaka, and they employed as agents and listeners male servants in brothels of the city. In the bath-house the spies themselves, disguised by their nudity, would sit immersed in the hot water with the ordinary customers, and would arrest one who made a remark critical of the government.

The censorship of books was more severe than it had been in Yoshimune's day, as witness the case of Hayashi Shihei, who was placed under arrest for writing a book on the need for coastal defences, and the punishment of the novelist Kyōden for an improper book, and of the colour-print artist Utamaro for painting "Spring pictures."

All these were oppressive actions of a trivial kind, probably ordered by busybodies of modest official standing; but on the whole the Bakufu treated the citizens with moderation, partly no doubt because they recalled the serious "smashing" riots of 1787 in Yedo and Ōsaka.

CHAPTER XVII

THE FURTHER DECLINE
OF THE BAKUFU

1. *Ienari and His Associates*

THE GOVERNMENT retained some measure of rational judgment and probity so long as men like Sadanobu and Nobuaki were influential; but in 1812 Nobuaki died, so that there was left in office no statesman of sufficient authority to keep a check upon the Shōgun Ienari and his disreputable companions.

Chief among these was Mizuno Tadanari, who now assumed the actual direction of policy, in so far as affairs of state as distinct from the Shōgun's appetites came under serious consideration by him. Tadanari was an adopted son of Tadatomi, a partisan of Tanuma Okitsugu. By flattering the Shōgun and Hitotsubashi Harunari, and by gaining the favour of the ladies of the Inner Apartments (Ō-oku—the Seraglio), he was able to form a powerful group which conducted a government by bribery not less flagrant than that of Tanuma's day. At its most prosperous it was joined by Tanuma's son, Okimasa, who became a Junior Elder (Wakadoshiyori) in 1822, and then a Chamberlain, until he retired to his father's castle at Sagara in Tōtōmi.

It was men of his type who assisted Tadanari in his work of influencing the Shōgun; and lest their methods should prove insufficient, Mizuno worked through the Seraglio, being himself a nephew of O-ume no Kata, Ienari's favourite concubine. Most of his partners had similar connexions with the Seraglio, sometimes because they had offered as concubines a daughter or a niece of their own.

The dimensions of the Seraglio and the extent to which it exerted a malign influence upon the conduct of public affairs may be measured by the number of its inhabitants. It is said to have included forty principal ladies ("sobashitsu") and as many as nine hundred female attendants ("jochū"). Ienari had one wife and twenty concubines, and is supposed to have fathered fifty-five children. The marriage of the girls presented a difficult problem, and since their weddings were celebrated in an extravagant fashion, the daimyos had to make frequent and handsome contributions.

That Mizuno seemed to the ordinary man to repeat all the faults ascribed to Tanuma is clear from some of the jibes current in Yedo, but

Ienari depended upon him and he was safe from dismissal. Ienari himself, an exhausted voluptuary, was guilty of the most extreme debauchery among all the Tokugawa Shōguns, indeed among all the leaders since government by warriors began. Yet he was loaded with honours by the Imperial Court, and his father (Hitotsubashi Harunari) was given the highest rank that could be conferred upon a subject.

As it may well be supposed, many of the daimyos followed the example of the Shōgun and lived extravagantly, giving costly entertainments, spending large sums on bribes and presents, and on new buildings. Their lavish habits naturally led to flourishing trade in the towns, and raised the standard of living of the citizens to a point which it had never reached before. The places of entertainment were crowded, the theatres and the restaurants crammed with customers. The houses of ill fame ("akusho," or "bad places," as they were called) increased in number, and even male prostitutes (known as "kagema") appeared. There were in the city of Yedo, it is said, no less than forty illicit quarters. The government repeatedly issued edicts forbidding these places and practices but to no avail.

Less reprehensible pleasure-seeking was, it appears, popular on such a grand scale that some Confucian moralists were appalled by the great audiences in the theatres of Yedo—numbering more than ten thousand in all, every day. This does not seem excessive in a population of over a million, but theatre-going was regarded as an indulgence, almost a vice, by the ruling class, partly because it was against the sumptuary rules and partly because some of the plays might travesty high life in military circles.

The disapproval of the moralists did not stop the citizens' feverish search for entertainment. It is difficult to explain this sudden increase in spending, but there must have been a great flow of money due to the release of savings and the minting of new currency. In 1798 the Bakufu's emergency reserve of gold and silver stood at over one million ryō, and by 1830 it had fallen to 650,000 ryō. This indicates an abnormal consumption which could not be paid for out of normal revenue. Furthermore the ordinary expenditure of the Bakufu for the decade 1822–31 showed a small favourable balance, as against a deficit in the preceding decade. It is true that this was due to currency manipulation during those years, with the inevitable result of inflation and rising prices. Yet although this seeming prosperity rested upon an extremely shaky economic foundation, it continued for some years because there were no serious calamities such as storms and plagues to reduce the crops. Consequently the high prices of rice and other commodities re-

Scene in Luchu gay quarter

mained steady, and there was no sign of disturbance in the markets of a kind likely to bring about agrarian revolt or urban rioting. The future looked bright. The country entered upon a period of wild spending.[1]

The reckless addiction to pleasure of this decade or so has been described by one Japanese historian as like dancing madly on a volcano. There was perhaps some excuse for this rashness. The current freedom from catastrophes and from violent price fluctuation no doubt created a feeling of confidence. This was a brief spell of fine weather. The towns were quiet, and there were few rural complaints. Indeed many farmers profited by the wider extension of the money economy to their sphere.

But these pleasant conditions were fugitive. The volcano did erupt, for in the last years (1832–37) of Ienari's rule the miserable sequence of disasters recurred. Famine and disease were followed by peasant uprisings and "smashing" in the towns. The Bakufu was again in a precarious situation.

---

[1] This period of prosperity is usually referred to in Japanese works as covering the eras Bunka and Bunsei (1804–30).

2. Conditions in the Fiefs

The political system developed by the Tokugawa Shōguns cannot be described only in terms of the structure of the Bakufu. It must be considered as an organic relationship between the Shōgun and the fief, a relationship which thanks to the skilful exercise of power by the Tokugawa family was to survive without serious challenge for more than two hundred years.

The number of fiefs was about two hundred and sixty, and of these about two hundred were relatively small, with assessed revenues not exceeding 100,000 koku. Fiefs of 30,000 koku or less accounted for half this number of two hundred, and they were relatively weak, only with difficulty maintaining their independence and nearly all insolvent. A few, by careful administration, contrived to develop their resources, but in general the small fiefs could not keep out of debt, and their weakness was a fruitful cause of discontent, often lending to riots.

Nor were the great fiefs free from such difficulties, for their indebtedness tended to be proportionate to their size, and few of them had resources which could be developed without borrowing. Moreover the Fudai daimyos in particular were treated with a great lack of consideration by the Bakufu, often being moved from one province to another for supposed reasons of political strategy. These movements were very costly, as may be seen from the case of the Himeji fief, which was held by Matsudaira Akinori, who in a series of reassignments ordered by the Bakufu found himself transferred there in 1741 from his family's fief in Shirakawa in the far north. Already in debt, he attempted to raise funds in Shirakawa before leaving. This was in 1742, and the inhabitants of his fief opposed him, so that he could not make a move; and a few years later, after a poor harvest, they rioted, and three thousand men marched on the castle town.

There were similar troubles in other fiefs which had been transferred to new daimyos. In one case the rioters were so threatening that the daimyo called for help from the Governor of Ōsaka, who sent a force to suppress them, but not before they had done great damage. Such troubles as these rarely afflicted the Tozama daimyos, for the Bakufu was careful not to antagonize them.

Whether Tozama or Fudai, the very large fiefs usually enjoyed favourable economic conditions. They were able to develop their resources on a large scale, using their power to develop not only agriculture but other forms of production within their boundaries. Those which were virtually self-supporting could to some extent at least check

Table of Tozama Fiefs[2]

in order of assessed
revenue (kokudaka)

Kaga (Maeda)	1,022,700
Satsuma (Shimazu)	770,000
Sendai (Daté)	625,600
Higo (Hosokawa)	540,000
Chikuzen (Kuroda)	520,000
Aki (Asano)	426,000
Chōshū (Mōri)	369,000
Hizen (Nabeshima)	357,000
Inaba (Ikeda)	325,000
Ise (Tōdō)	323,000
Bizen (Ikeda)	315,000

the inflationary trend within their own borders. Such were the great domains of Satsuma, Chōshū, Kaga, and Owari.

Although the small Fudai daimyos were not powerful as vassals, it was they and their adherents who furnished the Bakufu with officials to hold the most important posts in the government, often on a hereditary basis.[3]

Conditions in the fiefs changed with the lapse of time, and perhaps the most powerful agency of change was the effect of an expanding economy, which faced the overlords and the vassals with new problems that they were not well equipped to solve, for the founders of the feudal society had legislated against change. In its origins the system over which the Shōgun presided was a strongly conservative feudal society supported by a strict division of classes and a transmission of status by heredity. In principle it adhered to established methods of government because it was hostile to change; but after the death of Iemitsu, the third Shōgun, in 1651, the maintenance of the old regime began to prove inconsistent with a natural development of the country in an era of peace.

The immediate causes of this change were the expansion of a money economy towards the close of the seventeenth century, and consequent changes in the character of rural as well as urban life. The urgent problem before the Bakufu was how to reconcile these new conditions with

[2] The actual product was in almost every case much higher than the "omote daka," or official assessment.
[3] For some details of the allocation of fiefs and the treatment of Fudai daimyos by the Bakufu, see Chapter V.

the maintenance of discipline in the warrior class; for the finances of the Bakufu were showing a deficit, and the livelihood of the samurai was endangered.

This indeed was the pattern, the trend which had been followed by the government soon after its formation, once the great treasure accumulated by Ieyasu had been reduced by emergency payments. There was an almost regular alternation between expansion and contraction in the finances of the Bakufu and, it followed, of many of the daimyos, at intervals of about ten years between, let us say, 1700 and 1820.

The fiefs varied in size and strength and in the nature of their products, but they had one characteristic in common, and that was the financial stringency which they had to face as the national economy developed the use of currency at a great speed. All but the strongest were forced to dispose of their rice at whatever price the brokers of Ōsaka and Yedo were prepared to offer. The self-contained character of the fiefs might have been preserved but for the rule of alternate attendance (sankin kōtai), which obliged them to maintain an establishment in Yedo at great expense. To meet their obligations they could not pay in rice, but must settle their bills in currency; and it was this necessity that developed and hastened the use of money in the financial business of all fiefs, and consequently throughout the country.

The welfare of the clan, the quality of its government, thus came to depend upon its adjustment to the currency situation. This was well enough in theory, but (the records show) all fiefs without exception suffered from serious financial trouble, because their adjustment had taken the easy form of contracting debts at high interest. This kind of economic disturbance was of course accompanied by political dangers, but the rulers of the fiefs took no positive steps to avert them, because they could still depend upon feudal discipline and also upon military strength to preserve a balance in case of internal commotion—an uneasy balance, it is true; but the supremacy of the warrior class was unchallenged.

The financial troubles of the daimyos were inherent in the Tokugawa system of feudal overlordship, and indeed they were in some cases apparent before the foundation of the Shōgunate. The situation grew worse during the following years, and by about 1700, less than a century after Ieyasu, it had become usual for expenditure to exceed revenue. Negative policies of retrenchment were not effective; but, as we have seen, the best-administered fiefs opened up new land to cultivation and encouraged an increase of local products for sale, being especially fortunate if they had a monopoly of one of those products. These efforts brought in more currency and were more useful than increasing taxation within the fief. But it was rare for such measures to balance the accounts of the daimyo, and there were few fiefs which did not resort to borrowing in order to supplement the money value of rice in store.

The persons who dealt in the produce of the fiefs ("kuramoto" or "kakeya" in Ōsaka; "ryōgae" or "tonya" in Yedo and Kyoto) were a useful source of money income, and in the neighbourhood of most fiefs there were usually wealthy merchants ready to do business.[4] Still the accounts did not balance, and many daimyos were driven to undignified economies. They reduced the number of men in their service and even went so far as to "borrow" from their retainers a proportion of their stipends, and (it is said) to sell to prosperous farmers the right to use a surname and to wear swords.[5]

For borrowing on a large scale the daimyo would even offer as security a lien on the next year's land tax (in rice), and the "rice notes" thus issued were regarded as currency in the market. But some daimyos even gave notes without backing, though this was against the rules of the Bakufu; and thus they caused confusion and alarm among lenders. A celebrated case which excited the money market in Ōsaka was the circulation of rice notes from the Kurume fief for nearly half a million koku, an amount which it could not possibly supply. The Bakufu was obliged to intervene with a guarantee, in order to settle the confusion caused by this irresponsible act.

The way in which the indebtedness of the daimyos increased is well illustrated by the case of the Toda family. Between 1750 and 1772 they borrowed from an Ōsaka merchant sums amounting to 453 kan of silver (about 50,000 oz. Troy), on which the interest by 1836 had amounted to nearly 500,000 oz. Another example of the wealth derived from moneylending is that of Masuya, the man of business of the Sendai clan, of whom it was said in 1790 that Sendai belonged to him, and Sendai's rice was his rice. His prowess is related in a work entitled *Masuhei Yawa,* or "Evening Tales of Masuhei."[6]

Part of the financial burdens of the daimyo was shifted to the backs of the unfortunate peasants. They were called upon to pay heavier taxes or to pay taxes in advance. In addition they were squeezed directly or

---

[4] The immensely rich Kōnoike Zenyemon was "kakeya" to at least five fiefs. The kakeya were often treated as retainers and given rice stipends. Kōnoike received in this way as much as 70,000 koku a year.

[5] The right known as "myōji taitō."

[6] *Keizai Taiten,* Vol. XIV.

indirectly by rich merchants, by landlords, by moneylenders, and rice brokers. At times the pressure was unbearable, and they burst out in riots of the kind already described. In the fiefs much depended upon the degree of control, tight or loose, exercised by the daimyo, but in any case in this period the agrarian rising (hyakushō ikki) was almost chronic. It was most frequent in the small and middling fiefs, where the power of enforcement was not enough to prevent rash ventures by farmers with a grievance.

The policy of isolation pursued by most fiefs, by keeping them out of the main stream of development in the rest of the country, naturally resulted at times in a certain stagnation and even decay. At best it gave rise to internal dissension and in extreme cases to armed conflicts. Among the most flagrant examples of the weakness in the political structure were the violent quarrels between leading families or branches of families in some of the great fiefs. We have already seen a classic instance in the strife within the Sendai (Daté) fief in 1671; and during the early years of the eighteenth century similar succession disputes broke out into violence in other parts of the country.

Notable among them was one which almost destroyed the great domain of Kaga, the richest in Japan, assessed at over one million koku. So badly was it administered that by 1703 it was heavily in debt, owing capital and interest amounting to over 22,000 kan of silver (equivalent to about 2,600,000 oz. Troy). The questions of policy raised by this immense liability gave rise to violence of a degree hitherto unknown under Tokugawa rule. Two main factions struggled for as long as thirty years, and even after they came to terms there were riots in Kaga territory, not without reason, since the total debt had risen (by 1767) to more than 50,000 kan, and no way of dealing with this burden had been devised. The dispute did nothing but reveal a rotten administration by corrupt officials.

No description of the commercial undertakings of the Kaga fief would be complete without reference to the remarkable smuggling which was carried out by a merchant named Zeniya Gohei, who resided in the harbour town of Kanazawa and is said to have owned (about 1850) two hundred vessels and to have a capital of three million ryō. The administration of the fief, after turning a blind eye to his operations for some time, decided to confiscate all his possessions. He was imprisoned, and died in gaol, while his sons and his manager were crucified. The charge against him was that he had committed some offence in regard to a small reclamation scheme, but this was obviously a dishonest excuse. The exact truth is not known, but it is clear that the clan authorities wished to lay their hands on his wealth, and were not scrupulous in their choice of an excuse. Much of Zeniya's trading was quite legitimate, consisting of the carriage of goods to and from the Hokkaidō; but his enterprise shows that the desire to engage in foreign trade was growing fast.

Zeniya's case is of special interest, because it contradicts the view of some writers that in the first half of the nineteenth century the rich merchants exercised great political power. There is not much truth in this; for, from the time of Yodoya onwards, the Bakufu never hesitated to punish those of whom they disapproved.

Similar troubles to those of Kaga affected Akita and Kurume and (among smaller clans) Tsushima, Koga, and Matsuyama in Dewa. This last provides a striking example of misgovernment. The principal retainers fostered a revolt against the daimyo for his oppressive measures, which included not only extortion from the taxpayers but also a forced levy upon the retainers themselves. The daimyo issued rice notes in excessive amounts and in general drove the economy of the fief to the verge of collapse. The retainers were obliged to sell their possessions, and famine was avoided only by calling upon a related clan for help.

Many more examples of such deterioration could be cited. What caused it is not clear. It is probable that the system of fiefs designed by the first three Tokugawa Shōguns was fundamentally unsound, since it gave autonomy (qualified, it is true) to a large proportion of the territory of the whole country. In theory every daimyo was a vassal sworn to obey the Shōgun, but in practice the Bakufu had no constructive policy and did not interfere in the affairs of a clan unless there was evidence of danger to Bakufu interests or Bakufu prestige. The key to Bakufu policy in this matter was a desire to keep the peace. Its agents kept a watch upon the vassals in order to be able to deal with symptoms of unrest or disobedience before they reached a stage where drastic action would be called for.

But whatever the attitude of the Bakufu, it is clear that in many fiefs there was an urgent need for reform, and in fact the years from about 1750 onwards did see an improvement, due not to a special effort at the behest of the Bakufu but as part of a general tendency which characterized government under Yoshimune and continued for a century or more, interrupted unhappily by periods of depression or distress. An examination of the history of some of the leading clans during the eighteenth century shows that serious efforts to reform were made by Akita, Yonezawa, Sendai, Aizu, Shirakawa, Matsushiro, Owari, Okayama, Aki, Chōshū, Matsue, Higo, Satsuma, and Kii (Kishū). These were not all entirely successful, since success depended first upon the natural resources of the fief and upon the good sense of the daimyo and his senior retainers (the kashin), who were as a rule the effective administrators; but in general it may be said that the policy-makers were capable men, inspired by Neo-Confucian ideals. In most fiefs there were also thoughtful young samurai who felt that the system of which they formed a part had reached a critical point, and some of them were prepared for startling changes. This situation can be best explained by concrete examples.

An interesting case, which incidentally throws light on the way in which the great fiefs developed, is that of Yonezawa, the castle town of the great Uesugi family. Originally it was the Aizu domain, worth 1,200,000 koku, but after the battle of Sekigahara it was reduced to 300,000 koku, and then in 1664 to 150,000 koku. Despite these reductions the daimyo and his councillors continued on the former scale of expenditure, and the fief became insolvent. Its burden of debt was further increased by a reckless financial policy, and still further by famines which ravaged the northern provinces in 1755.

At this stage the people of the fief rose in revolt and engaged in "smashings" on the castle town. The government of the fief was one of exceptional weakness, and by 1764 its situation had become so critical that the daimyo (Uesugi Shigesada) decided that he must hand the fief back to the Bakufu. On the advice of his father-in-law, the powerful daimyo of Owari, he abandoned this project and resigned in favour of his adopted son, Harunori, who in course of time made progress by very determined action, which included the execution of certain Councillors (Karō) who had opposed him. Under his guidance and that of his successors the fief prospered. Firm disciplinary methods were introduced to increase production all round and to maintain a high standard of conduct among the samurai. Despite repeated blows from famine and plague his improvements turned out to be permanent, and in 1830 Yonezawa was praised by the Bakufu as a model of good government.

An instructive example of reform measures in another clan is that of Akita, where great efforts were made to improve the quality of its administration and to encourage profit-making industries, such as the manufacture of paper, pottery, and textiles, and the development of mining, for which latter purpose, it will be recalled, the services of Hiraga Gennai were obtained. To carry out these plans required a large capital expenditure, but Akita had no reserve and was obliged to borrow from wealthy merchants within the domain. With good fortune most of the projects could probably have been thus carried out on a satisfactory scale, but the desired reform was never accomplished, for by 1832 Akita was in distress, this being the year of one of the three great famines in Tokugawa history, the famine of the Tempō era (1830–44). The debt of the Akita fief in 1828 had reached 460,000 ryō.

Of prosperous fiefs the most important were Kishū and Higo. These were known as the Dragon[7] and the Phoenix. Kishū was one of three collateral houses of the Tokugawa—the Go-Sanke—and Hosokawa of Higo was one of the most powerful families in the country.

The Kishū fief, after some of Yoshimune's reforms about 1716, had endeavoured to improve its finances by increasing production in agriculture and manufactures, but by 1760 it found itself heavily in debt. In an attempt to increase revenue it oppressed both peasants and townspeople, causing serious riots. It then turned to borrowing on a large scale to finance its developments. Here it found no great difficulty. Thanks to its proximity to Kyoto and Ōsaka and its possession of rich lands, it was able to raise capital, which it used partly for commercial purposes and partly for developing its material resources, notably the great Kumano forests. In the period from 1750 to 1800 it made great profits and was thus in a strong position to deal with the expanding monetary economy.

Higo had extensive domains, which included a portion of the adjacent province of Bungo. Partly under the influence of Yoshimune's reforms its organization was already improved by about 1750. It had one special advantage, in the quality of rice which it grew, for "Higo mai" (Higo rice) was a standard of quality on the Ōsaka exchange. Like most fiefs it had overspent, especially in the early part of the century, and owing to its internal quarrels it lost the confidence of the great merchants and moneylenders, to such a degree that Kōnoike resigned his position as its agent ("kakeya"). This situation obliged the daimyo (Hosokawa Shigekata) to revise and develop the economic structure of his domain. He succeeded in restoring it to solvency and to prosperity. These results were achieved partly by improving the condition of the peasants, whom he assisted by loans and in other ways; while samurai who had no employment were encouraged to work in their homes at spinning and weaving.

To summarize the reforms in the fiefs of which the foregoing cases are examples, it may be said that politically their special purpose was

---

[7] Strictly speaking not a dragon, but the Kirin, another mythological monster.

to concentrate governing power in the hands of the daimyo, to improve discipline, and to strengthen the daimyo's control of inhabitants of every class. In the economic sphere their object was to increase and diversify production, and by employing experts to develop existing industries such as mining.

The reforms described above were concerned primarily with protecting the fiefs against the financial dangers which increasingly threatened them during the eighteenth century as the national economy developed along lines that were not consistent with their independence. In other words, strictly speaking these were not reforms but efforts to restore previous strength by adjustment to new circumstances. It was not until after this task had been completed that administrators could turn to the kind of social and political reforms which were to occupy the attention of some fiefs well after the turn of the century.

It will be seen that on balance the so-called Tempō Reform attempted by the Bakufu must be regarded as a failure, whereas by contrast the contemporary reforms in a number of important fiefs were, at least from the point of view of the reformers, to be regarded as fairly successful. The failure of the Bakufu reforms may properly be ascribed to the essential rigidity of the structure of Tokugawa government, and of course to the decline upon which it had already entered in the eighteenth century. Moreover it is clear that the strengthening of the fiefs was bound to bring about a relative weakness in the authority of the Bakufu.

3. Chōshū and Satsuma

More interesting from an historical point of view than the clans discussed above are the two great Tozama domains of western Japan, Chōshū and Satsuma, which were to play leading roles in the last days of the Bakufu.

Chōshū, covering the two provinces of Nagato and Suō, once governed by the great Ōuchi family and then by the Mōri, had as a single fief increased in size threefold since Sekigahara, and in the Tempō era had an actual revenue close upon one million koku. Despite efforts to economize (which included withholding part of the stipends of the senior retainers) expenditure increased year by year. Loans from rich merchants met the deficit for some time, but by 1840 the debt was 85,000 kan of silver, an immense sum. Attempts were made to divert a large proportion of the earnings of farmers and traders into the clan treasury, but this involved depriving them of profits not only from the production of rice but also from the sale of such articles as paper, wax, salt, and indigo, of which the daimyo assumed a monopoly.

This policy of the clan government angered farmers and traders to such a degree that from about 1830 to 1837 there were almost continuous uprisings. That of 1831 was particularly violent and plunged the domain into disturbance on a scale previously unknown. It was followed by certain measures of reform, although it cannot be said that these were due to the uprisings; and indeed the word "reform" here is somewhat misleading. Certainly the peasants had grievances, but the conditions of which they complained were not due to maladministration but rather to natural disasters that had plagued the country with famine from 1832 to 1836. It is important to recognize these causes, since some modern historians are inclined to take an ideological view of the risings and to describe them as revolutionary.

On the simplest economic grounds the government of the fief could not fail to recognize the danger of the situation. In 1840 the daimyo, Mōri Tadachika, selected an able samurai of middle rank, Murata Seifū, to put things right. Under his guidance the clan monopolies of trade were abolished, and monopoly rights on salt, saké, cotton, and other important products were sold to merchant guilds. Other financial measures were introduced to encourage production, such as loans at low interest to samurai, farmers, and traders. Advantage was taken of the position of the fief at the entrance to the Inland Sea through the Straits of Shimonoseki by providing berths and anchorages in Chōshū waters to vessels carrying goods from Echigo or Kyūshū to Ōsaka. Market fluctuations in Ōsaka were carefully watched, and goods were shipped accordingly.

There was a division within the fief between a conservative party which was in power and a progressive party consisting largely of samurai of medium rank; but the conservative party was not in principle against the policy which Seifū had devised and followed. All parties were united in pressing on a development of enterprises which would increase the strength of the clan. This movement received a strong impetus from the anti-Bakufu sentiment which traditionally pervaded the Tozama fiefs and was particularly strong in Chōshū. In fact Chōshū may be said to have led in this antagonism, though it should not be supposed that at this time Chōshū or any fief planned the overthrow of the Tokugawa government. What they all aimed at was the greatest possible degree of independence in regard not only to the Bakufu but also to other daimyos, and for that purpose it was necessary to develop both the human and the material resources of each domain to the greatest possible extent.

The so-called Tempō Reform of Chōshū was in fact not a political or social movement but a phase of economic planning designed to increase production. In this respect the "reform" was successful, and the wealth of the clan continued to grow. There were internal dissensions, but on the whole the traditional discipline of the samurai was maintained.

By mid-century the fief was in a strong position as to both military preparation and the spirit of its fighting men. It might be supposed that with a debt of 85,000 kan of silver its financial position was precarious, but Chōshū had hidden resources of long standing. It held important reserves and a sinking fund which could be used to balance accounts when needed. This was the fruit of careful administration and foresight; and it enabled its leaders to purchase modern military equipment on a large scale and so to play a decisive part in the stormy national politics to follow.

Changes similar to those of Chōshū took place in the other western clans, notably in Satsuma, a powerful fief assessed at 770,000 koku. It was rich, since it produced valuable commodities and also had a monopoly of a profitable trade with the Luchu Islands. Yet by 1820 or thereabouts it was heavily in debt, partly because of contribution to public works on behalf of the Bakufu, but mainly because of the free spending of the daimyo, Shimazu Shigehide. Satsuma's example illustrates clearly the operation of the rule of alternate attendance at the Shōgun's court, which was devised to keep the daimyos under surveillance and to encourage them to spend great sums in keeping up their style during their residence in Yedo.

Shigehide's extravagance had obliged the fief to raise loans in Ōsaka and Yedo amounting to over 70,000 kan of silver, on which the interest alone was greater than the total annual cost of administration of the fief. Senior retainers had urged Shigehide to introduce thoroughgoing economies, but without success, and their leader, Kabayama Hisagoto, was obliged to commit suicide. Upon Shigehide's retirement the clan suffered from internal quarrels, and the need for reform became urgent. The debt had reached five million ryō, and there was no prospect of repayment.[8] The great moneylenders refused further advances, and

---

[8] The gold ryō in the Tempō era had a purchasing power of the order of .75 koku of rice in Yedo.

Satsuma could no longer meet even its current obligations to the Bakufu or—still more serious—to the retainers and even to the workmen, who were kept waiting for their pay. The debts of the Satsuma establishment in Yedo for several years had remained unpaid, and the clan could barely find cash for travel expenses between Kagoshima and the capital.

In this difficult situation Shigehide called upon a Chamberlain named Zusho Hirosato to carry out a complete reform of the finances of his fief. Zusho's method of disposing of the problem was of an engaging simplicity. He proposed to the creditors in Ōsaka a repayment of the debt of five million ryō by annual instalments of twenty thousand ryō over a period of two hundred and fifty years—in fact a cancellation of the debt. This the creditors naturally scorned. Zusho thereupon, in a convenient display of the warrior's contempt for the merchant, took the acknowledgements of debt presented to him and tore them to pieces, which he burned. Thus Satsuma in effect declared itself bankrupt, and was at last able to proceed with a reorganization of its finances without regard to past liabilities. The creditors were helpless.

Satsuma continued to make great profits from trade with the Luchu Islands, which strictly speaking was smuggling, since the Luchus supplied articles obtained by trade with China and other Asian markets. The fief's most lucrative business was the sale of sugar from the Luchus and other islands south of Kyūshū.[9]

It will be seen that the reforms in these great fiefs were not of a liberal nature. They could in no sense be called anti-feudal. On the contrary they were designed to strengthen the feudal character of each domain in its conduct of economic and social affairs. It is true, however, that most of the measures introduced for that purpose were assertions of autonomy, and to that extent were denials of the authority of the Bakufu.

It will be noted that the departure from feudality had proceeded farther in Chōshū than in Satsuma, possibly because in Chōshū the attempt to create monopolies had been defeated by popular sentiment, and in 1831 by rioting, which had forced reforms upon the government of the fief.

4. Domestic Problems of the Bakufu

The man who was coming into power at this time was Mizuno Tadakuni, soon to be chief adviser to the new Shōgun, Ieyoshi. It was

---

[9] The Satsuma men drove hard bargains. They bought sugar at the rate of three "go" of rice for one kin of sugar, and sold the sugar in Ōsaka at four times that price.

evident to Mizuno that he could not safely proceed against persons of high rank, though it was clear that dissatisfaction with the Bakufu was spreading in the fiefs. He therefore decided to arrest only a few men of less importance, among them Watanabe Kazan and Takano Naga-hide, both samurai of good standing, accomplished scholars, and true patriots. These two were cruelly punished and persecuted, and ended by taking their own lives (in 1841 and 1850 respectively). Their history shows clearly how strong a feeling was aroused among men of probity by the obscurantist and erratic policy of the Bakufu.

A study of their lives leaves it in no doubt that quite apart from foreign intrusions the end of the seclusion policy was already in sight. One of the arguments against seclusion, rarely used except by the scholar Sakuma Zōzan (1811–64) and a few others but perhaps the most cogent of all, was the need to sustain the national economy, which had always been subject to crisis because Japan could not import food in time of famine. If we look at the history of Japan from 1840 backward for a century or more, we can see it as a sequence of famines between intervals of plenty—the Kyōhō famine (1732–33), the Temmei famine (1783–87), Tempō famine (1832–36). And in addition to these major disasters there were numerous failures of the harvest in different parts of the country, due to regional calamities such as floods, droughts, epidemic disease, or insect pests.

The Tempō famine grew worse in 1833, and conditions were more serious than just after the Temmei famine, when most fiefs had arranged storage of supplies against emergency. Now the reserves were barely sufficient to keep people alive for a short time. Peasants and townsmen were aware of this position, and without delay they began risings and "smashings" which were both violent and extensive. They spread from Ōsaka to distant provinces, north, east, and west, attacking especially merchants dealing in rice or cotton, some of whom were buying for storage and not for resale. In a revolt starting in Kai province in 1836 the crowd of peasants marching along the highways was said to have extended for over twenty miles.

It will be remembered that during the eighteenth century there had been several so-called "reforms" that were in fact efforts to restore normal conditions after periods of disaster. These continued into the nineteenth century, the latest being the Tempō Reform attempted by Mizuno Tadakuni, who became the senior member of the Council of Elders in 1841.

During the lifetime of the deplorable Shōgun Ienari it was not possible for Mizuno to take any independent political action, but he had

prepared himself for high office by much study, regarding Matsudaira
Sadanobu as a model statesman whose example he ought to follow. At
first his progress was slow, and he had to resort to bribery. His opportunity, however, came after the death of Ienari in 1841, when Ienari's
son Ieyoshi, already titular Shōgun, assumed the government. Ieyoshi,
whose term of office lasted until 1853, was no more than nominal ruler,
and the problems of administration were now largely in the hands of
Mizuno. The position which he had to face was one of great difficulty.

Whether through famine or misgovernment, the cities were seething
with unrest during the first decades of the century, and the citizens engaged frequently in riots which were the counterpart of the peasant
uprisings. Indeed it is not easy to distinguish peasant uprisings from
the revolts of townsmen, many of whom were refugees from deserted
villages. The day-labourers, the small shopkeepers, and the unemployed
vagrants joined in wrecking the houses of the moneylenders and rich
merchants in a dozen or more of the largest towns. In 1837 riots stimulated and organized by one Ōshio Heihachirō broke out with violence
in Ōsaka. Their story is worth telling in some detail because it reveals
a current of feeling against the Bakufu and its officers which overflowed
throughout the country.

Ōshio was a scholar who had held a post as police-court magistrate,
but sold his books to help the poor and planned with a score of his
friends to lead a great demonstration against the city authorities, whose
indifference angered him. They were to start fires in the town and raid
the houses of the rich. This they did with some success, for they destroyed a number of buildings. But the city authorities had got wind
of their intentions, and troops from the garrison of Ōsaka castle were
called out. Bitter fighting ensued, in which the rioters were overcome,
but not before thousands of houses and stores had been fired during a
struggle which lasted two days. Ōshio escaped to the countryside, but
returned after a few days. His hiding place was discovered by the
police, whom he cheated of their capture by setting fire to the house
and committing suicide.

The failure of the wardens of one of the greatest Tokugawa castles
to prevent such an outbreak made them appear ridiculous to the citizens, who circulated malicious jibes about them. Attention was called
with particular glee to the two City Commissioners who led the attack
on Ōshio's partisans. They were on horseback, but fell off when their
mounts shied at the sound of gunfire. News of the rising and of such
incidents as these spread over the whole country and encouraged similar revolts in other towns. For want of planning on a national scale, they

soon came to an end, but not before proof of the incapacity of the Bakufu had been made clear to many patriots eager for reform, while the
townspeople for their part took note of these absurdities of the ruling
class.

A manifesto by Ōshio referred to the high price of rice, but also
dwelt upon the oppressive treatment of the populace by the officials
whose habit it was to use force rather than persuasion. It also pointed
out that rice was shipped to Yedo, while people in Ōsaka were starv-
ing, but none was sent to Kyoto, where the Emperor resided. It is worth
noting here that like Ōshio most of the reformers were followers of the
Ōyōmei school of philosophy, which stood for independence of mind
and was frowned upon by the official Confucianists.

Ōshio's example was followed by reformers in other parts of Japan,
notably in the neighbourhood of Niigata by Ikuta Yorozu, a disciple of
the great scholar Hirata Atsutane, who was cordially disposed to Western learning.[10] Yorozu's rising took place in 1837, a time when famine
was widespread.

The measures of reform introduced by Mizuno Tadakuni were pre-
ceded by certain changes made in the administration of some of the
most important fiefs. This movement was not specifically directed
against the Bakufu, but arose from the pressure of samurai of modest
rank who were dissatisfied with the policy of their elders, the senior
retainers (kashin). The best and one of the first examples of men of
this type—they were called "shishi," or public-spirited men—is Fujita
Tōko (1806–55), a samurai in the service of Tokugawa Nariaki, the
daimyo of Mito who held advanced views and carried out administrative
changes on the advice of Fujita and others from about 1832. It is said
that some of the reforms introduced by the Bakufu under Mizuno were
suggested to him by Nariaki. At about the same time similar reforms
were introduced, as we have seen, in their domains by the leading Tozama daimyos, Satsuma, Chōshū, Hizen, and Tosa, whe were (in common with the Bakufu) alarmed by current trends in both domestic and
foreign affairs.[11]

The reforms in question were political, primarily economic rather
than social. They reaffirmed traditional principles, and they did not
relax normal restrictions upon the life of the fief. They aimed at retrenchment. Taxation and other burdens were increased rather than

[10] For a description of Hirata's beliefs, see Donald Keene's *The Japanese Discovery of Europe* (London, 1952).
[11] A most valuable account of the part played by Tosa is in Professor Marius
Jansen's *Sakamoto Ryoma and the Meiji Restoration* (Princeton, N.J., 1961).

lightened, but the conduct of affairs was to fall into the hands of men of the type of Fujita, who held that external dangers could be met only by internal stability and firm decisions. This was in effect an attack upon the Bakufu as well as a call for enlightened government in the fiefs, in other words for government by men like Fujita himself.

Mizuno was not unsympathetic to the views of Fujita and his party, but he could not tolerate the support openly given to them by Nariaki, which amounted to an attack upon the Tokugawa government by the head of one of the great Tokugawa houses. Nariaki was accordingly ordered into domiciliary confinement by the Bakufu in 1844.

While these problems were occupying the attention of such reformers, Mizuno was faced with urgent and specific, rather than theoretical, issues. At first his progress had been slow, but his opportunity came in 1841, when Ienari died at the age of sixty-nine. He was impressed by news of the Opium War, in which English warships had easy victories. In a letter to a friend he said that Japan must take note of this, and consider the possibility of an attack by foreign warships. To meet such dangers it was essential to put the government of Japan upon a firm basis. This was the kind of reform which he envisaged and which is known as the Tempō Reform.

He proceeded to subject to a strict discipline certain officers in the Shōgun's entourage and a number of women in the inner apartments, dismissing nearly a thousand persons in all. His reform was undertaken in the name of the Shōgun Ieyoshi. It was much more drastic than its predecessors and especially severe in its treatment of the cities. Like most such reforms it began with an attempt to impose a rule of frugality and economy. The sumptuary orders issued for that purpose were as usual disobeyed. Most of them were absurd. Female hairdressers, for example, were forbidden under a penalty of one hundred days in gaol for the coiffeuse and house arrest in manacles for the client. No doubt Mizuno issued some orders in general terms, and these were carried out by men like the City Commissioner Torii Yōzō according to their own fancy. Torii, a sinister character who hated foreigners and foreign learning, employed spies and informers and was reviled by the citizens, who not without justice described him as a viper and a demon. Many delicacies were forbidden and even the Shōgun was deprived of some of his favourite dishes.

It would seem that the experience of governing a small fief was not a good preparation for ruling a great nation. Mizuno had administered Karatsu and Hamamatsu, but he had no understanding of the complex relation between urban and rural societies. One of his first blunders was an attempt to drive back to their villages peasants who had drifted into the towns to escape from regions suffering from famine, particularly in the northern provinces. His efforts to control trade, far from reducing and stabilizing prices, had the opposite result. He dissolved the merchant guilds (kabunakama), hoping to break monopolies, but he could not overcome the resistance of the great wholesale dealers and was obliged to abandon his policy. His methods were too drastic, and so disturbed the markets that prices rose and merchandise was not forthcoming. These and similar decisions made by him aroused the anger of crowds, who attacked his official residence. He was obliged to resign in disgrace in 1844.

Tadakuni can scarcely be blamed for his failure to carry out the reforms which he planned. Powerful interests, both political and financial, were against him, and it is therefore pertinent to an enquiry into the contemporary scene to examine some of the abuses which he endeavoured to abolish. For this purpose the most revealing documents are accounts of the Bakufu's examination of the affairs of certain rich merchants and their political connexions. Tadakuni's own conduct was investigated at the same time.

Among the most striking of these cases is that of Gotō Sanuemon, whose career affords ample justification for Tadakuni's economy campaign. Gotō was arrested and taken before the Hyōjōsho, the supreme judicial organ of the Bakufu. A search of his house revealed that he possessed immense quantities of gold and silver coins, and that his household (apart from his wife and children) included six concubines, twenty maidservants, and thirty-two manservants. He was the son of a peasant and had come to Yedo as a youth taking humble jobs and at length finding employment in 1820 in the Mint. Thereafter he became immensely rich, by methods easily conjectured, while his brother also, being employed as a broker, made a great fortune.

Men of this kind belonged to the party of Torii Yōzō, and had no connexion with Tadakuni; but soon after their cases had been decided, the official investigation was directed to the affairs of Tadakuni and his satellites. The verdict of the court of enquiry was to the effect that his misdeeds while in office must be punished. His revenues together with buildings and other effects were confiscated save for a small sum to support him while in domiciliary confinement; but the nature of his offence was not specified, doubtless because his trial was not a judicial but a political move.

In the following year (1845) Torii was similarly impeached. He was accused of numerous offences, including the disclosure of official secrets. He was clearly guilty of corruption and disloyalty. He was a congenital xenophobe, and it was he who caused the persecution of men like Watanabe Kazan and Takano Nagahide. The court which tried Torii declared that his conduct deserved the severest punishment, but was lenient enough to sentence him only to exile.

CHAPTER XVIII

BREACHES IN THE SECLUSION
POLICY

1. *The Arrival of Foreign Vessels*

WE HAVE SEEN that in 1825 the Bakufu, stimulated by reports of landings on Japanese soil by foreign seamen in search of water and fuel, issued to all daimyos whose domains bordered on the sea an order to drive away by gunfire any foreign ship approaching the coast, and to arrest and kill any members of its crew who should come ashore. This order did not prevent occasional visits to Japanese ports by vessels bringing castaways for repatriation or attempting to trade, for in 1837 a small, unarmed vessel, the *Morrison,* chartered by American missionaries, was fired upon at Uraga and again at Kagoshima, where she tried to land some Japanese castaways. Nobody was hurt, but the Bakufu policy was criticized in Japan as likely to cause reprisals by powerful foreign ships; and it was subsequently relaxed, to such a point that in 1842 local authorities were instructed to supply foreign ships with food and fuel and to "advise" them to go away.

Foreign warships were naturally not welcome, but they were not turned away. In 1845 H.M.S. *Samarang* (a surveying vessel) entered Nagasaki harbour and was, according to its officers, treated with courtesy "by the gentlemen of Japan." There was much fear of English warships after the news of the Opium War reached Japan. The defeat of Chinese troops, the subsequent Treaty of Nanking (1842), and the compulsory opening of Canton and other ports to foreign trade were so alarming that the Bakufu hastily endeavoured to improve coastal defences and to increase the efficiency of the seaboard garrisons. Two companies of infantry and artillery were equipped and trained in Western fashion.

In 1844 the King of Holland sent to Japan a careful description of the recent trend of international politics and advised the Japanese government to abandon its policy of seclusion. But the Bakufu was stubborn. A French warship arriving in 1848 was not so well received as H.M.S. *Samarang,* because it had called at the Luchu Islands, where its captain had proposed a treaty to the King and had landed a missionary. Both these acts were highly displeasing to the Bakufu, but since the Luchus were under the control of the daimyo of Satsuma, it was left to him to deal with the situation at his discretion. He might have made a pact with the French, for he was anxious to trade, but he confined himself to arranging one transaction, the purchase of arms and machinery to be delivered at the Luchus. This was an offence against the laws of 1639, being a definite breach in the seclusion policy, and Satsuma's action testified to the weakness of the Bakufu.

2. *The Nature of Seclusionism*

The attitude of the Japanese government towards the pressure of foreign countries desiring a right of entry into Japan for their nationals raises a general question as to the nature of seclusionism in Asia. It has been suggested that the Neo-Confucian doctrines of Chu Hsi influenced the minds of high officials in Japan and disposed them to adopt a seclusionist policy like that of the Ming dynasty in China; and it is no doubt true that those doctrines were powerful in forming the political ideas of the Shōgun's advisers for the better part of the century after the foundation of the Tokugawa government. But the example of the Ming policy can only loosely be described as an important element in the growth of the Sakoku, or Closed Country policy, adopted by Japan in 1639.

For one thing the Ming policy was not uniformly seclusionist. China had never been entirely secluded or isolated. Her geographic situation, with extended land frontiers and a coastline of great length, made complete isolation impossible in practice. Nor indeed did China forbid foreign relations. On the contrary, she had regular if limited contacts with other countries, either by trade or by tribute, overland with countries of Central Asia and South-East Asia and (after the Treaty of Nerchinsk in 1689) relations with Russia which permitted trade and religious missions to Peking.

It is true that after the great Ming voyages of 1405–33 China withdrew into seclusion and her people were forbidden to leave the country or to communicate with foreigners. At first sight this appears to have been a firm policy of closing the country like that of Japan in 1640. But in practice these prohibitions were not obeyed. Indeed it would have been impossible to close the land frontiers, nor would it have been of any advantage to China. As for the maritime provinces, the edicts prohibiting ships and men from leaving China were usually disregarded, with the connivance of local officials. They led only to smuggling and piracy. By contrast the Japanese seclusion laws were ruthlessly enforced, and, as we have seen, they prevented both emigration and immigration.

Obviously the reason why the seclusion laws of Japan were completely enforced was that it was an island country with a firm central government determined to preserve its own institutions and to resist the pressure of Christian propaganda, which the Tokugawa rulers associated with plans of aggression by Portugal and Spain.

It seems at first sight that seclusion is most common in countries which are difficult of access, either islands distant from a mainland or territories which, like Nepal and Tibet, are in remote mountainous regions; but all states, great or small, are jealous of their separateness and tend to limit the entry of foreigners. This is true of many parts of South-East Asia and notably of Korea, which was seclusionist for fear of China, and certainly not out of a wish to exclude the Chinese cultural influence that was dominant among the literati. Korea's experience of Mongol rule in the thirteenth century, and of Chinese and Japanese invasions in the sixteenth, was sufficient to account for her desire for political isolation, and it was no doubt as a measure of protection that during the Tokugawa era she sent regular embassies, which were received with great ceremony by the Shōgun's government.

3. Anti-Seclusion Opinion

Although the pressure of Western countries was one cause of the gradual relaxation of the edicts, no less important at this time was a pressure from within, exerted principally by scholars, because it was they who most desired to associate freely with men of learning from abroad and to acquire knowledge of Western ideas in general and Western science in particular. We have seen that the pursuit of Dutch studies had already in the eighteenth century created a body of scholars anxious for the opening of the country, chiefly because of their interest in science, principally medicine but also astronomy and other branches of learning. Every learned man who visited Japan under the employment of the Dutch Factory at Deshima was plied with interminable questions by Japanese thirsting for knowledge, from Kaempfer in 1691 to Siebold in 1823–29.

In the first decades of the nineteenth century these studies were pursued so widely and with such enthusiasm that the Confucian scholars took alarm and intrigued against advocates of the new learning, charging them with subversive designs. The authorities not unnaturally were inclined to suspect the advocates of change, some of whom openly charged the government with ignorance and incompetence, and paid the penalty of execution for their courage.

Among those who played a leading part in the introduction of scientific knowledge was a remarkable man named Sakuma Zōzan (1811–64), a samurai from a northern fief who devoted himself mainly to military science, including gunnery. As late as 1841 he began to enquire closely into the question of national safety, and he presented a memorial on coastal defence which shows that he and men of his stamp were alarmed by the weakness of their country. He was at first inclined to take an isolationist line, but he gradually came round to admiring Western people for their enquiries into the real nature of the universe, and he ended by believing in an international society. By then he was in prison for an offence against the exclusion law, and there he was to remain until 1862. Not long after his release he was murdered by antiforeign fanatics.

Other men of standing who were against the exclusion laws were punished for making their opinions public, in particular a group of scholars who formed a club and issued what the Bakufu regarded as a seditious pamphlet, which was widely circulated. In 1838 the "Demon" Torii recommended the arrest of its members, against whom he brought false charges. The Shōgun's chief adviser, Mizuno Tadakuni, hesitated to take direct action, knowing that they were in touch with important persons in the powerful clans of Mito and Satsuma and even in the Bakufu itself. But in the end a harsh policy prevailed.

Among the victims of this persecution was an important figure already mentioned—Watanabe Noboru (known also by his pen name as Kazan), a versatile poet and painter and a leader of opinion in favour of learning from foreign countries. He was imprisoned on false charges and condemned to death, but the sentence was commuted in 1840 to domiciliary confinement for life. He committed suicide in 1841.

The growing political and economic independence of the great fiefs naturally diminished pro tanto the authority of the Bakufu and made it difficult for Yedo to dictate a national policy in foreign relations as well as in domestic affairs. At the same time, although the fiefs could not follow closely the cultural trend of the great cities, they did come under its influence. The study of Western ideas and institutions began to penetrate learning in the fiefs and played an important part in forming public opinion. Thus, for example, as the Bakufu defence policy was based largely upon foreign models, most of the daimyos followed its lead. The daimyos of Satsuma, Hirado, and other clans were said to be afflicted by "Rampeki," or the Dutch Craze, and the government of their domains took on certain foreign characteristics.

This development was not new, for, as we have already seen, such

Mission from the Luchu Islands to Satsuma

scholars as Maeno Ryōtaku and Sugita Gempaku had held important posts in their respective clans more than half a century before, and most of the leading fiefs, more than fifty in all, had schools for the study of Western medicine and military science, especially gunnery. These studies became of urgent importance as the danger of foreign aggression seemed to increase.

4. *The End of Seclusion*

The first half of the nineteenth century was a period of great maritime expansion by the leading European powers and by the United States of America. Notable among these activities was the development of whaling in the North Pacific Ocean by vessels based on San Francisco. It was principally these vessels which were driven ashore or put in at Japanese harbours for shelter or supplies; and reports of ill-treatment of members of their crews began to reach America in the 1840's.

It was owing to a developing American interest in the Pacific trade as well as to a desire to protect shipwrecked seamen that in 1845 Com-

modore James Biddle, acting under instructions from Washington, took two warships into Yedo Bay and proposed the opening of trade relations. To this démarche the Bakufu returned a flat refusal, and Biddle withdrew; but it was now clear that preparation must be made to meet further efforts by foreign governments to break into the seclusion of Japan. The crucial issue was not however reached until the year 1853, when (on July 8) Commodore Matthew Perry appeared with four warships in the harbour of Uraga. The Bakufu was prepared for his arrival, having received word from the Luchus, where he had first called on May 26, and where he had stayed for several weeks in practical occupation of the islands.

His mission was plain. He carried a letter from the President of the United States and his own written statement that his government had friendly intentions but was determined to secure good treatment for distressed American seamen and facilities for navigation and trade. He made no threat, but one was implied when he said that he expected a favourable reply next year, when he would return with a larger force. His strategic position was strong, for Yedo, the Shōgun's capital, was vulnerable, not only by bombardment but also by blockade, since the bulk of its food supply came from Ōsaka by sea and could easily have been cut off by enemy action.[1]

The Bakufu was well aware of these dangers, and when Perry returned to Japan in February 1854 with a more powerful squadron, he had little difficulty in negotiating a treaty despite the evasions and delays of the Japanese delegates. Though somewhat vain and overbearing, he was an able and impressive negotiator, showing great determination. Signed on March 31 at Kanagawa, this treaty opened two ports (Shimoda in Izu and Hakodate in Yezo) to limited trade, and provided for American consular representation in Japan. It was followed by similar agreements with Great Britain (October 1854), Russia (February 1855), and Holland (November 1855).

While the negotiations with Perry were in progress at Uraga and elsewhere, the American officers on shore leave found the countryfolk whom they encountered friendly, good-tempered, and much interested in their strange visitors. There were very few unpleasant incidents and no conspicuous anti-foreign sentiment, except what was expressed by the surly looks of some samurai on guard duty. The Japanese negotiators, in intervals between sessions, showed great good temper and a convivial spirit, stimulated at times by the strong liquors which were among the gifts brought by the American mission. But what interested them most were mechanical devices and lethal weapons, in particular revolvers; and it is not surprising that after this visit the coastal defences at Shinagawa and other strategic points were rapidly strengthened.

Political reactions to the Bakufu's policy were, as might be expected, various throughout the country; but in general, both in Yedo and in the leading fiefs, it was felt to be essential to promote the study of foreign countries. The Bakufu led the way when in 1855 a "school for foreign studies," the Yōgakusho, was opened (at the foot of the Kudan Hill), and in 1856 an office for the study of foreign documents was opened, also in Yedo. It was styled Bansho Shirabedokoro. Teachers and candidates for teaching posts were drawn not from Bakufu domains but from those fiefs in which foreign studies had already been organized. This was a period when village schools (terakoya) were opened or enlarged in great numbers; and other evidence shows that in most fiefs there was a remarkable growth of elementary education, approved by the daimyo's officers but usually initiated by the villagers themselves.

---

[1] In fact during the ten days of Perry's stay, the transport of rice from Ōsaka to Kyoto was interrupted, by fear rather than by danger.

It was at this juncture, too, that the Bakufu, faced with an unprecedented situation, felt obliged not only to consult the Go-Sanke and the Tozama daimyos but also to ask the opinions of the Fudai daimyos and the hatamoto. This new departure revealed the weakness of the Bakufu in its relations with both great and small vassals. Even more remarkable was the action of the Bakufu in reporting current events to the Imperial Court and asking for advice and direction. This was a significant step, for it betokened a change in the attitude of the military society towards the Throne, a change which had been foreshadowed a century before when the doctrine of loyalty to the Emperor had been proclaimed in Kyoto by Yamagata Daini and others.

Now in many fiefs the same doctrine was professed by the leading spirits, who stood for what was called Shinnō or Sonnō, reverence to the Sovereign. Their motive was in part a desire to break the authority of the Bakufu, and also at times no doubt to justify their own insubordination within the clan. The cry of Sonnō was to play an important part in the last years of the Bakufu, and it is therefore pertinent here to retrace on broad lines the history of relations between the Shōgun and the Emperor.

It may be asked why the Shōguns did not abolish the Throne, which depended upon them for its very existence. History gives the answer. After having been forced to abdicate by Yoritomo in 1198, ex-Emperor Go-Toba challenged the Hōjō Regents in 1221. He was defeated and banished, but a successor approved by the Regents was appointed. Upon the defeat of the Kamakura government the idea of abolition was proclaimed by some of Takauji's generals, but Takauji himself thought it wise to preserve the Imperial office, although he did not hesitate to imprison and exile the Emperor Go-Daigo. Throughout the war between the northern and southern Courts the monarchy was fully recognized, and successive Ashikaga Shōguns, though at times treating the Court with scant respect, admitted that they derived their office from the Throne.

Nobunaga's attitude towards the Emperor was one of great reverence, and more than once he found it prudent to claim that he was acting on behalf of His Majesty in his campaign or in his civil policy, as when he stopped military operations against Kōya-san at the Emperor's request in 1581. Hideyoshi paid great respect to the Emperor, entertained him in the Jurakudai and regarded himself not as a Shōgun but as a Regent carrying out the wishes of the Sovereign. The oath of loyalty to the Toyotomi family signed by the daimyos in 1588 was sworn in the Emperor's presence. Ieyasu, while depriving the Throne of all political power, made generous gifts to the Court and recognized its importance as a fountain of honour. Iemitsu's attitude towards the Throne was less respectful than that of Ieyasu, but although he meant to intimidate the Emperor by marching to Kyoto with a great army in 1634, he treated the Court liberally and showed no signs of wishing to abolish the Imperial rule. Ienobu, who followed Tsunayoshi, took steps to improve relations between the Court and the Bakufu, and made handsome grants to the Emperor's household.

The truth is that the tradition of reverence for the Sovereign was still powerful in all ranks of society throughout the country, and no Shōgun dared to arouse the opposition which an overt act of disloyalty would have aroused. It would not only have deprived him of support but might also have provided a powerful rival with an excellent reason for revolt.

5. Anti-Foreign Sentiment

The cry of "Sonnō" called for an attitude rather than a policy, although it was part of a movement hostile to the Bakufu. It gained in importance when it was coupled with a call for positive action to resist the pressure of foreign powers insisting upon a right of entry to Japanese ports for their merchant ships. Now the cry was "Sonnō Jōi," which means "Revere the Sovereign, Expel the Barbarians."

There is little to show that there had been in the past, or was at that time, any widespread and genuine xenophobia in Japan. Indeed the record of friendly feeling for foreigners is most creditable, from the days of St. Francis Xavier (ca. 1550), who said "These people are the delight of my heart" to those of the captain of H.M.S. Samarang, who in 1845 praised "the refined and polished urbanity of the gentlemen of Japan."

The animosity of which the cry of Jōi seemed to be an expression was a feeling deliberately stimulated by the enemies of the Bakufu, and it increased in force after the year 1854, when Perry's warships dropped anchor in Yedo Bay on his second visit. In all the great Tozama fiefs any reason for opposing the ruling Tokugawa family was gladly seized upon, and this was true also of the Mito fief, which was governed by a member of the collateral branch traditionally hostile to the Shōguns. Its leader at this time was Tokugawa Nariaki, who did his best to embarrass the Bakufu and also to stir up feeling against it at the Imperial Court. Fortunately, the President of the Council of the Rōjū, a very able man named Abe Masahiro, persuaded the daimyos to agree to the terms accepted by Perry in 1854.

Before long the anti-foreign party had more ground for complaint than was afforded by the mere signature of a treaty, for in accordance with the terms of the treaty of 1854 (known as the Kanagawa Treaty from the name of the place where it was signed) the United States of America sent a consular representative to Japan, Mr. Townsend Harris, who arrived in an American warship in 1856. He was not at all welcome, and the Japanese authorities begged him to go away, but he insisted on carrying out his mission. His instructions were to extend the scope of the existing agreement (which was a simple treaty of friendship), and he carried with him a letter from the President, which he intended to hand to the Shōgun in person.

For some months he lived in discomfort at Shimoda, where he met with the most baffling obstruction and made little progress, since, unlike Perry, he could make no threat of force. Fortunately for him, the most influential member of the Council of State was a man who favoured a policy of opening the country, Ii Kamon no Kami. Ii was opposed by a powerful group led by the daimyo of Mito, Tokugawa Nariaki, a somewhat two-faced nobleman whose ambition was to discredit and overthrow the Bakufu. However Ii's position had lately improved, and by 1858 he was able to carry out his own plans and to agree to what Mr. Harris had requested in the name of the American government.

Mr. Harris had proposed, when at last he had access to the Shōgun's officers, a Convention opening Nagasaki to American ships, granting rights of residence in the two ports of Shimoda and Hakodate, and in other respects giving effect to the terms of the 1854 treaty. This important approach was followed by an unprecedented step on December 7, 1857, when Harris was received in Yedo Castle by the Shōgun in person. This was a concession which the Bakufu would not have dared to grant, even under Perry's most determined pressure; but conditions had changed in the last few years. Not only had the Bakufu become able, if only momentarily, to reassert its authority, but also it had received some serious warnings from the interpreters in Nagasaki, who reported that a British squadron had attacked and burned Canton because the Chinese government had failed to carry out its treaty obligations. The Dutch Commissioner in Japan (Donker Curtius) repeated this warning and advised the Bakufu to put an end to the evasive tactics of its officials.

There was no doubt about the incompetence of the Bakufu in its conduct of foreign relations at this juncture, though it must be remembered that it was confronted by a most complicated and harassing situation. A very able and far-sighted Tokugawa adherent, Katsu Awa, wrote of this situation from his personal knowledge: "From the day of Perry's arrival for more than ten years our country was in a state of indescribable confusion. The government was weak and irresolute, without power of decision." Fortunately, thanks to the influence of Ii Kamon no Kami (who by that time had become Tairō), a treaty with the United States was signed on July 29, 1858, aboard an American warship at anchor in Yedo Bay, and it was followed shortly by similar agreements with Great Britain, Holland, Russia, and France. They all provided for extra-territorial jurisdiction and a fixed customs tariff, conditions which greatly limited the autonomy of Japan and in the long run were to breed great animosity against the Western powers.

As was to be expected, the action of the Bakufu in giving way to foreign pressure was violently criticized by the anti-foreign elements, whose policy was summarized in the phrase "Jōi," or "Expel the Barbarians." Their motive was not entirely patriotic, for many of them were aiming at destroying the Tokugawa hegemony rather than at protecting the country.

It was not only Mito and other great vassals who opposed the new treaties, for the Shōgun's officers in Kyoto found that the Court could not be persuaded to agree to them. There was a strong anti-foreign feeling in the capital, coupled of course with its normal hostility to the Bakufu, which Mito sedulously inflamed. He was a most intemperate man, who when the Bakufu asked the opinions of the great vassals on the proposals of Harris said that those who had negotiated with him should be ordered to commit suicide, and Harris himself should be decapitated.

This represented the extreme "Jōi" attitude, for on that occasion most of the daimyos consulted were, if not in favour of foreign intercourse, at least not firmly opposed. The attitude of the Throne was ambiguous, but it raised no open objection to the 1858 treaties. They were sanctioned and came into force in July 1859, when foreign diplomatic envoys took up residence in Yedo. At the same time the new port of Yokohama was opened to foreign trade and residence. Yet it is clear that, despite the successes of the Bakufu in reaching a peaceful agreement with the foreign powers, most members of the ruling class throughout the country were opposed to its foreign policy. Ii Kamon no Kami was therefore obliged to take steps to restore the government's prestige and save its authority. He decided to promote a movement for what was called "kōbu gattai," or the amalgamation of civil and military power, which, it was hoped, would arrest a growing antagonism to the Bakufu not only among the great feudatories and the more active young Court nobles, but also in the lower ranks of samurai and among influential merchants and landholders.

At this stage there was no concerted movement among those who wished for the downfall of the Bakufu, or at least for a severe reduction of its powers, and indeed Shimazu, the leading Tozama daimyo, had in 1856 arranged a marriage between his adopted daughter and the Shōgun. The parties to this agreement had different views on national policy, but they felt that all the military houses should present a united front to the Court. The Court, on the other hand, did what it could to encourage dissension among the feudal leaders, and in this it was successful. The Kōbu-gattai movement failed, for the Bakufu had already lost its primacy when it referred the question of Perry's treaty to the Emperor and asked the vassals for advice.

When the treaties came into force and the foreigners took up residence in the open ports, the cry of Sonnō Jōi resounded throughout the country, and a number of murderous assaults upon foreign merchants or their servants were committed in or near Yokohama, usually by rōnin. In 1860 (when a Japanese mission had gone to Washington to ratify the American treaty) there were frequent conspiracies against the Bakufu, particularly in Kyoto. The Regent, Ii Kamon no Kami, took vigorous steps against his enemies. Among them Mito (Nariaki) was punished by disgrace; and in revenge Ii was murdered by Mito and Satsuma clansmen on a snowy morning in March 1860 as he, with his escort, was about to pass through the Sakurada gate leading to the Yedo castle.

After Ii's death the attack upon the Bakufu was continued by Satsuma with the approval of the Court, and attacks upon foreigners grew more frequent and serious. The secretary of the American Legation was attacked in Yedo, and in 1861 the British Legation was attacked by Mito samurai.

The weakness and indeed the bad faith of the Bakufu were revealed when it was discovered after Ii's death that, doubtless in a quandary, it had agreed with the Court to fix a date for the expulsion of foreigners. At that time—in June 1862—a diplomatic mission was in London asking the government there to agree to deferring the opening of further ports, owing to anti-foreign activities in Japan. In that same summer the Shōgun, at the command of the Court, agreed to journey to Kyoto to consult with the nobles as to the future government of Japan and the appropriate time and method for expelling barbarians.

This journey, which took place in March 1863, was a further act of submission and entirely without precedent in the relations between the Shōgun and the Throne. Hitherto no Shōgun had visited Kyoto since Iemitsu's demonstration of force with 300,000 troops. The Bakufu had always given orders to the Court through its deputies there. Now, shortly after the Shōgun's arrival, the Court instructed the Bakufu that all foreigners were to be expelled and all ports closed; but the Bakufu pleaded that such action was premature and indeed dangerous. The Court reluctantly withdrew its order, and the proponents of Jōi were of course enraged. Murderous assaults were common. The members of foreign diplomatic missions and foreign residents in general were in danger, and an Englishman riding along the highway was killed by a Satsuma retainer near Yokohama. The British government, unable to obtain satisfaction from the Bakufu since Satsuma remained obdurate, ordered the bombardment of Kagoshima by British warships, and this was carried out in August 1863.

It is convenient at this point, before concluding the tale of the dying struggles of the Bakufu, to examine the reasons for its rapid decline.

First among these was the growing hostility of the Court, of the great Western clans, and of needy samurai; but perhaps more important was a widespread discontent in the civil population, particularly the middle-class merchants and farmers. The rich merchants of Yedo and Ōsaka, such as Mitsui and Kōnoike, always kept a watchful eye upon political trends, and they were not slow to notice signs of weakness in the Bakufu and to improve their relations with Satsuma, Chōshū, and other flourishing daimyos. But these changes of policy, though important, were slow to operate. Much quicker was the growth of discontent among farmers.

In the last decade of the Bakufu there were constant uprisings and "smashings," which were violent protests of peasants against landholders. These were not organized attacks upon the Bakufu, but they stimulated antagonism to feudal rule not only among peasants but also among samurai of the lower ranks. It cannot, however, be said, as is sometimes suggested, that such risings had political aims, nor did they have any direct political effect beyond underlining an already existing anti-feudal feeling.

One notable uprising of this nature took place in 1853, when the peasants of ninety villages in the Nambu domain, numbering in all 15,000 men, swarmed through the countryside proclaiming a doctrine of equality. In 1859 there was a similar rising in Shinshū, where bands of peasants from numerous villages proclaimed that an appeal to force was now the law of the land. But such expressions of popular discontent were spontaneous outbreaks, without organization or continuity.

The position of the Bakufu now grew weaker day by day, and it lost its control over the vassals when it relaxed the rule of alternate attendance. The great daimyos withdrew to their fiefs. The two most powerful Tozama chieftains, Satsuma and Chōshū, were in open revolt. In June 1863 Chōshū shore batteries fired upon an American vessel anchored off Chōshū territory, and the straits of Shimonoseki were closed for more than a year, until in September 1864 a combined force of American, British, French, and Dutch warships attacked the Chōshū defences and captured their guns. Chōshū gave way, agreeing to pay an indemnity; and it is much to the credit of the Chōshū leaders that most of the clansmen were soon on friendly terms with the foreigners. The same is true of the Satsuma leaders after the bombardment of Kagoshima. The truth is that both these clans were more antagonistic to the Bakufu than to the foreigners, partly because they were confident of their own strength in domestic affairs and partly because they saw the futility of the exclusion policy.

At this time the two clans were at odds, and Shimazu had more control over his refractory rōnin than his Chōshū rival. A majority of the Chōshū men atempted to "rescue" the Emperor from the Bakufu, by a rising in Kyoto, where they had a large contingent. This rising was checked late in 1864 by Bakufu troops with the assistance of Satsuma and other clans. The Chōshū leaders submitted and a settlement was in sight, when the Bakufu, with its now usual rash judgment, decided to destroy the Chōshū clan entirely. In this attempt it failed disastrously. Satsuma gave assistance to Chōshū by furnishing war material, and the Bakufu was placed in a most awkward position. The Shōgun led his troops as far as Ōsaka, but the loyal vassals were slow to respond to his summons. His force did not march again until July 1866, and it was everywhere unsuccessful. This was a fatal blow to the Tokugawa regime, for the Shōgun had now been defeated by a single Tozama vassal.

In August 1866 the Shōgun Iemochi died in Ōsaka. His successor, Hitotsubashi Keiki, took office and appealed for unity, while the Bakufu struggled to maintain its dwindling authority. But in the autumn of 1867 he resigned, and a provisional government was formed in which no member or adherent of the Tokugawa family was included.

There was a brief civil war in which the Shōgun's forces were defeated without much trouble, and the whole country submitted to the rule of the Emperor early in 1868. This was the end of the feudal society which Ieyasu had founded two and a half centuries before.

It was also the end of a millennium, during which the people of Japan lived a sequestered but not isolated life, thanks to the surrounding sea and to the distance separating their islands from the Asiatic mainland. They could at will accept or reject the influence of China and other parts of Asia, if need be by resort to arms, as they did to repel an invasion of Mongols in 1281.

In these favourable circumstances they could apply their energies to developing the natural resources of their country and improving its government. Both of these tasks presented great difficulties, for during the Middle Ages civil strife was endemic. Nevertheless, by the beginning of the seventeenth century, a substantial degree of political unity had been achieved, and after 1615 the whole of Japan was at peace under the government of the powerful warrior family of Tokugawa, whose successive chieftains kept their feudal vassals under control and established the rule of law.

The history of the subsequent era shows the country to be firmly, and on the whole justly, governed, despite occasional disorder. There is a continuous effort, both national and local, to increase the production of foodstuffs and other commodities, and population grows apace. Manufacture vies with farming. Town life develops, transport is improved, and a prosperous merchant class tends to displace, or at least to compete with, the military caste, whose poorer members fall into distress if they cannot find civil employment. By the beginning of the nineteenth century the authority of the central government is being challenged by the great feudatories. Pressure from Western countries, whose ships are now freely navigating in Eastern waters, gradually breaks down the old policy of insulation, and by 1853 the feudal government is obliged to agree to open ports to foreign ships. Japan has now to enter the international society. The feudal hierarchy presently collapses, and in 1867 the rule of the Throne is fully restored.

APPENDIX

THE VILLAGE AND THE FAMILY

Students of sociology may find some points of interest in the following details, which are supplementary to the account of village life given in Chapter VIII.

The peasant family in the Yedo period was of several kinds, but in its legal aspect the basic unit was the family of the hon-byakushō. His family was rather large, particularly in the later period, consisting as it did of lineal and collateral relatives together with persons who were not related to them by a blood tie. The main household, thus composed of several families, might easily consist of about twenty members in all, exclusive of young children.

It was these families that cultivated the soil, gathered the harvest, and paid the tax. Consequently the main household included a number of persons who were not blood relations but in fact the servants of the head of the household. They were described generically as genin (underlings), and specifically as nago, kamado, hikan, or local variants of those names. But they were not mere servants, for they were regarded as members of the family. With all the other members they formed one large family living under the orders of the head of the whole household—the patriarch, he might be styled.

As the family of the hon-byakushō increased in numbers, or as its holding of land increased, or as agricultural techniques developed, it became necessary, or at least desirable, to reduce the main family (honke) by dividing off branches, which were given land and could form new, independent branch families (bunke). The branch family, however, was not always able to support itself independently, and some of its members had to take outside employment as day labourers. Branch families might be one or more in number, according to the scale of the main family, and several branches around a nucleus formed by the main family would constitute a group which had the character of an extended family.

Not only did a main family and its branches subsist jointly, but there also had to be a real and not a nominal relationship between them all. It had to be a close relationship because a corporate effort was essential in the cultivation of the land that they possessed, which depended on the common use of irrigation water, of untilled grassland, and of male and female labour in the busy seasons of planting and harvest.

There were important reasons why a main family alone could not complete the farming processes. While at the head of a group consisting of branch families under his control, the hon-byakushō also had to be in close touch with other hon-byakushō. Farmers could not exist independently, and it was the various relationships between farmers' families that brought them into a permanent association—the village.

The scope of the village increased, and changes took place in the nature of their association, until the daimyos to whom they were subject constructed a system of villages and fixed their boundaries. Within those boundaries the hon-byakushō were the legally recognized members of the village. In practice the members of one village frequently formed associations with the members of other villages, thus extending a community of interest over a wide area.

After the Genroku period, changes took place in the character of the farmers and their villages. Some of the crops they grew were now articles of commerce (either in their natural form or as the material of handicrafts) which could be sold at a profit. Thus the land required a new kind of management. The branch families held only small areas of land, but their earnings from this kind of handicraft were considerable, and they tended to cease joint subsistence with the main household. Moreover, even without the land which was theirs to cultivate, the able-bodied members could earn a living as day labourers. Thus there developed a class of landless peasant. In such circumstances the group of main family and branch families tends to split into two parts, big farmers and small farmers; while the association of one main household with another main household becomes loose with the passage of time.

Within the family composed of persons related or not related to the head by blood ties, an order of age and sex was established. There was, it is true, also a rank or order dependent upon blood ties, but it did not take precedence over other orders. The order within the family always expressed a feeling of the relationship between parent and child (as, indeed, did the relationship between main family and branch family). This was customary and traditional rather than legal.

The Composition of the Village

The following is a much-abbreviated version of an official return of the farmers, their families and property, made in Haraguchi Mura, a village in Higo, in the year 1633 (in *Dai Nihon Kinsei Shiryō I*). The first entry is that of the Shōya, or Headman.

Holder: MAGOEMON   Assessed yield: 50.35 koku

Family (18 members in all):

Shōya (Magoemon)	Two nago (Zenbei and Heizaemon)
1 wife	2 wives
2 sons	1 father
2 daughters	1 [illegible]
1 wife of son	1 nurse
1 female servant	1 daughter
1 male servant	1 son

Livestock: 2 oxen, 3 horses

15 buildings (measured in ken—1 ken = 6 ft.):

2 x 6 dwelling	2 x 4 food store
2 x 5 kamaya (kitchen)	2 x 5 storehouse
2 x 4 children	2 x 4 dwellings for nago (2)
1½ x 4 shrine	1½ x 3 kamaya (2)
2 x 4 stable	1½ x 3 stables (2)
2 x 4 dwelling	1½ x 3 kariya? (lodging)

Next come entries of similar particulars for the remaining families in the village, beginning with that of the Shōya's eldest son. And, finally, the return is summarized by the signatories as follows:

Total yield .... 714.4 koku
Total persons .... 209 (120 males, 89 females)

Classification of Male Members of the Village

Shōya (headmen) 2
Kimoiri (agent) 1
Parents and grandparents of holders 19
Boys under 15 27
Boys over 15 11
Hayakushō (farmers) 22
Nago 29
Genin 6
Sakugo (servants) 3
Total males 120

Horses: 44   Oxen: 22
Buildings (including storehouses and stables): 178

The total number of hon-byakushō families in this village was twenty-five. This may be taken as an average size. A larger group in the same district was Takehazama-machi (called a machi, or town, instead of a village because it was strung along a highway). Its composition was as follows:

Total population:
   Females 242
   Males 287
                               529
Livestock:
   Oxen 62
   Horses 105

The adult males were:
   Shōya 2
   Hyakushō 47
   Nago 67
   Genin 63

The whole consisted of 49 holdings, ranging in assessed yield from 5 koku to 34 koku. The total assessed yield was of the order of 1,000 koku.

BIBLIOGRAPHICAL NOTE

The chief primary sources consulted in preparing this volume are:

Tokugawa Jikki.
Tokugawa Kinreikō, first series, Volumes I–V; and later series, Volumes I–IV.
O Furegaki, collections for the periods Hōreki, Kampō, Temmei, Tempō.

A handy guide to sources is *Shiryō ni Yoru Nihon no Ayumi.* Useful modern works are:

Nihon Kinseishi, Volume II, by Itō Tasaburō.
Yedo Jidai (in *Iwanami Shinsho*) by Kitajima Masumoto.
Hansei by Kanai Madoka.

The relevant volumes of Tokutomi Sohō's magnum opus, *Nihon Kokuminshi,* contain most useful primary and secondary source material and interesting, if dogmatic, commentary.

Murdoch's Volume III, like all his work, is vigorous and pointed; but he died before it was completed, and it was "revised and edited" by unqualified hands. It is a pity that those who prepared for publication this volume of over 800 pages furnished it with a very poor index.

INDEX

A

Abe family: Tadakatsu, 14; Tadaaki, Rōjū (1633–71), 53 f., 56, 63; Shigetsugu, 92; Masahiro, 236
Adams, Will, 5, 10
Agemai (offered rice), 157, 162
Agrarian risings, 106, 168, 180, 183–87, 193, 240; Shimabara Revolt, 37–38, 42, 179; mentioned, 214, 219, 222 f.
Agriculture: products, 96, 109, 120, 126; increase of production in 17th c., 106–10, 115; development under Yoshimune, 157–58
Akita fief, 216–17
"Alternate attendance" system, 20 f., 27, 47 f., 58, 212, 240
Animals, laws protecting, 131, 134
Anti-Christian activities, 39–44, 80; and Ieyasu, 5, 7, 13; ban on books, 25, 168–69; and Christian rōnin, 34; Shimabara Revolt, 37–38, 42, 179. *See also* Seclusion policy
Anti-foreign sentiment, 236–40
Aoki Konyō (1698–1769), 170, 188
Arai Hakuseki (1656–1725): as historian, 14, 139, 149–50, 163, 188; early career, 85, 146–49; and currency reform, 134 n., 140, 142–44, 154 f., and Ienobu, 138–41; mentioned, 145 n., 159 n., 169, 177; portrait, PLATE 10
Artisans, 6, 29, 30–31
Asaka Tampaku, 94, 150
Asano family, 19, 78
Ashikaga Shōguns, 15, 72, 113, 235
Astronomy, 169–70
Azuma Kagami, chronicles, 17

B

Bakufu, 54, 62, 92 f., 113, 152; foundations of, 3–4, 12, 16, 33, 70, 73, 111; foreign trade; 5, 35, 37, 144,
146; organization of, 10, 14, 19, 25–27; relation to Throne, 17–18, 27–28, 138, 140–41, 198–99, 235–36, 239–40; and daimyos, 20, 46–54 *passim,* 61–67 *passim,* 157, 210–18, 241; administrative system, 21–24; social system under, 29–32; and peasants, 30, 99 f., 106, 167, 179–80, 183–84, 240; and anti-Christianity movement, 40–43; seclusion policy, 40–41, 228, 233–37; and rōnin, 56–57, 59; and nonconformists, 78–81; the expanding economy, 120–29; and merchants, 127–29, 182–84; financial problems, 142–44, 155–66 *passim,* 194–97, 208; Minamoto, 160; hostility towards, 177–79, 231, 236–41 *passim;* domestic problems of, 221–27; mentioned, 8, 16, 52
Bakufu Orders (*O Furegaki*), 160–61
Bansho Shirabedokoro, foreign documents office, 234
Banzan, *see* Kumazawa Banzan
Banzui-In Chōbei, 60, 60 n.
Bashō, *see* Matsuo Bashō
Biddle, Commodore James, 232–33
Bribery, 159, 175–76
Buddhism, 70, 72, 131, 133; and anti-Christianity movement, 42, 44; Amidist (Jōdo) sects, 69; decline of, 69, 76 f., 82; Zen, 69 ff., 82; Ikkō sects, 115; mentioned, 6, 15
Bugyō (Commissioners), 5, 22, 24, 27
Buke Sho-Hatto (Rules for the Military Houses), 16, 47, 55; of 1615, 7–8; of 1631, 34; of 1635, 20, 27, 34, 37, 48, 75; of 1683, 132; of 1710, 139–40; sample clauses, PLATE 6
Bushidō, 13 n., 78
Bussangaku (science of production), 190, 191 n.

C

Calendar reform, 169 f.
Caron, François, 43
Censors (*Metsuke*), 23, 48, 176
Census (18th c.), 187
Chamberlains (*Soba-yōnin*), 22, 131, 140, 174
Chaya Shirōjirō, 10 f.
Chigyō-tori (recipients of land revenue), 49–50
Chikamatsu Monzaemon (1653–1724), 105, 151, 153
China: trade with Japan, 5, 6 n., 35, 37, 42, 45, 116, 144–45; influence on Japan, 8, 29, 38, 130–31, 242; and anti-Christianity movement, 38, 44, 168–69; Coxinga, 67–68; and Great Britain, 228, 235, 237; Ming policy of seclusion, 229 f. *See also*, Chu Hsi philosophy; Confucianism
Chō (measure of area = 2.45 acres), 96 f., 96 n.
Chōnin (townsmen), 117, 129
Chōshū fief, 218–20, 240 f.
Christianity, *see* Anti-Christian activities
Chu Hsi philosophy, 69–81 *passim*, 84–86, 94, 132, 192, 200
Chu Shun-shui, 83, 95
Chūgen (manservants), 59
Cocks, Richard, 41
Code of One Hundred Articles, The, 4 n., 93, 172
Coinage, 5 n., 140, 143, 161 n., 164 f., 198, 220 n.
Confucian college, 132, 199–200
Confucianism: Neo-Confucian ethic, 15, 69–93, 117–18, 216, 229 f.; Wang Yang-ming (Ō Yōmei), 74, 84, 86, 224; of the Analects, 80; Kogaku-Ha, 80
Copper, 145, 163, 177, 182
Corvées, 64, 100, 197
Cotton, 109, 120, 163
Council of Elders, *see Rōjū*
Court, *see* Throne
Coxinga, Chinese commander, 67–68
Currency: debasement, 134, 143, 153, 165; reform, 134 n., 140, 142–45, 161–62, 197; mentioned, 163, 208

D

Dai Nihon Shi, history, 94–95
Daigaku Wakumon, treatise, 79, 79 n.
Daikan (Deputies), 12 n., 23, 52, 101
Daimyos, 3–7 *passim*, 24, 46–52, 124, 235; Fudai, 14, 24, 131, 155; and Bakufu, 16, 19–20, 46–54 *passim*, 61–67 *passim*, 157, 210–18, 241; Tozama, 25–26, 43, 224, 236
Daishōjingi-Gumi (Pantheon Band), 59 f.
Daté family, 19, 47, 49, 63–67, 176, 213 f.
Daté Sōdō (Disturbance), 66–67
Davydov, Russian officer, 203 f.
Dembei, Japanese castaway, 202
Deshima, 37, 42, 116
Dogs, protection of, 134
Doi Toshikatsu, 14, 18, 22, 26, 29
Dojima Exchange, 125 f., 126 n., 163–65
Dokushi Yoron, history, 149
Dutch craze (*Rampeki*), 189, 231
Dutch studies, *see Rangaku*

E

Echigoya shop, 115, 184
Economy edicts, 151, 160–61. *See also* Sumptuary rules
Elders, *see Rōjū; Wakadoshiyori*
England, *see* Great Britain
Escheatment, 3–4, 33, 56
Exclusion policy, 35–39, 231
Exports, *see* Trade

F

Family relationships, 88–90, 245–46
Famines, 185 f., 193, 217, 219, 222
Farms and farmers, 29, 96–100, 108–9, 120, 166–68. *See also* Peasants
Fiefs, 49–52, 210–18. *See also Daimyos*
Fields, wet and dry, 96, 104–5, 158
Five Human Relations, 73, 76, 80 f., 84
Five-Man Groups (Gonin-gumi), 30, 30 n., 100–103
Forty-Seven Rōnin affair, 92–93, 134
France, 228–29, 238, 241
Franciscans, 40 n.
Fuchimai-tori (stipendiaries), 50 f.
Fudai, *see Daimyos*